HERE IS THE GOLDEN GATE

BY THE SAME AUTHOR

Fiction

THE NINE BRIDES AND GRANNY HITE
THE FREEDOM SONG

Nonfiction

TREASURE EXPRESS
SILVER STAMPEDE

With Frank J. Taylor

SOUTHERN PACIFIC
THE EARTH CHANGERS

HERE
IS
THE
GOLDEN
GATE

ITS HISTORY, ITS ROMANCE
AND ITS DERRING-DO

By Neill C. Wilson

WILLIAM MORROW AND COMPANY
NEW YORK • 1962

ACKNOWLEDGMENTS

Thanks are extended to Anne Roller Issler for permission to quote from her book, *Happier For His Presence,* the Stevenson poem on page 129 herein; and to Francis P. Farquhar, Marshall Maslin, Thomas Crowley, Rear Admiral Allen Winbeck and the U.S. Coast Guard from top to bottom, including Capt. B. P. Clark, Captain of the Port; Karl Kortum, Tom Wheeler, Lionel Shatz, Charles E. Regal, Josephine Duffield and all the many others who assisted this book.

N.C.W.

To
Nancy Jane and Mary Louise

CONTENTS

1. THE WAITING CLEFT   3

2. SHIPS THAT MISSED THE PORT   7

3. THE GREAT DRAKE MYSTERY   13

4. FIRST BEHOLDERS   19

5. THE SHIP THAT DIDN'T MISS   24

6. THE CIRCLE CIRCLED   32

7. A GATE RECEIVES ITS NAME   39

8. THE GOLD SHIPS   44

9. THE NAMESAKE STEAMSHIP   51

10. THE INCREDIBLE CLIPPERS   57

11. BELLIGERENT STEAM   66

12. HONEST MEIGGS AND HIS WHARF   74

13. THE GATE'S TWO HINGE-POSTS   79

14. DISASTERS IN THE GATE   89

15. GALLANT RESCUES—
    A FEW OF MANY   98

16. FATEFUL DEPARTURES   107

17. GUNS OF THE GATE   116

18. ON THE BEACH   122

19. SOUTH SEA PERFUME   131

20. THE LUMBER FLEET   141

21. INTO THE SUNSET   147

22. THE FISHING FLEET   154

23. FERRIES ACROSS THE GATE   162

24. LITTLE BOATS, ALL BUSINESS   169

25. SOME SALTY PERSONALITIES   176

26. THE ROCK   189

27. TWO LANTERNS   195

28. THE WEATHER MAKER   199

29. A POET AND HIS BRIDGE   203

30. THE MOUNTAIN ABOVE   209

31. BEYOND THE HEADS   214

32. THE ALWAYS READY COAST GUARD   220

33. HOME FROM THE SEA   228

34. THE WINDS OF CHANGE   233

    INDEX   237

LIST OF ILLUSTRATIONS

(between pages 70-71)

"It's a wild headland. Point Reyes' Light . . ."

"Her original name was *Balclutha* . . ."

"And then . . . came Captain Josiah Creesy's *Flying Cloud* . . ."

A steamship and a whale pile up on Lands End.

A modern steamer makes a slight mistake.

"The fog comes in—an army of ghostly sky-riders . . ."

Mile Rock, "the lonesomest lighthouse in America . . ."

"An unspoiled and unique forest . . ."

(between pages 198-199)

"The lantern keeper at Alcatraz is lonesome . . ."

Point Bonita from the South.

Point Bonita from the North.

The Golden Gate, San Francisco, before the Bridge (1932).

"So the Fort was saved . . ."

The Gate entrance is shaped like a bell.

"The nearest neighbors to Farallon light keepers . . ."

HERE IS THE GOLDEN GATE

1 : THE WAITING CLEFT

THE Golden Gate is at Longitude 122° 31′ W. The sun rises upon it three hours before reaching the line out in the Pacific Ocean where today becomes tomorrow and West becomes East. Its latitude is 37° 48′ N., squarely upon the belt of man's migrations out of Central Asia and the starting point of Columbus. The belt contains Samarkand, Ararat, Izmir, Athens, Seville, Washington, Tokyo and Peking.

The Gate has had powerful impact upon men's imaginations. It has been a magnet, a goal, a singing harp, a journey's end, a jumping-off place into new adventure, and it still is. It has beckoned tall ships, reckless men, gay and avaricious ladies, Yankee plowboys and counter-jumpers turned miner, Mississippi River card sharps, Southern pistol-packers, Botany Bay cutthroats, happy sons of the Hawaiian sun and the Mediterranean moon, coolies of the Orient who had lived ten thousand years without hope and suddenly found it, Chinese slave girls imported like sacked rice, dimpling Japanese picture brides, French chefs, Scots bankers, German institution-founders, skillful Jewish authorities on feminine vesture, talented actors, journalists of gusto, musicians, opera lovers, vintners, cup-lifters of awesome scope, prospective suicides in abnormal quantity, and a new race of emancipated land-tillers addicted wholly to the spacious life and the machine.

3

By sea the Gate is 2,074 sea miles from Honolulu, 7,519 from Yokohama, 8,029 from Hong Kong, 7,602 from Sydney and 4,000 from Panama. There was a time when it was 17,000 from New York, but the Isthmian canal cut that in half. It is 5,000 from Tahiti but you detour by way of Honolulu unless you have a yacht.

The best way to approach the Gate still is by ship on the sea. Rewarding, though, is the approach by motor car from the north. Then a vision of startling loveliness bursts upon you as you come out of Waldo tunnel and see orange-red bridge towers and shining waters directly before you and the window panes sparkling on the opposite hills. Though maybe the bridge towers will be wreathed in cloud, or the pavement swamped in fog of car-length visibility, full of ghostly headlights, dank with smell of kelp and salt, and moanful with the blasts of steamship whistles passing directly below your floorboard.

But the sea approach is the true homing. In clear weather Mount Tamalpais, north of the Gate, becomes visible while you're 60 miles away. The first welcoming committee down on the sea is that group of dark rocks, the Farallones, which fascinated early navigators and have had almost no visitors since. The Lightship is picked up three miles outside the bar. The ship channel through the bar has almost as many bells, horns, whistles and lights as Market Street on New Year's Eve. High hills rise to 1,000 and 2,000 feet on the north, a long sandy beach stretches to the south, and black rocks and surf embroider the Gate entrance at both sides. From January to May the hills on your left are grey-green, splotched with purple lupin and lemon-yellow mustard. Then they wither to bright or tired straw.

The Gate entrance is shaped like a bell. Its heads are Point Lobos and Point Bonita. "Lobo" in this case means "sea wolf" and "Bonita" means "pretty." Draw romantic conclusions if you desire; but Bonita was originally Bonete because it looked like a Spanish clergyman's hat.

Cliff House and Seal Rocks are beneath Lobos on the right. Two and a half more miles and the traveler is gliding under Golden Gate Bridge. Soon he rounds Telegraph Hill and is solidly in the Bay.

Among the many things that the Gate does, it marries the Pacific Ocean to river waters that have eloped from California's great central valley. The waiting place of these brides, San Francisco Bay, extends 50 miles inland and 40 south in a rough right-angle of three connecting bays. In comes the bridegroom, riding his tide, and out they all pile with the tide's turn. Nor are these bridal rivers dainty about it: they hit the incoming sea with 2,000 to 5,000 cubic feet of water per second in arid summer and up to 200,000 and even 500,000 in winter, which is about the volume of the once un-dammed Colorado River at titanic flood. Meeting them is the whole tidal and breaker power of ocean, gathering in an outer funnel 35 miles wide, narrowing to three miles at the Heads and then to one mile in the narrows under the Bridge. Switching metaphors, the Gate is a kind of washing machine that goes through four cycles daily, each cycle with its own surge, speed and timing.

San Francisco flanks the Gate on the south for seven or eight poignantly picturesque miles. From Point Lobos where sea lions bark to Fisherman's Wharf where seagulls creak, the far scene is of rough cliffs and handsome mountain, the middle scene is one of water and ships, and the near one is of parks, golf courses, the wooded Presidio that originated before the town, and steep hilly descents that curl the toes of cable-car riders and squeamish motorists.

The Gate is strictly three-dimensional. It has length, narrowness and startling height. It also has a fourth dimension, which is in the mind of the beholder: a sense of spell.

As if so much beauty just can't be real. But it is here, it is here.

In early days the Gate played hard to catch.

Masters of New Spain from Cortez onward sent occasional ships exploring up the coast. California was a mysterious land named for a domain in a Spanish novel and fictionally inhabited by Amazons and griffins. The venturing ships soon ran low on water and provisions. They desperately required a harbor where they might restock and repair. They found five harbors, of sorts, in the 150-mile coastal stretch to which the Golden Gate is central. But that slender seaway into the one big, safe, naturally well-stocked harbor they didn't find. The angle of water view inward between the Gate's guardian headlands is only 60° of arc and most of that finds two bulky bay islands in the way. Pleated cliffs and the two inner islands give the effect of a solid mainland wall. The river waters that pour through have already dropped much of their silt. And shore rocks give a formidable approach; summers often bring veiling fogbanks; winters bring sheeting rain.

So the early mariners made do with two of the semi-havens, Bodega Bay and the one now called Drakes Bay. They avoided as too dangerous of entrance the long slim shallow Tomales Bay and the somewhat exposed Bolinas Bay. They found with rejoicing, and then lost, Monterey roadstead. The Golden Gate they knew not.

Throughout the sixteenth, seventeenth and much of the eighteenth centuries the Gate kept the secret of its existence. Requisites for its discovery and revelation to the world—clear weather, a calm sea, ship proximity, a skipper's determined curiosity and political conditions favoring a public announcement—for 233 long years simply never came.

2 : SHIPS THAT MISSED
THE PORT

THOSE mailed Conquistadores who tumbled out of Spain on the heels of Columbus and seized much of the Americas, were among the bravest men who ever lived. But they didn't love the sea. When everything from Mexico to Peru had fallen to their falconets and crossbows, they sent a Portuguese navigator to examine the Pacific Coast of North America.

Juan Rodríguez Cabrillo, tough and capable, set out from a primitive port 350 miles west of Mexico City on June 27, 1542. He commanded two crude little vessels that a modern salt would hesitate to cross San Francisco Bay in. They had been hewn out of the jungle by lubberly hands and the scanty iron in them had been brought over from the Gulf of Mexico on men's backs. They were short, plum-shaped caravels—craft with high stern-castles and lateen rig aft of square-rigged foremasts. The word *caravel* still rings in mankind's ear with a romantic chime. But they were mere chips on the waves. Cabrillo's crew were men pulled from the military guardhouse and any Indians who could be grabbed. A rope was put in their hands, a heavy boot to their tails, and they were sailors. Cabrillo did have one man of his own stripe with him: Bartolomé Ferrer—Ferrelo in some manuscripts—as "pilot," or second in command.

So Cabrillo put forth in his *San Salvador,* Ferrer or Ferrelo in the even smaller *La Victoria.* It took the tiny ships
three months to make the 1300 miles to the site of San
Diego. Touching there, Cabrillo became the discoverer of
Alta California. Pressing onward, he was tossed by November weather. South of Monterey Bay, where the Santa Lucia
Mountains shoulder up the landscape, "All the coast run this
day is very bold; the sea has a heavy swell and the coast is
very high. There are mountains which reach the sky, and
the sea beats upon them. When sailing along near the land,
it seems as if the mountains would fall upon the ships." The
journals of sixteenth-century seafarers do not spare the emo-
tions of the reader. Terror suffered is terror shared.

After much sickness and suffering, Cabrillo's two-ship
command reached a point opposite Monterey Bay (some as-
sumptions say Point Arena, farther north), and came about.
At the moment, flesh and bone could stand no more. While
seeking anchorage at San Miguel Island off future Santa Barbara, Cabrillo fell to the deck and shattered a leg or arm. He
died from this or unknown causes and was given Channel
island burial.

Pilot Ferrelo, whose one-deck *La Victoria* had been the
often-separated companion of the flagship, then took over. It
was January, 1543. Spain's king and New Spain's viceroy had
expected a voyage of discovery carrying much farther than
so far achieved. Well then, they would have it. Bartolomé
Ferrelo, as tough and brave as they come, drove his two
prows and his reluctant men northward again. They reached
a latitude about opposite the southern edge of Oregon. Their
course had carried them westward of the Farallone Islands
that guard the Golden Gate—too far out at sea to give view
of that cleft in the hilly shore. Brutal storms blew them about
and Ferrelo finally ordered the return home. Again he passed
the Gate without seeing it.

The cleft continued playing hide-and-seek. Spain ordered

an annual shipping run between the Philippines and Mexico. The westbound route from Mexico had favoring winds and currents along the twentieth parallel and was followed for the next 250 years. The return trip carried north, then across from about opposite the northern tip of Japan to Cape Mendocino—the blustery fortieth parallel. A fleet of four ships and 400 men, initiating this run, made the eastward, homebound passage in 1565. Its smallest vessel, a 40-tonner, cut loose while in Philippine waters and went off freebooting on its own, then led the 500-ton flagship and the other two on that first lunge along the Roaring Forties. When Skipper Arellano raised the mighty jut of Cape Mendocino, a cleaver of land that neatly splits wind and weather, he hurriedly veered south. He made Acapulco ahead of his angry admiral and safely tied up to a tree. He had set the eastbound route that the Spanish were to follow for the next quarter of a thousand years. He, like Ferrelo before him, had missed the Gate.

The Philippines became a staging place for goods from Japan, Ceylon, India, Persia; for spices from the Moluccas, gums from Cambodia, silks from China, and gold and silver from Cebu and Luzon—all transported across the Pacific to a sighting of the California coast, thence south to Acapulco, and by land to the Gulf of Mexico and onward to Spain. Stately wind-ships of 300 to 500 tons, gorged with spices and treasure, with square sails and castled sterns three and four stories high, they spent two or three months going and six or seven months coming. Ready to trade or fight, they carried small cannon and, in the earlier days, stone-hurling catapults. Their beam was one-third their length. Waddling pompously, they made the tremendous voyage every year until 1815. Along with tinkly *caravel* the sonorous phrase *Manila galleon* tolls in man's ear with a romantic booming. Many and many of those beflounced dowagers of the sea passed the waiting Golden Gate, hurrying home for the fleshpots of New Spain. Just as they never discovered the Hawaiian Islands outward-bound, so did they likewise never discern the Gate as they returned.

In 1579, those floating treasure-warehouses attracted the eye of a gentleman named Francis Drake.

Frankie Drake didn't love Spaniards. A decade before, they had mauled him and his redoubtable uncle John Hawkins at Vera Cruz most treacherously. Barely escaping with his life, Drake had crossed the Isthmus of Panama afoot to spy out the chances of recouping his fortunes on Spanish gold bullion coming up from Peru. From a perch in a tree he saw the Pacific. To quote his comrade-in-arms John Oxenham, he "besought Almighty God of His goodness to give him life and leave to sail once in an English ship on that sea." Sail it he did. With Queen Bess's blessing he ultimately put out from England in the 100-ton *Pelican*. He renamed it *Golden Hinde* (the heraldic crest of one of his sponsors) when his vessels reached the Pacific. Drake, "master thiefe of the unknowne world," had aboard "expert musitians, rich furniture," the queen's own gifts of dainties and perfumed waters, and table articles and many cook-room utensils made of pure silver. Persons whom he didn't cutlass down he meant to dazzle. The perfumed buccaneer plundered settlements and Spanish ships from Chile to Mexico. Off Nicaragua he captured papers and charts showing the Spanish route home from Manila to Mexico. Drake made straight north, intending to intercept a galleon. At about the Oregon line, puffs of Alaska-born weather sent him reeling. Wrote the chaplain aboard, "The very roapes of our ship were stiff, and the raine which fell was an unnatural congealed and frozen substance . . . in 38 deg. 31 min. we fell in with a conuenient and fit harborough, and June 17 came to anchor therein."

Opinion as to this location has the scholars divided, for latitude-reckoning in that day was inexact. Was it the Bay of San Francisco inside the Golden Gate? Or one of several minor bays to northward? A considerable authority, George

Davidson, has pronounced in favor of a sheltering cove and lagoon under Point Reyes Head, well outside and beyond the entrance pillars of the Gate. There, or at one of the rival sites, Frankie had nailed a "Plate of Brasse" to a post, named the region New Albion for its white cliffs, claimed it for his Queene, and stayed thirty-six days. While his ship was being repaired he explored inland. If his haven was the so-called Drakes Bay, he was blocked off from view of the Gate and its vast harbor by only the bulk of Mt. Tamalpais. But he contented himself with viewing startled Indians and "fat deere," and sailed away. Next day, July 24, 1579, he went ashore upon the Southeast Farallon. Drake was apparently the first European shipmaster to set foot upon a portion of the future City and County of San Francisco—the Farallones being today in that jurisdiction. The rock was then and is now a great place for gull's eggs and sea lions. But the day of Drake's visit was foggy. The Gate, far away and low on the horizon at best, was invisible.

Whether Drake had really penetrated the Gate is a historic riddle that will be discussed further a few pages onward.

The next explorer, sixteen years later, was a Portuguese in Spanish harness named Sebastian Rodríguez Carmenho. He missed sighting the Gate but reached Latitude 41° north, opposite the site of Eureka. Carmenho—Carmeño to the Spaniards—was flung back by storms. His *San Augustín* struck under Point Reyes and went to pieces. Sixty-seven survivors took to a longboat and a canoe made of a single tree and set out for Mexico, 2000 miles away. For the second time in this voyage they passed the Gate without seeing it. They were west of the outrider Farallones and low on the sea's surface. They made ten leagues on that potentially significant day without discovering anything worth noting. Both cockleshells reached home after hardships almost beyond belief. The haven where Carmeño had left the bones of his *San Augustín* —now called Drakes Bay—and the general open roadstead below Point Reyes, he had named Bahía de San Francisco. The name was to be transferred by later Spanish explorers to the bay inside the Gate.

Eight years more brought Sebastian Vizcaíno out of Mexico by sea. His mission was of another stamp. He planned to bring back to New Spain's viceroy much information about the two Californias, Baja and Alta, which were to be colonized and Christianized by him if possible. In swap for his efforts, he was to have the pearl-fishing concession.

Broken rudder chains aborted his first effort. He made another try. This time, with his *San Diego, Santo Tomás* and *Los Tres Reyes*, he discovered Monterey Bay, a "famous" harbor, "sheltered from all winds." He reached Cape Mendocino's latitude and a bit further, was driven back by scurvy, short provisions and antic seas, and looked in at Carmeño's little cove. The wild shape of the Farallones kept him west of those rocks both going and returning. His sheaf of thirty-two coastal reconnaissance charts went into burial in Mexico City archives, not to be exhumed for two centuries. His cartographer on that voyage of 1603 had noted Monterey Bay, the Farallones, the cove under Point Reyes Head and the bay now called Humboldt north of Mendocino Cape. Some of his men had been on the previous voyage with Carmeño. But no lookout of Vizcaíno's command had perceived the gash in the cliffs that was the Golden Gate.

Though Manila galleons and perhaps other ships passed from time to time, the veiled lady was to continue to hold her mantilla to her face for the next 172 years.

3 : THE GREAT DRAKE MYSTERY

THE Spaniards were rough; none rougher. And Frankie Drake thoroughly enjoyed contending with them. He was a man for the times. He matched any don at courtesy. He seized ships, apologized for the trespass, gave clothing and provisions to the captured crews. He dined politely, even jovially, with all; even with one of his lieutenants who had leaked his plans to the Spanish. Dined, and over the wine gave Tom Doughty his choice of being beheaded or cast to the natives of Patagonia. And after the cigars, personally attended to the beheading.

We can deduce something of what the *Golden Hinde* looked like. At 100 tons' burden and with what we know of sea architecture of her time, the *Pelican* was probably under 100 feet in length and over 20 feet in width. She had high covered decks. She had double sheathing, stout sails and tackle, and seven armed portholes on each side. She was extraordinarily crammed and crowded, what with eighty-six men, much baggage for her officers, eighteen pieces of bronze and iron artillery, ammunition, stores, and constantly swelling treasure. But just what was Drake up to in the Spanish-claimed waters, anyhow? What orders did he have from his Queen? Was he, like Frémont 267 years later, a bearer of secret instructions that had no more justification than the "manifest destiny" aspirations of a young nation beginning to feel its strength? Did he really expect to sail around the north of North America from the west? Did he seek lands for England? Or was he just the piratical partner of a sovereign who needed another sovereign's treasure? Did Drake know he was going to "encompass" the globe via the "Portuguese" route found by Magellan's men?

Other questions arise. How serious was the claim he made to "New Albion," the California coast and hinterland at the point where he repaired his ship? And just where did he land and sojourn for those six weeks? If he actually entered the Golden Gate and anchored in the bay behind it, it seems probable that he became thoroughly serious about New Albion— so serious that he, or his Queen and her ministers, presumably suppressed or destroyed his entire log, reports and store of carefully drawn and painted maps, lest the Spanish learn about the excellent harbor that their Ferrelo had missed.

Drake still had with him a Spanish bark captured off Nicaragua. The two vessels, after turning back possibly at Latitude 48°, (more likely at 42°), sought haven; and at somewhere around Latitude 38° the voyagers found a "faire and good baye with a good winde to enter the same" and landed, beached and overhauled the *Golden Hinde*, and built defenses. They abandoned the prize which had been taken off Nicaragua and they erected a post and put a memorable plaque upon it, claiming everything around for Good Queen Bess. One pictures the leather-armored English, the naked and wondering Indians, the raised swords, and the falling hammer that nailed the plate in place; the rush by the Indians for the abandoned bark after the *Hinde* had sailed away, and the riot too around the Plate of Brasse, which well may have ended as a souvenir around a Miwok chieftain's neck. Or perhaps was left there by the Indians on its post, a thing to be worshiped, a memento of the white gods who had mysteriously appeared and departed.

Careful scholars have beaten their brains weighing the evidence and the probabilities of each of several bays being the one that Drake put into. Henry Raup Wagner concluded that it was Bodega Bay. This, a shallow harbor afterwards much used by the Russians, is 45 miles northwest in an airline from the Gate. George C. Davidson, who spent almost half a century with governmental surveys of the Pacific Coast, firmly endorsed Drakes Bay, so-called, only two-thirds as far from the Gate. Other students have peered into Trinidad Bay far at California's north; into Tomales Bay just south of Bodega; into Bolinas Bay right in the anteroom of the Gate itself; and into and through the Gate. They have compared the lay of the lands, their headlands and sandspits and estuaries, with the descriptive notes of Fletcher, Drake's chaplain, even to the speech and customs of the Indians and habits of the local ground squirrels and moles—all described by Fletcher. And each of five coastline indentations has come up with its adherents. Public acceptance rallied for some time behind the arguments of Professor Davidson, and the cove under Point Reyes became "Drakes Bay" by general acceptance. When, of a sudden, all hell broke out among the scholars.

Someone had picked up an inscribed chunk of brass on the north shore of San Francisco Bay that tallied exactly with Chaplain Fletcher's description of the "Plate of Brasse" Drake had affixed to a "faire great post," claiming the land for England in 1579. This is what the discovered plate said:

BEE IT KNOWNE VNTO ALL MEN BY THESE PRESENTS
IVNE 17   1579
BY THE GRACE OF GOD AND IN THE NAME OF HERR
MAIESTY QVEEN ELIZABETH OF ENGLAND AND HERR
SVCCESORS FOREVER I TAKE POSSESSION OF THIS
KINGDOME WHOSE KING AND PEOPLE FREELY RE-
SIGNE THEIR RIGHT AND TITLE IN THE WHOLE

LAND VNTO HERR MAIESTIES KEEPEING NOW
NAMED BY MEE AN TO BEE KNOWNE VNTO ALL MEN
AS NOVA ALBION

FRANCIS DRAKE

(Hole for
silver
sixpence)

This plate, about 5 by 8 inches, rough-hewn and angularly
engraved as if by mallet and chisel, was found by a picnicker
in the summer of 1936. The place of its discovery was a hillside between San Rafael and Corte Madera Creek. The finder,
Mr. Beryle Shinn, reported his discovery; and there was a
rush of savants to the spot, and elaborate arrangements were
made to test the plate's authenticity. It was turned over to
metallurgical experts at Columbia University—California
professors not wanting to seem pre-prejudiced—and given
every test conceivable, including the age test by Carbon 14
and a chemical analysis of the patina. Other scholars compared the spelling with Elizabethan writings. An Elizabethan
sixpence was found to fit exactly into the hole that had been
made for the sixpence that bore the Queen's countenance.
Finally, and with more than a little excitement, the revered
Herbert E. Bolton of the University of California pronounced
the conclusion: the plate is genuine.

But did that settle the question of what bay Drake put
into? Was it finally and for all time proved that he had anchored off Corte Madera Creek in San Francisco Bay and on
that nearby shore had erected fortifications, careened his
Golden Hinde for cleaning and caulking, and laid claim to
a stretch of land that would be forever England?

And, after sailing on across the Pacific, around Africa, and
home, and sharing his Spanish loot with his Queen and receiving knighthood, had he or the Queen concluded to burn
his papers and maps and say naught of the great discovery?

For England, compared to Spain, was still very weak and would remain so until Captains Howard, Drake, Hawkins, and others, and a good rousing British Isles storm, a few years onward, should destroy the Spanish Armada.

The issue seemed resolved. Drake had sailed in through the Gate.

Whereupon a chauffeur named William Caldeira came forward to state that he had picked up a likely chunk of brass in 1933 about a mile and a half east of Drakes Bay; that he had carried it around and finally tossed it out near the place picnicker Shinn found it.

That really muddied the pellucid waters. Interviewers grilled Caldeira. It was rather generally decided that whatever piece of metal he had toted about and discarded was not the piece found by Shinn. And anyway, how did it get up the hill from that roadside, and under a rock? Francis P. Farquhar, meticulous authority and recent president of the California Historical Society, sums it up for these pages: "The evidence [of Drake's landing place] is not conclusive as to either place, but certainly there is at least as good reason to believe that Drake entered San Francisco Bay as that he remained north of the Golden Gate. It is most unfortunate that the chauffeur's story has been given so much credence. In my opinion, it is completely irrelevant and unsubstantiated and ought to be thrown out the window. Walter Starr, in a review not yet published [March, 1962] has, in my judgment, shown conclusively that Caldeira, if he had any plate at all, did not have the plate now in evidence as the authentic plate left by Drake. Caldeira's story has been successfully refuted, and there can be no verdict that Drake missed the Gate. I think you should emphasize the possibility that Drake did come through the Gate and leave Drakes Bay as an unproved alternative."

Search for the "great and faire poste" has gone on, but without much hope. Wood doesn't last as long as brass. But meanwhile, nagging doubts about Corte Madera Cove persist. Wherever the "faire poste" stood, would Indians have left the plate there? Might it not have come down and traveled from hand to hand for considerable mileage? Does it seem really likely that the proud and geographically sensitive Drake, who painted realistic maps of the coast as he journeyed past, would have kept mum about a harbor so well endowed with wood, fresh water, game, friendly aborigines, safety from storms, and room for all the ships of the seas? Is it possible that not one of Drake's men would have tattled of this find after the Armada was dispersed, but before the sensational voyage was written up by contemporaries?

So the riddle of Drake's landing place remains. The Gate always has been a tease. If he missed its surf-pounded, fog-drenched headlands, he later had lots of company.

Anyway, Elizabeth wasn't strong enough to colonize New Albion. The great post presumably stood awhile, then rotted. The plate fell off, and where it fell nobody exactly knows. What concerned Elizabeth, soon after her admiral got home, was the Invincible Armada of 129 vessels sailing toward her from Cadíz. It was bent upon destroying England. Up, Howard! Up, Hawkins! Up, Drake! Up, all you mariners who serve the Queen's eighty little ships! Up, farmers and your pitchforks! Up, you North Sea and Irish Sea winds!

And the Armada was blown to bits by gales and gunpowder. England was safe. Drake was slain seven years later in another attack upon the Spanish Main. Dreams for "New Albion" died with him. Whether he found the Gate or missed it no longer matters except to the romantically minded and the historically curious.

For effective discovery by ship, even if Drake actually got there, the Gate still had 193 years to wait.

4 : FIRST BEHOLDERS

AFTER scores of years of occasional probing for information of the North American west coast and for a rumored route around the continent which Spaniards called Strait of Anian and Englishmen the Northwest Passage, the Spanish heard alarming news. According to their ambassador at St. Petersburg, the Russians were on Alaskan islands off the west coast of North America. With designs on Alta California? The area had never been reconnoitered except by sea; had not been colonized by the Spain that claimed it.

The viceroy of New Spain at Mexico City ordered out men and ships. The governor of Baja California, Don Gaspar de Portolá, who was a captain of dragoons and a sound military man, volunteered to lead a land expedition. With him would go priests, soldiers and some Christianized Indians. The destination would be Vizcaíno's highly extolled Bay of Monterey.

The two supporting ships got away first, from La Paz in Baja (Lower) California. Rendezvous with the land party would be at the halfway point, Cabrillo and Vizcaíno's San Diego Bay, which had been waiting for more Spaniards for two centuries. The crews as usual were conscripts and unhappy Indians. Provisions were coarse, the meat brine-soaked. Adverse currents and head winds held the little

19

vessels offshore for weeks. Scurvy killed and disabled. They made San Diego with only sixteen of ninety men left fit for duty.

The land party of forty soldiers, thirty Indians, clerics and supply trains had marched from Baja California in two divisions. Governor Portolá led one, accompanied by the elderly president of the missions of the peninsula, Fray Junípero Serra. The other band was led by Capitan Fernando Rivera y Moncada.

Provisions and the hearts of the men were low when all united at San Diego. But a mission was erected, the first in Alta (Upper) California, and the march recommenced. The sixty-five explorers reached Monterey Bay without recognizing it. Vizcaíno's description had been too lyrical. They pushed on. Sixty miles farther north, on Tuesday, October 31, 1769, they crossed a steep ridge near the sea and at about 700 feet elevation beheld a headland 35 miles away. It was Point Reyes. They also saw some whitish cliffs, probably Point Bolinas. They did not see the strait below and to the right of those cliffs. It was cut off by the hills and ranges that now hump the streets of San Francisco. Mount San Bruno lay to the northeast, between them and the bay. They camped that night on a lagoon behind San Pedro Cove. Two days later a detachment of hunters under a sergeant clambered over the backbone range of the San Francisco peninsula and saw the southeast arm of San Francisco Bay. Portolá decided that this was the water, reaching down the coast from Point Reyes Head, which Cermaño had named Bahía de San Francisco.

Sergeant Ortega and a detachment made a jaunt around the new bay's south end. They reported that a great arm of water swung inland. That discouraged Portolá from trying to circle his find. He had discovered a new harbor and a big one, but his men were reduced to eating acorns, and winter was nearing. Besides, this bay didn't at all resemble the description Portolá had been given of Monterey Bay. The latter was the port he had been sent to capture. His men voted to backtrack for San Diego. He concurred.

He had missed the sea entrance to his big bay—that is, the Gate—by 13 miles and the accident of a few intervening hills.

It is astonishing that Portolá, who was one of the later Conquistadores, and whose imagination worked overtime when it came to scenting dangers and hardships ahead, had so little imagination left for the find Ortega had made. The bay was salty. Why didn't he taste it, smell it, observe its tides, explore farther, bid his men live on game and fish? Evidently the soldiers were atrocious shots, inept wilderness men. Their flight from an acorn diet and the fancied perils of winter snows would be ludicrous today to a band of well-led Boy Scouts. But California in 1769 was unknown land, consequently full of terrors. The explorers had set out from just-established and ill-supplied San Diego without even one good meal under their belts, and no contact had been made up here with an expected supply ship. So the party hurried back, down the general route that was soon to become flowery El Camino Real to muleback padres. The exploradores ate mule on the way. As San Diego was neared, the Indian choremen deserted. They stole good Father Serra's spectacles and his robe. They borrowed or dragged from the expedition's leader, Don Gaspar, his leather coat, waistcoat, and pants. Captain Rivera had already got back to that pioneer Spanish settlement in Alta California and he brought out fresh horses and, it is hoped, more habiliments.

But the image of that marvelous Bay of Monterey, which Vizcaíno had painted in men's minds, still danced in Portolá's bearded head and in Viceroy Bucareli's. Don Gaspar, with grim determination, set out again. His party included the Father Crespi, Captain Rivera and Lieutenant Fages who had been along the first time. Father Serra, who was resolved to found a chain of missions in the new land, arranged to go by sea. This overland party did identify Monterey Bay when they reached it, in the spring of 1770. With supporting thunder from a ship's cannon, they took possession. They built a mission, Alta California's second, and its first presidio, and made Monterey the capital of the province. His assignment completed, Don Gaspar returned to Mexico and thence disappeared from history.

Captain Rivera remained at Monterey as California's governor. Two years passed. Father Serra agitated for more missions. One, he felt, should be erected on the bay Ortega had found. In March, 1772, the now Capitan Comandante Don Pedro Fages and Father Juan Crespi set off for another look at that sheet of water to northward. The two leaders, twelve soldiers, two servants and a packtrain went over the hills and through the valleys to about the point on Coyote Creek where they'd last seen the big "estero" in '69. They followed its southeastern shore to a creek they named San Antonio and a plain dotted with oaks and backed by redwoods, the present Oakland. They went on, climbing the slopes a bit. When their line of vision was no longer cut off by Yerba Buena (Goat) Island, they looked into the inner end of the Golden Gate. They named it "La Bocana de la Ensenada de Los Farallones"—the Mouth of the Bay of the Cliffs. It was Thursday, March 26, 1772.

Next day, continuing north, they crossed the future campus of the University of California at Berkeley and ascended a little way up the slopes of Grizzly Peak. From there they saw through the Golden Gate and onward to the Farallones' ship-like sails of rock. This writer lived in Berkeley as a boy of ten and had much the same view and, though he'd never heard of the two ancients Fages and Crespi, knew much the same thrill every time he looked down Bancroft Way.

Crespi and Fages had taken the veiled lady squarely in the rear. Two years later, Captain Rivera took her on the flank. He marched from Monterey to Portolá's old farthest camp, behind Point San Pedro. He continued over the intervening ridges this time and up the long sands south of the sometime Cliff House, and ascended Point Lobos. And there she was.

Captain Fages and Father Crespi had returned to Monterey after reaching the south side of San Pablo Bay and the delta of the two inland rivers. They'd looked into the great Central Valley and across to the white-tipped Sierra Nevada. They'd reached home after sixteen far-ranging days. Theirs were the first European eyes, Drake and his men's possibly excepted, that ever had beheld the Golden Gate.

And, unless by Drake, it had not yet been observed or entered from the sea.

5 : THE SHIP THAT DIDN'T MISS

THE new bay was called Port of San Francisco because all who had so far seen it were convinced that it was part of the "port" given that name by the shipwrecked Carmeño in 1595. Father Serra, pursuing his project of a mission to St. Francis on the imposing bay, needed soldiers to protect his missionaries. Fages, the new acting governor, wouldn't give him any. Serra made the painful sea journey from Monterey Bay to Mexico and took the matter up over Fages' head. Don Antonio Maria Bucareli, viceroy of His Catholic Majesty Carlos III, was a man of fire. He backed Serra's enterprise by ordering out soldiers, friars and a wholesale lot of farmers, artisans and their families who would stick and grow up with the country. Expeditions were organized to the Golden Gate country by land and sea.

Leader of the land party was Don Juan Bautista de Anza, comandante at Tubac and as able a Spaniard as ever buckled sword to leather armor. He made a reconnaissance trip to Monterey in 1774 by way of Gila Valley, Colorado Desert and the pass north of San Jacinto Mountains. Now knowing the route and its hazards, he prepared carefully for the colonizing march. He hand-picked a hardy band of Sonorans and Sinaloans who were used to poverty and could subsist on anything. There were to be wives; there were to be children.

24

Wise in matters outside the military, he even laid in a supply of ribbons for the women's hair. The party of 240 got away to a great jingling of bells and shouting at mules in October, 1775, for a rugged journey that was to take four months. They proceeded by tributary valleys of the Gila into present Arizona, crossed the Colorado at low water, and pressed on over desert that was below sea level and between mountain ranges that looked like the picked bones of dinosaurs. They made it over San Gorgonio Pass, down San Gabriel Valley, and up coastal valleys to Monterey without a single loss, and with four more subjects of King Carlos who were born on the way. Anza left the band at Monterey temporarily and pushed on for the Golden Gate, which he reached on March 23, 1776. Father Font of this reconnaissance party cried, "The port of San Francisco is a marvel of nature, and may be called the port of ports."

Anza picked out a site for a presidio high above the Gate's south shore. Three miles inland, on a streamlet that fed into a lake connected with bay tidewater, he chose a site for the mission. Then, ill and worn and his work well done, he headed back for Monterey and Tubac. In Juan Bautista de Anza the fading Conquistadores had once more flowered brightly, and this time without cruelty or greed.

In the shallow unhealthy harbor at San Blas, the sea expedition had prepared and launched itself. In part its task was to explore the dazzling new cleft and bay and in part to ascertain what the Russians might be up to. The Northern Mystery, the elusive Strait of Anian to the Atlantic, now had this companion worry.

There would be four vessels: one to go as far as San Diego with supplies, one to survey the new port on behalf of Anza and his colonists, and two to go farther north and see how far down the coast Russia had advanced. Preparing the three explorer ships had taken two years. It had been necessary to send to Spain for tools and iron, to Cuba and Peru for canvas, tackle and artillery. The largest vessel, the frigate *Santiago*, got away in '74. Her master, Juan Pérez, took her to 55° North, beyond the line of present British Columbia, but found no Russian settlements. He returned and the *Santiago* set out again with Bruno de Heceta in command and Pérez his pilot. The packet boat *San Carlos* and the 36-foot schooner *Sonora* were ready and they put off too. The *San Carlos* had the assignment of penetrating that cleft and bay opposite the Farallones and making a thorough inspection.

It was March 16, 1775, seven months before Anza's large party got on the road. The three vessels were weighted down by all the supplies they could stagger under, and even by an alternate set of names. The *Santiago* was also *El Príncipe*. The *Sonora* doubled as *Felicidad*. The other name for *San Carlos* was *Toysón de Oro*, or Golden Fleece: a prophetic alias. The Spanish imagination still soared in the naming of things, and the long California coast is forever richer for it.

Trouble arose on the *San Carlos* the night before sailing. Her master, one of six naval officers sent over from Spain, went insane and tried to shoot up the ship. He was subdued after keeping one of his friars at gunpoint all night. The command was transferred to Juan Manuel de Ayala, who'd had the *Sonora*. The *Sonora* was given to Juan Francisco de Bodega ye Quadra.

There have been handsome murals painted of the *San Carlos* in subsequent years. The muralists made her a small version of a Manila galleon, high-castled, square-rigged, with every topsail, stunsail and pennon blowing and heraldic crosses glowing on her canvas. She was not quite this majestic. She was deemed too small for the contemplated farther trip north of the Gate, though the *Sonora*, which was assigned with the *Santiago* to undertake it, was only 36 feet long. The *San Carlos* was a modest little goleta, a two-masted fore-and-after with a rag of topsail to her foremast and a squaresail to a removable stick forward of that. On a goleta, the stern-castle was cut down to a mere poop.

Her trip from San Blas to the tip of Baja California and northwestward was rough. One of the double-barreled pistols left by the maniacal former commander went off and shot her new captain, Juan Manuel de Ayala, in the foot. While he lay in his bunk aching and tossing, and water went low in the casks. A pot of pitch caught fire on the deck. For moments it threatened the vessel. The sea alternately becalmed and tossed the little craft. Eventually its crew sighted kelp, seals and ducks and began to watch for land. The 24th of June brought the Farallones up on the horizon. For the present condition of his ship, Ayala had come too far. He was not ready to try conclusions with the rocks, shoals and currents of that indentation on the mainland. He came about and made for the Monterey settlement. He arrived there next day, having been 101 days at sea.

Ayala and his *San Carlos* stayed at tiny Monterey for a month, mending sails, repairing the ship's bruised skin, taking on food and water, and building a "launch," or deck boat, out of a redwood tree on Carmelo River. On July 27 the oared launch pulled the vessel to sea until she caught the wind. The launch was lifted aboard. It too had bold business ahead. Sails filled, and the *San Carlos* was off for her date with glory.

On August 3, land was sighted again. It was Point Año Nuevo, north of present Santa Cruz. At 1 P.M., Point Reyes was raised. All that night the packet boat zigzagged up and down the coast, waiting for a favoring wind. Her wanderings continued the next day. At evening, being opposite the Gate, she lowered her launch that had recently been growing greenly behind Monterey's Point of Pines. She sent pilot José de Cañizares and ten oarsmen off into the strait in search of an anchorage. Sunset at his back filled the bell-mouth of the

Gate behind Points Lobos and Bonita. The launch did not return. At morning, the tide carried the packet boat out to sea but brought it back again. That evening, Ayala decided to wait for his pilot no longer but to set this prow straight into the cleft. Though a strong wind from the west-southwest filled his sails, the outpouring current allowed him to make not more than a mile and a half an hour. Continual sounding with a 20-pound lead on a 60-fathom line could not find bottom. Winds made him fear for his rigging. There was a constant drift toward rocks. A moon rose. The narrows of the strait neared and there were strong eddies under the high north cliff, a new Charybdis under a dread new Scylla. If he heard siren voices through the splash, they were the shouts of amazed Indians whose village was a mile or two around the corner. But he pressed on, sheering away from that tall Lime Point which he named Point San Carlos. Near an opposite headland his lead struck sandy bottom and of a sudden the wind stopped. An anchor was hurriedly dumped and made fast to the mainmast. The tide changed and the *San Carlos* rode lightly in 22 fathoms. She was in a bight just inside Fort Point, off the soon-to-be Presidio.

At that hour, down in New Spain's province of Sonora, Captain de Anza and his 240 colonists, soldiers and priests were organizing for their 1200-mile trek which would start in two more months.

Sea Captain Ayala's wounded foot hurt woefully. The pistol bullet had gone in between two toes and come out under the big toe, and he had known nothing but anguish and fever for weeks. He didn't know what had become of Pilot Cañizares and ten men, nor what the redskins ashore would do. But he had sailed through a gorgeous Gate, that moonlit summer evening of August 5, 1775, and he had found snug anchorage. The brave if dingy sails were furled. The watch was set. Captain de Ayala wrote up his log to the effect that he had arrived inside the Port of San Francisco and was in a fine-looking harbor which seemed commodious.

Matters were all right with Pilot Cañizares and his men. They had tried to come out to the packet boat but currents had pushed them back to shore. With a better tide they came aboard next day. The next forty days were spent examining the bay from end to end and around its shores. "It is true," reported Skipper Ayala to Viceroy Bucareli by subsequent letter, "that this port is good . . . healthful, though cold . . . Indians constant in their good friendship." Pilot Cañizares ended his peripheral survey with the southwestern or inner Peninsular beach which would later know the Gold Rush city of '49 and the downtown San Francisco of today. Did the pilot-mate of the *San Carlos* or *Toysón de Oro* envision, a few decades onward, 500 ships anchored there and 40,000 gold-lured people ashore? The practical Cañizares did not. He simply reported to his commander that he had observed "a small slough [Islais Creek] navigable only by launches and two harbors [Yerba Buena Cove and Mission Bay] where vessels could anchor. On the more eastern one [Mission Bay] there is an Indian village, rough, like the ones in Monterey. This part seems to have better places for missions, though I did not examine it except from a distance."

On September 7 the *San Carlos* filled her sails again and pulled out. Charybdis caught her and sent her against Scylla, injuring the rudder and breaking three bolts. She limped into a cove for repairs. Then on for Monterey where she rejoined the frigate *Santiago,* and de Ayala reported to Father Serra ashore that the great "estero" his *San Carlos* had entered and surveyed was not one but many, with a single entrance, capable of holding all the vessels of Spain.

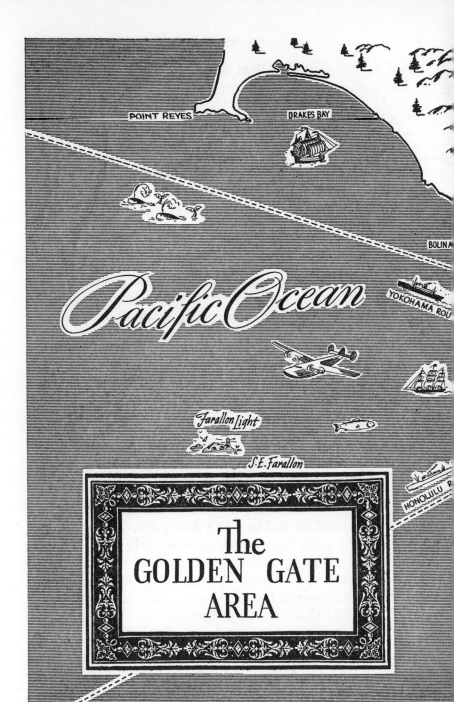

POINT REYES

DRAKES BAY

BOLINA

Pacific Ocean

YOKOHAMA ROU

Farallon Light

S.E. Farallon

HONOLULU R

The
GOLDEN GATE
AREA

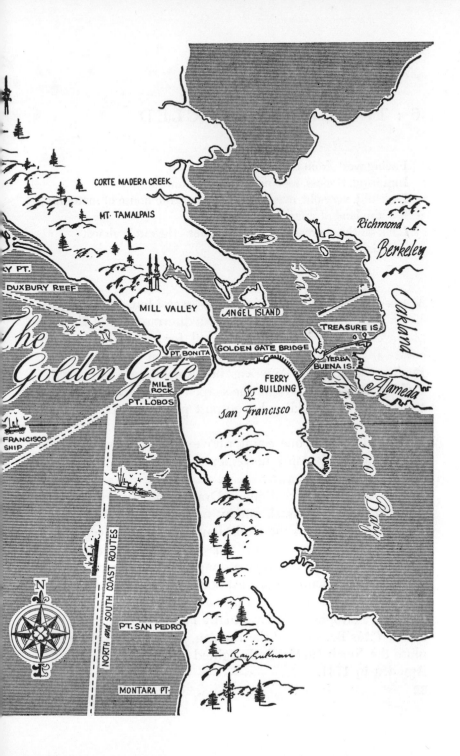

6 : THE CIRCLE CIRCLED

Facing west, from California's shore,
Inquiring, tireless, seeking what is yet unfound,
I, a child, very old, over waves, towards the house of maternity,
   the land of migrations, look afar,
Look off the shores of my Western Sea—the circle almost
   circled.

WALT WHITMAN's "child, very old" was Man. From Tigris-
Euphrates and Nile and Western Mediterranean and Europe
to the Americas he had quested until, for civilized man, ever
westward seemed the ordered way. When he reached the
farther shore of the Americas he turned south and north.
So here he was, by 1776, in the shape of Anza's doughty lieutenant Moraga, building his outpost presidio directly above
the Golden Gate.

There had been one countermove out of Europe, and in
this Gate the opposing movements were about to make a
globe-encircling juncture.

In 1578, just before Francis Drake paid his call to this
neighborhood, a Cossack outlaw named Yermak had led a
band eastward across the Ural Mountains and started a Russian thrust that carried across Asia clear to the Pacific. Furs,
freedom, silver and the ivory of long-frozen mammoths were
the lures. The hardy eastward-bound empire makers scattered harsh consonants as they advanced—Omsk, Yakutsk,
Okhotsk, Petropavlovsk. Eventually Peter the Great sent the
Dane, Vitus Bering, and the Russian, Alexei Chirikof, to explore the North Pacific. Both sighted the mainland of North
America in 1741.

32

By 1784 the Russians had a fur-trading station on Kodiak Island under the Alaskan Peninsula and fifteen years later the royally chartered Russian-American Company was headquartered at Sitka close in among the fjords of the Alaskan panhandle. Soon Sitka even had a brass foundry. It had an exceedingly aggressive manager in Alexander Baránof. The Aleutian Indians in his employ numbered hundreds and they were bold, skillful sealers and sea-otter hunters. In their sea-going skin canoes or bidarkas they out-vikinged the very Vikings. The furs they captured went back to St. Petersburg and Moscow to adorn sleek ladies and fine gentlemen, and into China to warm thin-blooded mandarins, and profits were excellent. Ships from Boston sometimes came into Sitka too, and bartered rum for peltries.

In an early year of its existence, Sitka almost starved. Its two supply ships were due, but one had been wrecked, the other blown askew. A Boston ship, the *Juno*, happened in.

An imperial inspector from St. Petersburg was at Sitka at the moment, painfully regarding the empty larder. He'd been wondering if it wouldn't be possible to obtain food from California. He bought the whole cargo of trading goods—mirrors, beads, pocket knives and calicos—of Captain Wolfe's *Juno*, and he chartered ship and skipper to take him down to the San Francisco Presidio to negotiate. He arrived off the Golden Gate on April 5, 1806. Since Spain was touchy about visitors to its domains, he was extremely uncertain of his welcome.

But the *Juno* ran the defenses of the Gate, which consisted of a couple of unloaded muskets. It anchored off the presidio and sent a boat ashore. The commandante, José Darió Argüello, was away. His son Luís was in charge, and he was less concerned with high policy than with his own boredom. Life out on the fingernail of Spain's most extended finger held but limited excitement. He invited the Russians to his home.

There Nikolai Petrovitch Rezánof, imperial inspector and

plenipotentiary of the Russian-American Fur Company, met Don Luís' sister.

Concepción Argüello, or "Concha," was sixteen. The life that was narrow for her brother was equally narrow for her. No historian has ever undertaken to disprove that she was beautiful. She was dark-eyed and slender, and she loved to dance. She loved even to be told about dancing. Nikolai Rezánof was a man of the world. He knew no Spanish, but with slender Concha's help he picked up what he needed. He told of court life, of balls and ballets and brilliant entertainment. And he had all that stuff aboard the *Juno* to give away. When the senior Argüello returned from Monterey, the little señorita's heart was a warm, throbbing bird in the visitor's hands.

Rezánof was there six weeks, improving his Spanish every minute. He captivated Concepción's sire. He won Don José's approval of a betrothal. There remained only to obtain permission of the Pope for the Castilian-blooded Catholic maid to marry outside her faith, and the friars of the mission over the hill promised to try for it.

Meanwhile Rezánof had to be off for Sitka, with the cereals and other foodstuffs he had obtained, and then on to St. Petersburg to report on Pacific affairs. The señorita must wait for his return.

So the *Juno* sailed out the Gate, Concepción Argüello watching and waving. Years passed. She became a nun. In later life she learned that her fiancé had died on his long homeward journey across Siberia.

There were scuffles between Spaniard and Russian at Nootka Sound on Vancouver Island, where both wanted trading posts. The English and the Boston men joined this fracas and both Spanish and Russians withdrew. Outposts of the two empires remained at Sitka and beside the Golden Gate, 2,000 miles apart. They soon were to come much closer.

Upon his return to Sitka and before embarking for his final journey, Rezánof had briefed Baránof quite thoroughly about the weak Spanish hold on California and had advised cutting in on a piece of it. Baránof already knew much of this from the Yankee shipmasters. The soil was said to be sunny and fertile, the sea teeming with otters. One of several partnerships Baránof made was with Captain Jonathan Winship and his vessel, the *O'Cain*. Baránof contributed one hundred Aleuts, including twelve women, in fifty bidarkas, and the *O'Cain* convoyed them south, first to Humboldt Bay and then to the Farallones. Off the latter, otter-killing was wonderful. Another Yankee ship, the *Peacock*, brought twelve Aleuts under a Russian. These based themselves on Bodega Bay, 42 miles north of the Gate and the sensitive Spanish. By 1809, forty Russians and one hundred fifty Aleuts were quartered there.

Three years later, Baránof was ready to throw his seahunters down the whole length of the California coast with a permanent base ashore, and no Yankee partners. He sent Ivan A. Kuskof, his tough one-legged secretary, at the head of a strong expedition. They put in at Bodega Bay, looked about and selected a stream bank 18 miles farther north for headquarters. Kuskof bought the thousand-acre site from the Indians for three blankets, three pairs of breeches, two axes, three hoes and some beads. On a bluff above the ocean his people built a 12-foot wooden stockade with blockhouses and gunports. A chapel, barracks, commandant's house and other structures, nine in all, went inside the palisade, which was about 100 yards square. Fifty other structures—wooden huts for Aleuts—went up outside. The Russians installed twelve cannon, later increased to forty-one. They built a shipyard. They planted potatoes and cereals and two hundred fruit trees. Kuskof's house had five rooms, glass windows, carpets and a piano. There were ninety-five Russians in the first band. With eighty Aleuts helping, they laid out another farm halfway down to Bodega Bay and a third back of that bay, which they called Roumainzoff.

The general outline and some structures of the headquarters settlement still exist. The Russians called the nearby streamlet Slavyanka. The Spanish, who were watching, called the Slavyanka settlement El Fuerto de los Rusos. Today it is known as Fort Ross.

The Spanish were more than uneasy about all this. In 1810 a Russian-partnered Yankee ship, Captain Bill Davis' *Isabella*, not only made Bodega Bay its hunting base but sent bidarkas into the Golden Gate itself, and the Spanish killed or captured some Aleuts. And there had been other trespasses. But until the Spanish thought of the trick of posting soldiers at all likely waterholes, they lacked the means of repelling invaders. Meanwhile, the Russians and Aleuts went busily after furs. Sea otter and seal were satisfyingly abundant. The sea otter is a short-legged, web-footed mammal about five feet long, his fur thick, glossy and fine. His pelt fetched $75 in Canton and, just possibly, a woman's promise in St. Petersburg. To slay him the Aleut sat in his bidarka far at sea for hours, perhaps for days, with a waterproof skin that was part of his boat drawn up to his waist, making him one with his craft. When the prey showed up, it was met by a bone-tipped harpoon.

The Russian-directed Aleuts killed thousands of otter. They set up an advanced base on the Farallones in the same year that they established Fort Ross. They built stone huts that were occupied by some Russians and from six to thirty Aleuts for the next twenty years. Being less than 30 miles from the Gate and its presidio, they were practically in the Spanish king's whiskers, but neither governor at Monterey nor comandante at San Francisco had any way of throwing them out. Five or six times a year, bidarkas would fight their way from Bodega Bay out to the lonely rocks, bringing wood, food, water, and kegs for sea-lion meat and oil. Once a year a new gang of men was landed and the old sojourners taken off. Farallon sea lions furnished the meat, blubber and oil that were caviar to the Aleuts. Each year the rocks furnished 3,000 to 7,000 pounds of salted sea-lion meat, besides 1,200 to 1,500 commercially valuable fur seal. Sea-lion skins and bladders were sent over to Fort Ross and made by the Aleut women into clothing and bidarkas.

Between 1812, when the Russians arrived in force, and 1841, when the sea otter had been virtually annihilated, the exasperated Spanish tried every means of coping with the interlopers except sending for an armada. They even tried merging 'em, since they couldn't lick 'em. For a time they shared in the profits in return for not shooting down Aleuts ashore.

Fort Ross never was a colony in the lands-acquiring sense, for it did not have Russian families. It was a business venture. But it was the largest collection of permanent houses north of the Gate, and it died solely because the Russians and Aleuts who occupied it weren't farmers and because the sea otter gave out. If some farmers had been sent, and they had gone over the hills a few miles, they could have produced potatoes, cereals and fruit that would have made every day in Sitka a feast day and some of the northern half of California forever Russian. So close were they to the Spanish and the latters' Mexican successors that their footprints on the Farallones were actually within the future City and County of San Francisco, as Drake's had been.

But the otter did give out, and in 1841 the Russians sold Fort Ross with all it contained to Captain John Sutter of Sutter's Fort over in the Central Valley. Down the coast and in through the Gate, and up the bay and the Sacramento River in a sailing vessel went cannon, tables, chairs, beds, windows, doors and that piano.

But two streams of civilization, marching around the globe, had met at the Golden Gate—with a kiss, between

Concepción Argüello and Nikolai Rezánof, and with musketry from the shore for those hunting bidarkas. And in the chapel at Fort Ross, a bronze bell hangs that was cast in Sitka, and in some of the Franciscan missions of California hang bells that were cast in Sitka too. So, in real fact, did questing man come full circle, not in the house of maternity, the land of migrations where he started from, but on his last shore west.

Entrance to the Golden Gate

7 : A GATE RECEIVES ITS NAME

SPAIN had been out of New Spain for a quarter-century. The green, white and red flag of an independent Mexico flew over the two Californias, Baja and Alta. Texas had shrugged off Mexican control and Alta California was on the point of doing so. Commodore Sloat was about to seize Monterey for the trespassing Yankees. Captain Montgomery was about to do the same at Yerba Buena Cove. And Captain Frémont of the United States Topographical Engineers had marched up and down Alta California with a view to tying up all loose ends of the grab. Like the roll-back of the Indians across North America, the seizure of Alta California was something to be accomplished first and apologized for later. The justification for it was that concept called "Manifest Destiny." And perhaps, in view of the fact that the discovery of gold had not yet seriously taken place, but very soon would, destiny was really involved.

On a June day in 1846, with Frémont and the power of the United States lurking in the background, the Mexican colors were pulled down at little Sonoma north of San Francisco Bay and a bunting of the "Bear Flag Republic" hauled up. Captain Frémont then bethought himself of ten Spanish cannon maintained by the Mexican authorities at the Presidio of San Francisco on the south side of the Gate. These guns,

39

and the escape of some defending Mexican forces from the north shore, brought the Frémont party pell-mell through the hills and around the marshes to Sausalito Cove. The hills had lost their vibrant green of spring but were bright with yellow-orange poppies.

A ship was in the cove, taking wood and water aboard at the spot where the *San Carlos* had restocked herself seventy-four summers before. This time it was the *Moscow*, a Yankee hide and tallow drogher, Captain William D. Phelps.

Frémont went into camp and Captain Phelps used the opportunity to look him and his famous party over. The lean, weathered Tennesseeans and frontiersmen from the upper Missouri were in blue wool and deerskin shirts and deerskin breeches and moccasins. Bowie knives bristled and rifles were handy. Fenimore Cooper would have loved them. Dan'l Boone wouldn't have sniffed at them. Davie Crockett and Jim Travis would have welcomed them with a cheer that last day in the Alamo. They had ridden through unmapped country across half of North America; and though the mountains around them may have got lost occasionally, they themselves never had. Their commander was a man of medium height, slender, black-haired, with deep-set hawklike eyes. He was on his third mapping expedition, his purpose further fortified by some secret orders from Washington.

Frémont told Skipper Phelps about the current politico-military picture and his present desire to cross the water and spike those Spanish guns. Phelps was all for it, and how could he help? By lending a boat, said Frémont, and some men handy with oars. Certainly, said Bill Phelps; and how about me coming along too? Fine, said Frémont.

The boat was well loaded. Besides Frémont and Phelps and the oarsmen there were twelve riflemen, one of whom—Kit Carson—was another dozen in himself. The craft set out on a two-and-a-half-mile row across choppy water with a six-knot current. Except for the greater distance of this oared foray, it was Washington crossing the Delaware all over again. And, famous painting of Washington to the contrary, both leaders probably had the sense to sit down in the boat. If Frémont hadn't, he'd have been tossed with a splash while on the weather side of Alcatraz Island, for there the swells are like elephants running under a rug.

Here the event occurred that was more important than the spiking of unmanned cannon at the little fort of El Castillo de San Joaquin at Fort Point. John Charles Frémont, from that bucking boat, took in the scene about him: the beflowered narrows, the waters rolling in from a quarter-way around the globe, their flashing blues and then the floral yellow and orange hues rising up, up behind cliffs and bluffs on each side. A thought came to this imaginative man who was not only engineer and military commander but vigorous pen-wielder. This parting in the Coast Range, this scene of splendor should have a name. And the appropriate name sprang to his mind. Or perhaps it sprang to his brilliant wife Jessie's mind later, when they wrote his report.

Frémont, Kit Carson, Bill Phelps and the others set to the business immediately at hand. They scaled the slope, spiked the ten guns by driving rattail files into their match holes. Alta California's almost nonexistent Mexican defenses were crumbling at all ramparts and this particular castillo's garrison hadn't stayed to dispute the assault. The work done, Frémont, Carson and party went on to other scuffles.

Swift events took their course: Winfield Scott at Vera Cruz; Zachary Taylor at Buena Vista; Chapultepec; the discovery of a good-sized flake of gold in a California mountain river. These things occurred in the nineteen months between Frémont's crossing of the Gate and the Treaty of Guadalupe Hidalgo. The latter confirmed the United States in its possession of Alta California and almost all else of old New Spain north of present Mexico. Four years and two months after Frémont's crossing of the Gate, Alta California became the

State of California, and Frémont one of its two first senators.
By that time, if he's tried that oared voyage again, he'd have
been in mortal peril from inrushing prows of ships in bewild-
ering numbers.

Frémont had been an honest mapmaker as well as a zealous
carry-outer of secret orders. Before California became the
thirty-first star, he submitted a "Geographical Memoir" of his
Third Expedition to the United States Congress. It paid due
regard to the Bay of San Francisco. Up to that time, the entrance to the big bay had been named only in general terms.
Those who entered or drew maps of it had used an unwieldly "La Bocana de la Ensenada de los Farallones"; "Entrance of the Famous Port of San Francisco" —also quite a
mouthful; "The channel leading to this spacious port"; "The
channel which leads into this beautiful and spacious bay"; or
plain "Entrance."

In his "Geographical Memoir," which the Senate published
in June, 1848, and the House in '49, Frémont recaptured that
vision he'd had while on his way to the spiking of the guns.
He recorded in a footnote: "Passing through this gate—called
Chrysopylae on the map, on the same principle that the harbor of Byzantium (Constantinople afterwards) was called
Chrysoceras (golden horn) . . ."

The underscoring and parentheses are Frémont's. His ac-
companying chart had it down, "Chrysopylae or Golden
Gate." Old Byzantium and modern Istanbul's Golden Horn, a
stream running into the Bosporus, is not outstandingly dra-
matic. The Bosporus or main cleavage between Asia and
Europe is much more the western gate's counterpart. But
Frémont's feeling for words was true. Golden Horn—Golden
Gate.

Frémont's trial shot of "Chrysopylae" soon was forgiven
and forgotten. The men of the Gold Rush adopted "Golden
Gate" with a whoop. With a thousand ships headed thither
and real gold the lure, why prate Greek?

So the cleft that had been missed by the early voyagers, including perhaps the *Golden Hinde,* and first sailed into by a vessel whose alternate name was *Golden Fleece,* was again at the business of prophetic nomenclature two years before gold itself was found in the back country and sensationally heralded. The triple coincidence is part of the curious mystique of the Gate.

Frémont was a man of ambition. He decided, later on, to make himself rich in lands and mines. He succeeded at first, then lost all. He determined to be President. Buchanan beat him. He marched as a major general in the Civil War. Stonewall Jackson's outriders trampled him. But in 1886, when he published his "Memoirs of My Life," he set down one item in capital letters: "I named it GOLDEN GATE."

The phrase glows, rings and bounces like a minted coin.

What the natural scene had suggested, that day in 1846 in a bobbing boat, history soon confirmed.

8 : THE GOLD SHIPS

FIRST vessel ever to enter the Golden Gate with any considerable number of passengers was the wind-borne *Brooklyn* on July 28, 1846. She was from New York for Oregon with 238 colonists, chiefly Mormons, under the leadership of a practical and worldly Latter Day Saint named Sam Brannan. San Francisco had been only three weeks under the Stars and Stripes. It was about as remote an outpost village as the globe afforded. But Sam took to it and Oregon lost a new citizen. It was Sam who, early in '48, proclaimed the gold discovery in his weekly newspaper. At that date San Francisco had about 800 people, 200 buildings of sorts and two wharves, also of sorts. It straggled over sands and barrens behind Yerba Buena Cove and was separated from the sea gate by Telegraph and Russian Hills.

East of the Rocky Mountains and the Missouri River, the young men of the nation of 23 million were home from the war in Mexico with tales to tell and robust energies still to expend. Life again was humdrum. Church twice a day on Sundays; the familiar mortgage once more to shoulder; again eyes to the furrow and the ledger—eyes that had viewed the floating islands of Xochimilco, the pyramids of Teotihuacan.

Sawmill carpenter Jim Marshall, in far-away California, found that gold. Others slipped out from San Francisco, San

44

José, Monterey, and came back with buckskin pouches of it. Word went east in military saddlebags. The news took six months or a year to seep through the thirty states. Then it burst with a prairie-fire roar. "I'm going, Ma." "Take care of the children and the farm, Molly." The boot and shoe factories of New England had been getting their cowhide from California in sluggish wind-ships such as the fellow—what was his name? Dana—had written about after spending two years before the mast. Now the hides, reshaped, started walking back on men's feet. Over the pass in the Rocky Mountains that the other fellow—Frémont—had put on his maps. Out into endless alkali deserts. Up and over more mountains.

The hide ships started back too. Some had been pushed up on tidal mud and never had thought to sail again. They and their betters, serviceable merchant and whale ships, found themselves being advertised in the papers. "FOR CALIFORNIA! The good schooner *Civilian*, 170 tons"—with a fine, lying woodcut of a full-rigged three-master—"of Chatham, will sail Oct. 20. She is owned by the 'Cochituate Company for California,' now nearly full. She is fitted up with Superior Accommodations, is a fast sailing vessel, and offers advantages equal to if not superior to any vessel that has yet been put up." Out of hundreds, the *Civilian*, which has here been mentioned at random, was almost everything she claimed. She got away from Boston a year behind many others, and swung into the Golden Gate after 142 days, which was excellent time. Her 70 people found 100,000 at the diggings ahead of them.

Weird and wonderful were the vessels that had brought many. Those brigs, barques, schooners and paddlewheelers —anything that could hoist sail or make steam—had headed out into the Atlantic and charged clear around the Americas without knowing where a spare yard of rope, barrel of pork or sack of onions was to be obtained. Some reached the Gate patched with planks hewn from the Amazon jungle, and sails

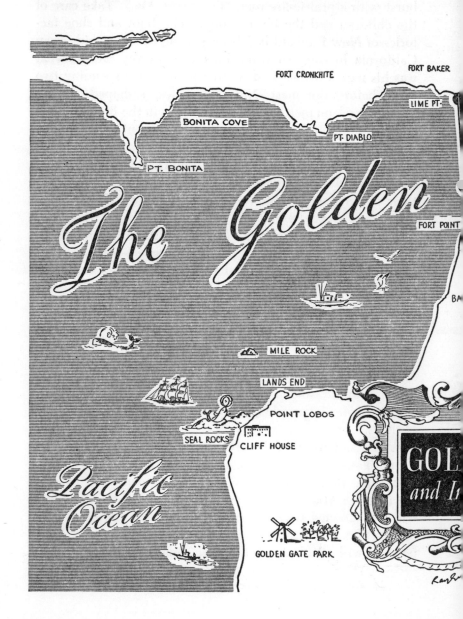

Sausalito

FORT CRONKHITE

FORT BAKER

LIME PT

BONITA COVE

PT. DIABLO

PT. BONITA

FORT POINT

The Golden

BA

MILE ROCK

LANDS END

POINT LOBOS

SEAL ROCKS

CLIFF HOUSE

GOL

and I

Pacific Ocean

GOLDEN GATE PARK

resembling lace. Some never did arrive, nor were ever heard from.

Sixty vessels departed New York for the Gate in February, '49; seventy sailed from Philadelphia and Boston; eleven from little New Bedford. Soon sails were filling from London and Liverpool and Valparaiso and Honolulu, Brest and Lisbon, Coromandel and Malabar. Sitka sent a ship down with a tiny steamer, the *Little Sitka*, on its deck. This was intended to make a fortune for its owners on the inland run to Sacramento. *Little Sitka* took six days and seven hours going the 100 miles up bay and river, and on its down trip was beaten by an ox team. Gold hunters found it faster to hire a rowboat.

As early as midsummer, '49, more than 200 square-riggers and schooners had already swarmed through the Gate. By year's end, 697 had arrived. Most of them never got off the beach. Officers and crews had gone over the side. The ships that had whipped the Horn were turned into stores, hotels and firewood.

A craft termed a "floating palace" was launched in New York for Hudson River holidaying. Her owners couldn't complete payment to her builder. Before she so much as had a trial trip, the sheriff came to the pier with attachment papers. The broad-beamed paddleboat was gone. The sheriff supposed she was out trying her machinery, so he waited. The *New World* was flexing her pistons indeed. Windows boarded up and hold and decks stocked with fuel, she was off on a two-ocean voyage with her skipper Ned Wakeman in the pilot house. She completed that bruising odyssey, every inch of it, and churned triumphantly into the Golden Gate in the spring of '49. Within, she again became a river boat and a stunningly successful one. Captain Ned was duly admired for his feat.

There was worthy Mrs. Eliza Woodson Farnham, a social worker who had spent four years as matron of Sing Sing Prison without losing her optimism. She decided, with reason, that what rowdy, masculine California needed was women, good women. She undertook to fill a brideship. She induced Editor Horace Greeley, Preacher Henry Ward Beecher and other eminents to endorse her, and made arrangements with a ship called the *Angelique*. Then she circularized for 130 intelligent, virtuous and efficient women to put to sea with her for the port of gold. Applicants were required to be over twenty, without ties, modest, chaste, and equipped with a letter of character from a clergyman, together with $250 passage money. These several hurdles, not to say girdles, proved too much for her spinster prospects. Eliza obtained only four clients, one of them her servant. When this certified virgin jumped ship at Valparaiso with a mulatto steward, Eliza went ashore to hunt down and excoriate, and the *Angelique* sailed without her. Its arrival in the Gate was a rueful one for the robustious males ashore. They had heard of its coming, and the *Daily Alta California* had whetted them with reports of a toothsome load of "Grade A spareribs."

The first steamship to poke between Points Lobos and Bonita was the *California*, a wooden sidewheeler of 1050 tons' burden. She set out from New York on October 6, 1848, cracked and repaired a cylinder cross-head while at sea, plowed through the Straits of Magellan, picked up 365 passengers of 1500 who were waiting clamorously at Panama, ran out of coal, finished with wood torn from her fittings, and steamed through the Golden Gate on a beautiful morning, February 28, 1849. There were five warships in harbor, and she threaded in and out among them, receiving salutes from all. Exulted the *Alta*, "The *California* is truly a magnificent vessel, and her fine appearance as she came in sight of the Town called forth cheer after cheer from her enraptured citizens, who were assembled in masses, upon the heights commanding a view of the bay, and in dense crowds at the principal wharves and landing places." The entire crew except one oiler boy deserted and made for the mines. She was ten weeks getting away, to return to Panama for more of those stranded Isthmus-crossers.

For the next six years, getting frantic gold-seekers up the Pacific Coast from Panama was the turbulent job of the *California* and her sister mail steamers. "Opposition" steamers also joined in the rich-quick business.

The greatest peaceful migration in history was occurring, and half of it was coming by land, half pouring in through the Golden Gate.

9 : THE NAMESAKE STEAMSHIP

PRIDE and excitement ruled at William H. Webb's great ship-yard on South Street in New York, that summer morning in 1851. The steamship that slid down the ways into East River was far larger and more sumptuous than most steamers on the Atlantic and twice as large as anything on the Pacific, for whose waters she was intended. She was 270 feet long, 40 beam, with depth of hold 21 feet, and three full decks. Her main saloon, when her cabinetmakers finished, would be grand enough for Buckingham Palace. She was built of selected, well-seasoned timbers and planks of the same sound-ness and sweetness that were going into *Challenge*, *Comet* and *Sword-Fish*, three new California clipper ships that were under construction at the moment in that same shipyard.

All autumn the shipwrights and machinists swarmed over her. Into her depths went not one but two mighty oscillating engines, with 85-inch cylinders and 9-foot stroke, connecting with a central driveshaft that in turn joined two huge wrought-iron paddlewheels, one on each side. Her coal bunkers were generous, but coal was not free and wind was, so she also had three masts, bark-rigged. She had cabins for 300 first-class passengers and sofas and steerage for 550 more. She had cost her owners, Pacific Mail Steamship Company, close to a quarter-million dollars. She was to join its other

51

steamers, *Tennessee* and *Constitution* and *Isthmus*, on the run between Panama and the port of gold. Her name befitted her destination. She was the *Golden Gate*.

She was off on her maiden voyage December 4, 1851, taking the sea track that was regularly patrolled by the steamers of various lines between New York and the Atlantic side of the Isthmus. She saw the last of them as they bent for the Caribbean. On she sped for the far eastward bulge of South America, her only companions the tall square-riggers, some as fleet as she, that trailed no smoke. She rounded the southern continent and put in at Panama seventy-two days out, gathered up her waiting quota of gold-seekers, and entered the Gate two weeks later.

The arrival of a mail steamer, then and for some years afterward, was a matter of great moment at San Francisco. As soon as one was sighted, the letter-hungry citizens queued up at the post office on the Plaza, or bought out the places of those already in line. A "telegraph" had been rigged at Point Lobos to flash any ship's first appearance on the horizon. Semaphore arms atop a two-story shack told, by code, what kind of vessel it was. Another semaphore on Telegraph Hill, watching a relay hill by spyglass, notified the town below. When Point Lobos signaled "mail steamer" this day, all poured out for hilltops and Plaza, for here came the new flagship of the mail fleet, the queen of the coal-eaters. The *Golden Gate* swept in past Fort Point and Black Point, rounded Telegraph Hill, and came to rest eighty-six days out from New York.

The *Herald* hailed her as "this magnificent steamer" and later, finding that description inadequate, called her "the steam clipper." She was praised for her "immense proportions," her "elegant accommodations" and "noble promenade deck." Fourteen months later the adjectives still were being strewn at her lively feet like roses. When she glided to her berth at Long Wharf for better than the dozenth time, the *Alta* exulted, "She came into dock like some dashing belle into a ballroom, fresh from the boudoir." When she set a new speed record up from Panama in April, 1853, of 11 days 14 hours, the *Alta* tied all its editorial whistles down to celebrate "a feat unparalleled in the history of steam upon the Pacific Coast."

Steamships of rival lines were mistaking rocks for whales and shoals for deep water and crashing or burning all up and down North America's west coast, but the vessels of the Pacific Mail were seemingly immune to life-loss. Back and forth they went, and the proudest of them was the *Golden Gate*. Immigration was at one of its flood tides that spring and summer. On May 22, 1852, she brought in 1050 passengers. For two years she tripped back and forth with ferryboat regularity, clearing about $800,000 for her owners. Briefly drydocked, she was at it again in the fall of '53, still dashing like the aforementioned belle from boudoir to ballroom without so much as catching a heel in her hem. She was joined by other new Pacific Mailers, the *John L. Stephens* of 2500 tons with two stacks and a walking beam, and the *Golden Age*, another big one from the Webb ship factory. But the *Golden Gate* remained the favorite.

But the route she traversed on her 8,000-mile roundtrips was no ferryboat course. It was over ocean: wild ocean. There could be storms, difficulties with machinery, shortage of fuel, food, drinking water. Sumptuous saloons are no comfort when a vessel is crowded with humans elbow to elbow.

On January 1, 1854, the *Golden Gate* left Panama with nearly 1,000 passengers and crew aboard. She bucked across the boisterous Gulf of Tehuantepec, where all the winds from the Caribbean pour through the low continental gaps and make playthings of ships on the Pacific. She put in at Acapulco after six rough days and picked up provisions and water and 200 tons of badly needed coal. The 305 miles she made next day put her master, Captain J. B. G. Isham, in high spirits. She was on schedule, he announced, and if this pace kept up he would present his passengers with the fastest run from Panama to Gate ever known. It was not to be. Four more days and the massive double oscillating engines stopped. The center shaft had snapped at a point that rendered one engine and its side paddle useless. She would have to continue on one wing.

Then followed a drama of the sea. While engineers cut through twenty inches of metal, the vessel heeled. For a time her milling passengers thought she would capsize. Sail was rigged to steady her and keep her from helplessly drifting. San Diego, the nearest port, was 500 miles onward. Finally her remaining engine throbbed again, the single iron paddlewheel churned, and she made her way like a wounded duck, zigging and zagging and taking seas aboard. Food again ran low. Water was rationed, half a cup per day per passenger. There was near-rioting.

She made San Diego. Water casks were filled; fifteen bullocks were brought to the beach and slaughtered; it was all the little port could do for her. The Gate that was her destination, that alone could mend her broken bones, was 800 sea miles onward. Limping, wavering and unwieldly, she continued her journey. It was a corkscrewing maneuver to keep to the harbor channel and she didn't make it. She rammed and stuck on the Point Loma shoals.

The little steamer *Goliah* was in port. It came up gamely and took the big queen's hawsers. It struggled to pull her off. Hawsers parted. Night came on, and the beginnings of a gale. The *Goliah* ran for cover; she could do nothing more.

The gale proved to be a rousing sou'-wester, a decksmasher. It bore down on the *Golden Gate* and wrenched at her planking. The passengers cowered in that saloon and, having previously half-died from fear of capsizing and the tortures of thirst, prepared to make a finished job of it. But first, as was the custom of those perilous seafaring times, they drew up and passed resolutions. They extolled Captain

Isham for his seamanly conduct in circumstances "which no human ken could anticipate or avoid." They paid tribute to their doughty ship, "this magnificent specimen of American naval architecture." No sooner seconded and passed than the ship underwent a convulsion which tore tables and chairs from their iron fastenings and sent them sliding. But, worthily, the "magnificent specimen" held together. Morning found her still alive. All day, gangs bailed and pumps strained. After a second pounding night, the gale blew itself out and the *Goliah* and two other vessels took most of the passengers off. The *Goliah* also took the precious mails. Two hundred passengers, game or broke, elected to stay with the gallant *Gate*.

San Francisco had sensed that something had happened to the overdue *Golden Gate*. When Sweeny & Baugh's semaphore at Point Lobos signaled a steamer, great was the relief. But it was only the *Goliah*, bringing 200 of the rescued passengers and those bags of mail. She'd left while the *Golden Gate* was still stranded; she had orders for spare parts and 100 skilled mechanics. The *Herald* headlined, ARRIVAL OF THE GOLIAH. THE GOLDEN GATE ASHORE! PASSENGERS AND MAILS SAVED!! PERILOUS POSITION OF ALL ON BOARD.

The hundred salvagers and the vessel's own crew got her off successfully, and once more she voyaged on one wing, zigging and lurching with what was left of her operational paddlewheel. Her welcome through the Heads of the Gate was a well-earned one, and after she returned from the Benicia drydock the *Alta* was able to announce "her lines and bearings as perfect as the day she was launched . . . we shall have the *Golden Gate* in all her former elegance, bearing no marks of injury, and with proof now firmly established that she is one of the strongest steamers afloat."

She was indeed, for the next eight years. She had come through all her voyages and vicissitudes without loss of a life from perils of the sea. The proud record was still shared by all Pacific Mailers, though they'd had wrecks galore. But then the luck ran out.

The *Golden Gate* cleared from her wharf and set out the Golden Gate on a midsummer day, Captain William H. Hudson on the bridge above the paddlewheels, and Fleet Captain R. H. Pearson also aboard. On Sunday evening, July 27, 1862, the sea was smooth, the heat of the tropics oppressive, the passengers languorous, the ladies lightly but elegantly clad. They were passing the Mexican shore so closely that they could see the picturesque rocks and green hills fifteen miles north of Manzanillo. At 4:30 P.M., with a thunderstorm approaching and relief from the heat in sight, there was a cry of "Fire!" A curtain of flame, starting in the kitchens, swept sternward. The helmsman at once set course for shore. The vessel's speed fanned the flames. They swept aft, preventing the launching of most of the lifeboats. Many persons plunged over and swam for it. Wind raised rough seas and lightning flashed. About 265 persons, including many women and children, perished.

In her ten years the *Golden Gate* had brought perhaps 50,000 people to the Golden Gate, and almost as many away from it. Her passing was a national calamity flamboyantly recorded by the color brushes of Currier & Ives.

10 : THE INCREDIBLE CLIPPERS

MARCH 30, 1849, brought an unusual early-spring crowd to the battery ramparts and the terraces of New York's Castle Garden. Reports of California gold had reached the Atlantic in such volume that one of the fine new China clippers had been diverted from that sure traffic in tea and silks and was now about to try for the Golden Gate. Her crew was aboard and, sober, drunk or just dizzy, were flinging out her canvas to the morning sun. A light, graceful, sharp and purposeful ship, that *Memnon*; off the ways at Smith & Dimon's only the year before; Captain George Gordon a driver; if anyone could bring the Pacific Coast to New York's doorstep, he could. Would he reach the Gate in five months, in six? Sharp commands came across the water, followed by a sailors' chanty. Anchor chains thumped. Main and afteryards were braced to the wind, five tiers of sail were laid to the sky, and the 1000-ton *Memnon* was off, first of her breed to try for the golden prize. On July 28 she entered the Gate, and her time was only three days more than the Gate's first steamship from the Atlantic five months earlier. One hundred and twenty days! Full-built ships—not clippers—took up to three-quarters of a year.

The harvest reaped by the *Memnon*, with an iron nail worth a pinch of gold dust, a quart of whiskey $25, and coffee

and sugar $3 a pound, was enough in freight tariffs to build
another like her outright. Small wonder every shipyard on the
Atlantic began to build clippers, those sleek fast pickerel of
the sea, for the California trade; or that the world's greatest
age of sail had just been opened. In ten amazing years, starting in 1850, with hammers ringing and keels splashing from
Maine to Richmond, 160 of the tall slim beauties hit the sea,
every one Golden-Gate bound. Elegantly fitted though they
were, and proud as princesses, they were not passenger car-
riers to any extent. They were freighters. They carried beef
and pork, its shippers hoping to reap $50 a barrel; they bore
cowhide boots, anticipating $50 a pair; and $10 or $15 picks
and shovels. The Golden Gate was their goal but the golden
fleece was already in their holds, if they could beat each other
to the frequently bare but often glutted market. It was a
voyage for the daring, the able and the lucky, and every trip
a race.

The time made by the *Memnon* was the record for one
year. Then the *Celestial*, built expressly for that wishbone-
shaped race course around the continents, stormed through
the Gate only 104 days out of New York. Yet even while she
was at sea, her time had been bettered by a full week. The
black-hulled, low-lying, rake-masted *Sea Witch*, 890 tons,
had driven her dragon figurehead to the Gate in 97 days,
whipping the ocean-to-ocean time of Pacific Mail's first three
steamships by 20, 16 and 5 days respectively.

Sea Witch is one of the immortals of Yankee clipperdom.
But even her fast time was soon to be beaten. Shaping up for
the twelvemonth following was the greatest maritime race in
history.

Stir was great and betting high in New York's Astor House
and San Francisco's El Dorado Bar, that spring of 1851.
Eight clippers of championship promise were about to cut
long white furrows to the port of gold. The time of each
from Atlantic departure point to Golden Gate would not be

known in New York until many weeks after arrival within the heads of the Gate, creating mounting suspense. For owners, designers and builders, fortune and glory were at stake. To everyone else in the eastern seaboard city it was a horse race for the gods.

First away was *Seaman*, a smart little 546-ton ship out of Baltimore. She had left two days before Christmas but was at sea when the new year started. She skimmed around the Horn before its season of heavy gales struck, caught the favoring winds of the Pacific, and dashed blithely through the Gate 107 days out. Sweeny & Baugh's semaphores on Point Lobos and Telegraph Hill gave her appropriate welcome.

Next in at the Gate was *Surprise*, the Boston-built masterpiece of Samuel Hall, gilded eagle flying at her prow. She had been through bitter blows but under the almost invincible Captain Philip Dumaresq she had tossed 16,308 miles behind her and had reefed topsails just twice. The freight on the merchandise in her hold grossed her owners $78,000, enough to build another like her. Arriving March 19, she was 96 days from Sandy Hook. Let anyone equal *that*.

Third in was *Sea Serpent*, 115 days plus a refitting delay at Valparaiso. She had carried sail that had all but lifted her out of the water, and had lost much of it and some spars off Tierra del Fuego.

Eclipse, 112 running days, came in three days later. She too had lost top hamper off the Cape. *Stag-Hound* followed, logging 107 running days. Six days out from New York she'd lost maintopmast and three topgallant masts and had been without considerable of her upper canvas for a dozen days.

Witchcraft backed her stays and dropped hook behind Telegraph Hill on August 11—103 days. These were sensational running times, better by two to four months than had been made by full-built, conservatively masted ships of '49. *N. B. Palmer* drove through the Gate on August 21 with a passage of 108 days. And then—

And then, on the last day of August, the last of the group to set forth but winner by a margin that was to be remembered for the next hundred years, came Captain Josiah Creesy's *Flying Cloud*. Three days out from New York she'd lost her main and mizzen topgallant masts and had sent replacements up. Next, she had sprung her mainmast and made repairs at sea. In thunder and lightning and raging winds her fore and main topsails split—Joe Creesy was no man to take a washing off the line for a bit of a squall—and again the mainmast sprung. Sullen sailors he'd clapped in irons were let out to help fist that leaping canvas. Cape Horn was covered with snow and the wind sufficient to blow the whiskers off a skipper's face, but around that mighty pylon of the globe the *Flying Cloud* sped. She turned in a single day's run of 374 miles, the fastest ever made up to that date under sail or steam. Joe could stand the pace but his chief officer couldn't. One more hatful of such wind and the ship would lie flat on a high mountainside of South America. When the officer began cutting the ropes with a knife to trade canvas for lives, Captain Joe clapped him too in irons, and when a fore topgallant mast toppled he sent up another. And here were the Pacific—the Equator—Latitude 37° North. "Six A.M. August 31. Made South Farallones bearing northeast ½ east; took a pilot at 7; anchored in San Francisco harbor at 11:30 A.M. after a passage of 89 days, 21 hours."

Flying Cloud, handiwork of Donald McKay of East Boston, the Duncan Fyfe of American shipbuilders, equaled that time again three years later, and *Andrew Jackson* from Irons & Grinnell of Mystic did it in 1860 as a salute to a dying age. After that closing year of a dazzling decade, most of the clippers, strained and weary, plodded the seas under shortened masts. *Flying Cloud* herself went out as a flaming torch at St. John, New Brunswick, in 1874.

Another great race of 1851 began in August, a three-ply affair in which *Typhoon, Raven* and (again) *Sea Witch* started all in the same week, were rarely out of sight of each other, and dashed in through the Golden Gate within a blanketing 48 hours—their times, *Raven* 105 from Boston Light, big *Typhoon* 106 and seldom-beaten *Sea Witch* 110, both from Sandy Hook.

Between these two sets of contestants there had been another, but her conflict had all been inboard. *Challenge,* from the Webb yards on East River, carrying 12,000 square yards of canvas and a 97-foot mainmast and with a hold measured for 2006 registered tons of cargo, was commanded by resolute old-school R. H. Waterman and manned by as ruffianly a crew as ever had to be quelled with a belaying pin. Fifty of the fifty-six, though they shipped as sailors, were the dregs of European and New York alleys headed for the gold fields. First day out, sea bags were searched and enough iron knuckle-dusters, bowie knives and pistols thrown overboard to serve a Central American revolution. Off Rio de Janeiro, Mate Douglas was attacked by four whose knives hadn't been discovered and the skipper, hearing the scuffle, snatched an iron pin and laid about as if it were a baseball bat. Score, two corpses. After that, all officers carried revolvers every time they stepped on deck. Off Cape Horn, three half-frozen sailors fell from the yards and were killed. With but six of his remaining half-hundred skilled enough to steer a ship, Captain Waterman drove on, shot into the Gate, rounded to and dropped anchor 108 days from New York.

Many another valorous passage was to ensue, but 1852 brought a record to stand for all time beside that of *Flying Cloud. Sovereign of the Seas* set it. She too was from the hand of Donald McKay. The man on her quarterdeck was Lauchlan McKay, a titan among titans and one to get several times the utmost out of any ship built by his brother. *Sovereign of the Seas* was a big ship, her hold stuffed with a 2,950-ton cargo, length 258 feet, breadth 44—a mighty platform built to carry stupendous sail. Launched in June, she sailed for the

Golden Gate in August and it was the only voyage she ever made there, for later she went into the Australian trade. But before that first round-trip voyage was finished, the feats she did! She arrived at the Gate in 102 days, earning $84,000; the flour in her hold fetched $44 a barrel. Then she swung out the Gate for the "Sandwich Islands," where she picked up sperm oil from the whalers, and headed home via Samoa and the Horn. On this leg in the southern latitudes, with Lauchlan McKay trumpeting orders to the highest yard, she ran off the amazing mileage of an average of 330 miles a day for eleven days, 378 per day for four of them, and on March 18, 1853, logged 411 miles in one 24-hour day. No vessel, sail or steam, had ever remotely approached that. *Sovereign* sailed for Malacca Straits in '59 and was wrecked forever.

To the Josiah Creesys, Bob Watermans and Lauchlan Mc-Kays of that decade of glory must be added another lustrous name and a gentler one, but equally as determined: Mary Patten's. She was the wife of Captain Joshua Patten of Maine. She was a beautiful lady, refined, soft-spoken and church-going, and she often sailed with her husband and darned his socks for him. She sailed with him in *Neptune's Car* in '56. Winter was all it was advertised to be, down off Cape Horn. Captain Patten had to toss his chief officer in the brig and keep to the quarterdeck all hours himself. He was the only one on duty who could shoot the sun, except his wife. From exhaustion and exposure, he fell ill and was stricken blind. Mary Patten, age twenty-four, immediately took command of the heavily masted, 1600-ton clipper. With the help of an illiterate second mate she handled that vessel for fifty days, besides nursing her dying husband. And she brought it into the Gate as neatly as "knit one, purl two." All the annals of the sea hold no finer achievement.

A railroad across the Isthmus of Panama, completed in 1855, gave the clippers freight competition that knocked down their rates. Prices in general plunged in '57, further disrupting the shipping business. Then came the Civil War, followed by completion of the Suez Canal and the first overland railroad, changing the world's traffic patterns. By '55 the clippers' brief day was fading and by '69 it was all over.

Sober truth is that those canvas kites converging on the Gate were not all white and gleaming. If they honestly reflected doings on the decks below, they often should have been grey or black. From Gold-Rush days right along to 1906, when old San Francisco went down in quake and up in smoke, bitter was the lot of fo'c'sle hands. Pay was low. Hours were unending. Brutality was frequent. So grim was the life that most young men preferred jobs ashore in almost any calling. To get crews, shipmasters east and west turned to the crimps. A many-port pattern of forced recruiting gained its name and its fanciest capers in the town beside the Gate: the pleasantry called shanghaiing. Many a man on the street or in a tavern was simply kidnapped. Knockout drops and trapdoors in saloon floors are repeatedly mentioned in old annals. However collected, gangs including various non-seamen were produced aboard ship just at sailing time. Thereafter, discipline was ruthless. Shipmasters possessed more power than Caesar's, and some of them abused it. New England captains whose drive and daring made their names legendary may have been plate-passers in church at home, but at sea they wore forked tails and horns. Men were slugged by bucko mates, triced up, flogged. In at least one hideous instance slow performers were shot while in the rigging, or lowered over the bows into wave after wave of icy water. No, all was not beauty on the *Rainbow*, piety on the *Crusader*, or glamor on the *Glory of the Seas*.

But during the two-decade reign of the Yankee clipper, one phase of human achievement reached zenith. From Persian Gulf dhows and Phoenician galleys it had advanced to Portuguese caravel and Atlantic packet. And then all at once, these five and six tiers of canvas, leaping for the cleft in the California coastline that had been discovered only one long life-time before!

There used to be a wide-verandaed brick building on Rincon Hill behind the San Francisco Embarcadero. It had been built in the Gold Rush as a marine hospital. When I knew it, it was a dilapidated pile furnishing food and shelter to sea-men. It had one treasure, a register of ship arrivals through-out the Clipper Age. The peglegged superintendent of the home, J. P. Fitzgerald, would bring it out and open it for me, a young waterfront reporter, and we would turn its pages and read those magic entries. How they filled the shabby office with fresh wind, tropic sun, stinging spray, howling gale and the quarterdeck trumpetings of iron-willed masters! Here, as if coming straight in through the Gate, were *Rainbow, Race Horse, Sea Witch, Challenge* and *Flying Cloud; Stag-Hound, Tornado* and *Witchcraft; Comet, Herald of the Morning,* beautiful *Typhoon*—she had been launched with all masts, spars and rigging in place and pennons flying. Here were *Flyaway, Mandarin, Sweepstakes, Young America.* Here came *Flying Fish, Westward Ho, John Gilpin, Twilight* and *Dashing Wave.* Here were *Houqua*: she foundered in a China Sea typhoon in '65; *Samuel Russell,* wrecked in Gaspar Straits in '70; *Trade Wind,* sunk by a collision in the Atlantic in '54; *Nightingale,* that ended up as a slave ship under the Brazilian flag; and *Phantom,* lost on Pirates Shoal in '62, whose skipper Henry Sargent made the 200 miles to Hong Kong in an open boat and obtained command of a bark there which promptly vanished in a typhoon off Yokohama.

We would read for an hour, then carefully put the register away. Tugs and liners and a few remaining windjammers would lie at the wharves below us. But none could take us on a cruise to compare with the voyaging we just had done, seated on the shoulders of the lady in white and gold drapery who figureheaded the *Sea Witch,* or riding the gilt neck of the great wing-spread eagle of the *Surprise.*

Head in the clouds, I'd get back to work, boarding and searching for news in every vessel from China Basin to Meiggs Wharf, and pausing to watch the carved bald head of Mayor Jim Rolph being affixed atop the wooden figure of the Earl of Clarendon. His Honor owned several ships of British origin and the winds of the sea still powered them. But I was looking for *Romance of the Sea,* that had departed the Gate for the coast of China fifty-two years before and never had been heard from since.

Clipper Ship

11 : BELLIGERENT STEAM

A CURIOUS incident, about as soundless as a cat's tread, occurred at a Golden Gate dockside one May night in 1854. A sheriff's deputy, who was on board the brig *Vesta* to see that she didn't sail without paying a $350 attachment, was asked to step below. For coffee, or settlement of the claim? Deputy followed messenger down the ladder. In the ship's cabin he was welcomed by several men, some of them decorated with old knuckle-duster and saber scars, some mere fuzzy-cheeked boys. One, a taut-faced hundred-pounder with a blond beard and a high voice, signed the deputy to be seated. He gestured his invitation with a pistol. The deputy knew him well; knew his awesome reputation. Running feet were heard overhead, the thud of rope, the chug and bumping of a hard-nosed tug. It was 1 A.M. Men paraded through the cabin, dragging bags and haversacks, looking for handy places for their bedding. Every one had a rifle and a couple of navy revolvers and a sheath knife. Cortez or Henry Morgan would have welcomed the lot. They numbered about fifty.

The sheriff's deputy decided that the creditor's $350 didn't matter. He drank his coffee, wished William Walker and his merry band well, and thankfully departed down a rope ladder to the tug when the *Vesta* was outside the Heads.

66

William Walker and his filibusters were off through the Gate, the van of 3,500 adventurers, to capture Nicaragua.

Filibustering was a popular sport in the '40's and '50's. Essentially it was a carry-over of what the Spanish had started in 1519 and wreaked from Mexico to Peru. It was freebooting, nineteenth-century model, which meant with Sharpe's breech-loading rifles instead of musketoons, and without the cassocked friars. In William Walker's case it had overtones of Montgomery Street and Wall Street business. It was part of a fight for control of the steamship traffic between the two coasts. Before he finished, 3,000 followers and others would be dead in the swamps and jungles, and Commodore Cornelius Vanderbilt would be owner of several currently competing steamer lines, including the first and longest-lived of them all, Pacific Mail.

To explain William Walker, it is necessary to sketch the steamship picture. Three long years before gold was discovered in an electrifying way in California, Oregon was attracting settlers. Covered wagons were grooving the Oregon Trail. The settlers had sent a petition to Washington asking for a steamship mail-service. This, in view of the small population, was like a shot at the moon. But Congress granted it. The Oregon country had just been won after hot dispute with the British, and the United States was determined to hold it.

So there was to be one line of steamers from New York to the Atlantic side of the Isthmus and another from the Pacific side up the coast, and the mailbags could fly, walk or swim the intervening fifty miles. George Law and others formed the United States Mail Steamship Company to operate the Atlantic leg. That on the Pacific went to W. H. Aspinwall, a New Yorker who was already doing business with the Isthmus. The combined mail subsidies were to be $440,000 yearly —an astonishing sum, for it would have bought almost every house, barn and rail fence in Oregon.

Aspinwall contracted to carry one steamer-mail a month. To do so he ordered the construction of three steamers. This was a solid year before any quivering of a westward gold rush. Portland was the destination. San Francisco, which was in territory just conquered, and which Mexico had not yet ceded by treaty, wasn't even mentioned.

But that unforeseen Gold-Rush passenger-traffic explosion took place while Pacific Mail's first steamer was still churning around South America. It quickly resulted in several savagely competing steamship lines from Panama north. These in turn soon had competition from an alternate route through Nicaragua. Cornelius Vanderbilt of New York had plans there for a sea-to-sea canal, and until his canal should be in being he had his Accessory Transit Company, which ran ships down to Greytown on the Caribbean, and inland steamers and connecting mule strings to San Juan del Sur on the Pacific, with steamships thence to the Gate. The route was shorter than the Panama way from Sandy Hook to Golden Gate by many miles. On paper, it appeared to offer more comfort for the traveler. Commodore Vanderbilt had an agent in San Francisco, C. K. Garrison, who did more than sell tickets. He was a steamship man of ability and Vanderbilt paid him, it was said, $60,000 a year. In '52 that sum would have paid off a sizable chunk of the national debt. Garrison was in banking as well as ships and forwarding. An old steamboatman from the Mississippi, he had another steamboatman, Charles Morgan, for banking partner in the New York and New Orleans ends of the business.

Privately, Garrison had a notion to possess that Nicaragua route for himself. In '54 he was forty-five years of age, a personable man with a long, slightly lumpy nose, hair that flared like a violinist's, a short neck and a chin that sank into his cravat. He had been mayor of San Francisco and given his salary away to the Protestant and Catholic orphanages. His popularity was great. His personal ambitions were sweeping.

His partner, Charles Morgan, no descendant of Henry the Buccaneer but worthy to pull on one of Henry's jackboots if he had to, was aware of these ambitions and in accord with them.

Cornelius Vanderbilt had won his handle of "Commodore" by running and owning ferry boats from Staten Island to New York. He had extended his steam operations by water and land. His high forehead held a scheming brain, his eyes were unsmiling, his side-whiskers flew like spray from the paddles of his new liner *Brother Jonathan,* his chin was blunt and solid as a billiard ball. He conducted prayers at nine every evening. The rest of his hours were less godly. He was no man to be pushed off a dime that he considered his'n.

Cornelius Kingsland Garrison in San Francisco; his partner Charles Morgan in New York; Cornelius Vanderbilt in New York. The scene of their approaching power struggle 2,500 and 3,000 miles distant from the countingrooms of either faction. Garrison-Morgan and Vanderbilt would be where the rattle of arms, the screams of wounded men, the smoke of sacked towns and the stench of death wouldn't be noticed.

William Walker was a Tennesseean who had won both medical and law degrees at twenty-one and tossed both aside. He had been a newspaper editor in New Orleans, had reached the Gate in 1850 and become editor of the *Herald;* and even newspapering in that era of pistol-packing journalism was too tame for him. He had already made one trial run. He had sailed out the Golden Gate with a hundred fellow adventurers to see if he could capture a couple of the states of Mexico. He did take La Paz in Lower California, then Sonora, and almost took Sinaloa before he was driven out, only thirty-four of his tattered band making it back across the border. Walker had returned to San Francisco and newspaper work, and spent two years perfecting the next adventure. When ready, he began advertising for three hundred "colonists" who would follow him to Nicaragua, where there was a convenient revo-

lution going on. His ads advised that his recruits would be
"liable for military duty."

The town by the Gate had its full share of restless men
who had failed at the placer mines, at business, or at sailoring,
and were at loose ends. Walker, the natural-born trouble-
maker, was a crackling leader. He had unquestionable military brilliance and the conscience of a wolverine. Nobody
objected to his organizing a band for the armed invasion of a
neighbor republic. If he wanted to rid the city of its rowdiest
malcontents, only Nicaragua was the loser. When the *Vesta*
sailed, Walker had able financial backers, for he was a good
talker and the enterprise handily suggested profits to come.
That he could be used in the steamship war was obvious. So
behind the *Vesta* were vessels with reinforcements. Nicaragua, with fertile lands and great mineral promise and an almost continuous water route from Caribbean to Pacific, was
a handsome prize and Walker was prepared to risk much and
pay high for it. His "army" was uniformed, each man was a
walking arsenal—those Sharpe's rifles used cartridge ammunition and worked fast and hit hard—and he had a brass band
to beguile the natives who didn't require shooting. He had
been in correspondence with one of the revolutionary fac-
tions. He would drive all before him from sea to sea. He
would be a second Pizarro.

Nicaragua, twelve degrees above the Equator, presented
to the Pacific a 200-mile shoreline backed by a façade of vol-
canoes. The *Vesta* arrived at San Juan del Sur and Walker's
"Falange Americana," reinforced with natives, marched at
once to attack Rivas, the country's largest town. The Sharpe's
rifles routed 1000 defenders, killing 150, at a loss of six Americans including Walker's second-in-command. Walker was
scraped by a ball across his left temple, gouging an eyebrow.
A few days later he killed 160, losing nine. He pretended to
retreat on San Juan, feinted Nicaragua's governmental forces

"It's a wild headland. Point Reyes' Light is at the northern end of Gulf of the Farallones, the anteroom to the Golden Gate. Drakes Bay is the cove at the top of the picture."

San Francisco Maritime Museum

"And then, by a margin to be remembered, came Captain Josiah Creesy's *Flying Cloud*," 89 days from Sandy Hook to Golden Gate.

San Francisco Maritime Museum

"Her original name was *Balclutha*. She was the last full-rigger of the large Alaska Packers' fleet."

A steamship and a whale pile up on Lands End.

A modern steamer makes a slight mistake.

"The fog comes in—an army of ghostly sky-riders; a charging, trampling herd of formless wraiths."

Mile Rock, "the lonesomest lighthouse in America, because only a sea biscuit throw from a lively city."

"An unspoiled and unique forest within four or five beeline miles of a major town. Just north of the Gate."

out of position, counterattacked, and stormed the capital city of Granada. This stronghold had been withstanding a siege of revolutionaries for thirteen months. Walker took it with fourteen casualties. The barefoot Nicaraguans looked upon this slight, tense, carnage-loving man out of the North with awe. Now he was "Walker the Liberator." He was also, by this time, Garrison & Morgan's private skewer poised for Vanderbilt's ribs. For a year and a half he ranged the country, military man one day, politician the next. Letters from his lieutenants went back to the San Francisco press and his successes did not lack Homers. The mosquitoes and cholera weren't mentioned. The steamship *Sierra Nevada* brought more recruits down from the Gate, and several heavy field pieces. In spite of losses he now had 200 American fighting men. Holding the capital, he installed himself as generalissimo of the little nation's army. For the present he did not interfere in any way with the lucrative transit of passengers between the oceans or with Vanderbilt's interests. Completely lulled, the Commodore went off to Europe on his yacht. When he came back, he didn't have stock control of his Accessory Transit Company any longer. His agents, Garrison & Morgan, had it.

When he realized what had been done to him, the Commodore erupted like Nicaragua's Momotombo volcano. "I won't sue you—the law's too slow. I'll ruin you!" he shouted.

Garrison in San Francisco and Morgan in New Orleans further strengthened their forces with men, rifles, artillery and shells. Walker's forces grew to 600, to 1000 Americans. Down from New York came Vanderbilt emissaries with counteroffers of size and glitter. Still unsure about where Walker stood, they proposed that he throw Garrison & Morgan out of Nicaragua in favor of a new Vanderbilt line. The little filibuster with the big sword then told them how it was. Since December '55 he had been working for Garrison and Morgan.

While Vanderbilt raged, the bedazzled Nicaraguans elected
General William Walker president of their republic.

Vanderbilt wasn't just blowing his whiskers. A gifted ma-
nipulator of men, steamships, railroads and governments, he
set the armies of Costa Rica marching on Walker, and he sent
men and munitions to help them. Walker defeated them at
practically every turn. He was a master tactician, perhaps
one of the best alive. But Vanderbilt was a strategist, and
while tactics win battles, strategy wins campaigns. He
pointed out to the British, who didn't love Walker, that
Walker was a threat to British Honduras. The British swung
a man o'war into Greytown harbor and nipped off all Morgan reinforcements that were trying to get through. Then a
new Secretary of War in Washington, Jefferson Davis, sent a
warship to lie off San Juan del Sur on the Pacific side and nip
off Garrison-sent reinforcements from the Gate.

The Costa Ricans claimed that Greytown belonged to them,
and fought hard for it. Hondurans and San Salvadoreans
poured into the fray. Walker found himself fighting Vanderbilt, Britain and much of Central America. With passenger
service across Nicaragua completely stopped, and help for
Walker not getting through, Garrison and Morgan threw in
their hand. With an army of 7000 marching against him, and
his own band decimated and redecimated, Walker retreated
on San Juan. The captain of the *U.S.S. Saint Mary's* took him
and his surviving 463, including 170 sick and wounded, to
Panama.

Vanderbilt had won his shortcut route back, but it was
valueless. The Panama Railroad had been completed and
there was no longer any need to trek by inland waters between Nicaragua's coasts. Vanderbilt moved swiftly over his
divided foes and snatched the Pacific Mail itself for his financial empire.

William Walker sailed once more. He attempted to seize
Honduras. He captured its chief town, Trujillo. Again a Brit-

ish warship appeared. Sharpe's rifles were no match for broad-side guns. Walker surrendered, was turned over to the Hondurans, and was shot.

The United States, in that swashbuckling era, had sent south a full gaggle of little Napoleons with waving swords. Walker's had been the deadliest. Central America was tired of the lot. So was the Gate.

Departure of a Steamship

12 : HONEST MEIGGS AND
HIS WHARF

HENRY MEIGGS was a kindly-looking man with a high forehead, Washingtonian nose and gentle mouth that constantly
wore a half-formed smile. His deep-set eyes had a brooding
look as if set on pious matters. But he was a money-maker.
At twenty-four he'd acquired a moderate fortune as a lumber
dealer and builder in New York. In 1848, at thirty-seven—
ripely middle-aged for that era, if not positively elderly—he
set sail for the Golden Gate with its first shipload of lumber.
Since a single board was worth several dollars at the gold
port, statements that he made 2,000 per cent on his venture
seem reasonable. And when he looked about and saw the
immense trees that were growing within a few days' haul of
sail, he began erecting sawmills.

That wasn't all. As an early-bird Forty-Niner he set up
what was perhaps San Francisco's first commercial laundry.
The prevailing rate for doing shirts was eight dollars a dozen
and a consignment had to travel clear to China and back, for
the argonauts were willing enough to wash silt for gold dust
but not at all interested in soshing each other's duds. Meiggs
(rhymes with eggs) saw a handsome profit going to waste.
He discovered a large pork-barrel that had come around the
Horn with a ship's provisions and bought it for eight dollars.
Then he located a hefty Australian woman with two strap-

74

ping daughters. He engaged the three to function as San Francisco's first washing machine. The gals, suitably peeled down, took turns in the barrel treading the customers' washing like vintners pressing grapes. Too much soda in the first batch ate chunks out of the clothes and burned the operators' feet, closing down the washhouse for days; but popular demand and a good-sized cheering section got them back into the tub and the Australian pistons again worked majestically.

Yes, Harry Meiggs was a natural money-maker, and widely admired for it.

What brings him into this narrative is the interest he took in the undeveloped North Beach section of the gold port, fronting on the Gate. This was a district about a mile north and west of the rising town, which had erected its shelters in the lee of Telegraph Hill. A considerable lagoon lay in Meiggs' way. But he saw a future for North Beach. He bought acreage there and erected a sawmill and a planing mill, and in 1853 ran a pretentious wharf out over Tonquin Shoal at the foot of "Lumber Street," between Powell and Mason. Sixteen hundred feet long, this wharf reached to deep water and became a landmark that endured for eighty years. Upon it, Meiggs' lumber schooners and sloops discharged timber from his logging camps and mills up the coast. The first important wharf that any vessel tied up to or passed on its way in through the Gate, it was three and a half miles inland from the Gate's portal and directly opposite Alcatraz Island. It is the site, in part, of Fisherman's Wharf of today.

The wharf represented a goodly outlay, and Harry Meiggs was equal to it. His sales of lumber to the growing metropolis were handsome, and were helped by the six successive townwide fires that leveled everything not made of brick. To grind out beams and boards fast enough, Meiggs erected a dozen mills. He grew portly. He was open-handed. His affability made him widely popular. He went into politics, became an alderman. He had been followed west by a brother, John C.

Meiggs, and he helped Brother John become town comptroller.

Harry's snowballing enterprises made him a busy borrower. The real estate he'd acquired around and below the north and west sides of Telegraph Hill didn't move quite as he'd expected. No doubt he also took other expensive fliers; it was a speculative age. But as his credit stretched, so did his smile. He was hail-fellow to everybody. If he worried, nobody guessed it. He sold quantities of lumber for sewering, side-walking and street paving. He took payments from the city in scrip. The bankers and merchants of the day readily accepted these city warrants as collateral for more borrowing. He got hold of a book of warrants that the mayor and the comptroller had signed in blank. These he filled in and cashed without any trouble, for he was widely known as Honest Harry. On a propitious day in 1855 he went sailing on the chartered brig *American*, which was stocked with foods and wines of the finest. He sailed out the Golden Gate, leaving behind him that wharf, those sawmills, an astonished brother, a city treasurer who had been personally duped of $20,000, his laundresses, and bankers and merchants who screamed that they had been taken for a million.

For decades that stretched on into the twentieth century, Meiggs Wharf continued to gather fragrant lumber shipments that came down from the north coast; to collect barnacles and borers; and to assemble legends. Many were the characters who spent their hours or even their lives there: sailors home from the sea, whitehallers, beachcombers, lookout men for the Marine Exchange, the men of the steamer *Bear*, which sailed annually for the Arctic to carry doctors and the flag and to read weddings, come summers, over the Eskimos who thought they needed it; the men of the Customs cutter and the Quarantine cutter; the Immigration men; and the local fishing fleet. So large did the latter become that a hollow square of fishing boat berths was built adjoining Meiggs Wharf and the wharf itself took on various extensions that ran broadside to the Gate, and so the smells of halibut, sole and crabs were added to the resinous perfumes of fir from the Columbia and cedar from Port Orford. In the 1930's, Meiggs Wharf was whacked out of shape by a construction of new docks including the immense Pier 45 and the present-day Fisherman's Wharf with its restaurants. The whole area where the crab cauldrons boil and the souvenir shops flourish is right atop the fill and piling that have effaced Meiggs Wharf, San Francisco's early-day front porch out into the Gate.

As for Honest Harry, it would be satisfying to one's sense of justice to state that he was pursued over sea and land by those three indignant washerwomen, and collared and dragged back; that he was hauled through the streets of the town he had bilked, and jailed in the prison brig at San Quentin Point.

It wasn't that way. Quite the contrary. He had run away from his debts, but he still could plan. He landed in Chile, some say with a fortune; Meiggs himself said with only $8,200, and when that was gone he had to pawn his watch. He took construction contracts for a couple of short-line local railroads. In five months he was Valparaiso's business leader. He tackled the building then of a 116-mile Valparaiso-Santiago line. He hired 8,000 men, divided the job into sections, put his superintendents and subcontractors on a dollar-a-yard bonus for beating the construction schedule, and had the railroad running in two years—well ahead of time. He was a good employer. He put up hospitals and decent barracks, organized a sound commissary, paid high wages. He became a South American hero. Peru sought his services. Would Don Enrique, the Norteamericano who got things done, kindly build a railroad up and over the Andes and down to the headwaters of the Amazon? Peru had the money. It had obtained a fat loan, $50 million, from Paris bankers for granting them a monopoly of its exports of guano.

Here was a project that figuratively and literally took the

breath away. Harry would, and did. He arrived in Lima, Peru, just as California's "Big Four" railroad builders, Stanford, Huntington, Hopkins and Crocker, were completing their Central Pacific over the Sierra. That first high-line railroad had climbed 7,000 feet. What Don Enrique undertook was to cross a range twice as high. He carried the line to a dizzy 14,665 feet, laying an iron thoroughfare between Peru and Bolivia. He created so many well-paying jobs that he headed off one or two South American revolutions. He was asked to build a second Andean-topping line to northward. That one really called for an iron horse with wings. It started at Callao, made the seven miles to Lima over Meiggs' own land, within sixty miles of the Pacific had climbed 15,300 feet, and continued on by precipice brinks, bridges and thirty-two tunnels to the crest of the cordillera at 17,000 feet. He wanted to reach the Cerro de Pasco copper and silver district by feeder line and continue the main line clear across Brazil to the Atlantic, but he didn't live to make it.

He had handled $120 million worth of construction contracts and built the highest standard-gauge railroad the world had ever seen. He had bought up and paid off all those fraudulent California warrants that he could locate. When Chicago burned up in 1871, he was the largest individual contributor to its refugees' relief. He died, an expatriate but still a citizen of the United States, in 1877. The California legislature had forgiven him for past errors and had cordially invited him to come home. The projects he had in hand didn't permit it. A grandee of Spanish America, he is buried under a big stone in Peru and is remembered with honor.

For the next sixty years after his passing, tides continued to swish past "Meiggs' Folly," as his wharf had been called when he built it.

Whatever his local sins, he was the man who brought the town out from hiding under Telegraph Hill and planted a part of it directly on the edge of the Gate.

13 : THE GATE'S TWO
   HINGE-POSTS

THE Gate's northeast corner, or "Head," is Point Bonita, a promontory of unbelievable thinness and delicacy under which the sea roars and tunnels completely through. This finger of black-brown rock thrusts out from Marin County for half a mile. At one point it is only as thick as a man's outspread arms and at another it recently disappeared altogether and has been replaced by a 165-foot suspension footbridge. Although its western or weather face takes the sea's brunt, its laughingly-styled lee face is also heavily battered. Outgoing tides and constant eddies gnaw at it. In present time the approach to the lighthouse out on the end was narrowed by erosion to a shelving trail, scarcely three feet wide, scratched along a thundering drop of 100 feet. The government spent $100,000 making life and limb again safe for something else besides goats.

The all-important lighthouse, fog signal and radio-beacon out on the tip are probably the only installation of the kind in the country which is approached, first of all, by a lengthy tunnel. This was hewn through the rock years ago by Chinese labor, working with pick, wheelbarrow and black powder.

Though the experience of reaching the tip of Point Bonita is one of great reward, it has to be something of a labor of

79

love. Difficulties for the visitor begin at the north end of the Golden Gate Bridge. A padlocked wire gate to a posted military reservation offers the first rebuff. Having turned away from that, the Bonita-seeker dives under Highway 101 toward Sausalito, finding only a ganglion of roadways and not much in the way of directions. (A Coast Guard officer in his search for the way to Bonita made the wrong turn at this point and found himself back on the bridge, which he had to stay on until he again reached the toll plaza and paid two more tolls.) But after the way to "Fort Cronkhite" is successfully picked out, the traveler finds himself in a one-way tunnel, low, narrow, ancient of days and half a mile long, beyond which a sign happily says "Welcome." It adds, however, a stern injunction about 15 m.p.h., which is always advisable to obey in a military reservation. The road thence runs westward through deep vales behind high hills. Here there is no view of sea or Gate, but plenty of evidence of a former large military population back in the 1940's when the heights bristled with guns. Eventually the road climbs up and over the hills on the left, its blacktop yields to a thrifty red shale, and white Coast Guard structures appear down yonder on a shelf above Bonita Cove.

If you go no further, your trip has paid off right here. You are looking on one of the most stunning sights you'll ever behold.

But you do go farther, of course. You go to the station headquarters behind the tall flagpole, and there's no doubt whatever about it: the chief bosun's mate who is Officer in Charge, and his crew of seven, are downright glad of some company.

From this shelf, all is view. The whole Gate is presented in one grand sweep. But on this side, only a handful enjoy the vista. The nearest neighbors, excluding the military people behind the hill, are over on Mile Rock a couple miles away, and they might as well be on the moon. Next nearest are the seals on Seal Rocks, three miles south, and the traffic over the long flat arch of the Bridge three miles east.

But Chief R. C. Hogenmiller and his little band don't get this scenery all the time. From one thousand to two thousand hours out of the year's 8,765, fog is in and the view is apt to be about like that at Adak. And in those hours, business at Point Bonita is deadly serious. The function of the station is not only to light the entrance to the Gate, but to holler. Of the many mechanical larynxes or clusters of larynxes that warn of Gate shoals and perils, Bonita's is usually the first to screech and the last to pipe down. It is strictly the main hinge to the Gate, and a squeaky one. The louder the better.

The place where Bonita emits its unbeautiful cry is out on the end of that half-mile finger of rock previously described. It is a tiny platform that holds a tall steel radio-beacon tower, a stubby light tower, a lookout room, and an engine room for the fog signal. The lookout room is always manned. It resembles the bridge of a ship. Its corner view is directly north and directly east. Watch is kept on four objects at about five miles' distance: a beach here, a bluff there, a rock or a buoy somewhere out yonder. When one of the objects becomes obscured, Bonita's high yodel cuts in, and Fort Point Coast Guard Station across the Gate is notified by telephone. Point Diablo on the north shore and a couple miles east is an unmanned light and fog signal under remote control by Bonita, and the punch of a button in the Bonita lookout room sets Diablo's hoarse voice going too.

The group command station for the whole Gate is at Fort Point Station just east of the Bridge. As the fog sweeps in, the cacophony of hoots, yowls, screams and bull-roars is picked up by Mile Rock, echoed back by Lime Point, flung at the dinmaker down at the base of the Bridge south tower, heaved for further relay out to midspan, pitched at the two ends of Alcatraz, and variously tossed back and forth like a basketball by Cavallo, Yellow Bluff, Angel Island, Treasure

Island, Goat Island and the Bay Bridge. Then, as the atmosphere clears, the horns subside one by one, until even Bonita is quiet again.

Bonita's 30-second sound cycle consists of a 2-second blast, 2 seconds silence, 2 seconds blast and 24 seconds silence. This signal is emitted by a high, single-note eardrum-piercer known as a super-tyfon, and may be likened to the dire shriek of a sea gull that has not only caught its leg in a shark's mouth, but has dropped its fish. It is the successor to a diaphone, or 2-toner, which was slightly more pleasant to hear but required a great deal more electrical energy to operate. In the little engine room below and forward of the lookout room a motor operates a compressor which jams 40 pounds of air pressure through a 1¼-inch pipe against brass diaphragm plates whose vocal protest to the ordeal is audible six miles at sea. It took similar pressure through a 4-inch pipe to operate the diaphone, so the saving is substantial. The high-pitched cry of the tyfon is nerve-rasping, even to householders across the Gate; but Bonita isn't talking to them, but to passing ships. And ships in fog off a rocky coast want a warning, not a Lorelei.

The first fog signal on Bonita wasn't a horn, but an 8-foot cannon with a 6-inch bore—an iron siege gun on wooden wheels, capable of throwing a 24-pound shot. But no shot was provided for it. Just powder, and an army sergeant who had no relief. In August, 1856, which was the foggiest month of a year that had a great deal of fog, Sergeant Maloney took up his lonesome job. His instructions were to fire that gun every half-hour whenever fog obscured the entrance to the Bay. He wrote to the lighthouse service two months later, "I cannot find any person here to relieve me, not five minutes; I have been up three days and nights, had only two hours' rest—I was nearly used up. All the rest I would require in the twenty-four hours is two, if I could only get it." But Sergeant Maloney stuck by his gun until the $2,000 annual cost for powder forced discontinuance.

The cannon, which is still in existence over at the Coast Guard base at Alameda, was superseded in 1858 by a bronze bell on a boat. A steam horn took over in '72, followed after many years by that doleful but almost melodious diaphone. Then came the super-tyfon, and there are traducers who do say that no wonder Point Bonita is shaking to pieces; not only the sea waves, but the very air waves are ripping at it.

The light on Bonita was placed there even earlier than Gunnery Sergeant Maloney's fog signal. It arrived in 1855, soon after Alcatraz was equipped with the first lighthouse on the U.S.A.'s west coast. Bonita's original light was set up on an elevation of 324 feet. As the prevailing fogs tend to ride in high, this was too much elevation; the beam couldn't reach the ships down on the water. Also, getting up to the light from the keeper's dwelling was like climbing a rocky flagpole. There were seven different keepers in nine months. The high location was abandoned and the present one adopted in 1877, 200 feet lower but still 124 feet above the water. The light at present consists of a 500-watt lamp equipped with a second-order Fresnel lens that produces 40,000 candlepower and is visible 17 miles at sea. It flashes 1 second, eclipses 2 seconds, flashes 2 and eclipses 15. It is "exhibited" from sunset to sunrise and also during daylight hours when the fog signal is sounding. The adjacent radio beacon operates on a frequency of 314 Kc., for use of those having radio direction finders aboard vessels.

For many years Point Bonita was not only equipped with light and sound, but with an often summoned lifeboat station. There were also such stations at two points on the beach south of the Cliff House, and at Fort Point. Helicopters, fast cutters and modern communications have made all but the one at Fort Point unnecessary, so today the life-saving station at Bonita is a mere melancholy relic of tumbled structures and rusty rails where the surfboat used to be launched.

But there were many daring feats performed, for Bonita has collected its share of wrecks in spite of lights and sound-makers. One of these occurred in January, 1915. The steamer *Eureka*, 315 tons, approached the Gate via the Potato Patch Shoals just north of Point Bonita and fouled her propeller with a dragging rope. Surfman Al Fisher of Bonita Lifeboat Station, patrolling the heights north of the Point, saw the lit-tle steamer overwhelmed by a giant wave and sent crashing against the shore rocks. He alerted his station. And up on the bench where the lightkeepers lived, assistant keeper Alex Martin saw the ship's flares, donned his heavy-weather gear, and caught up a coil of rope.

The midwinter evening was already as dark as midnight. Martin could see the vessel trapped in creaming surf. He did not make out the lifeboat holding almost all of the crew and assumed they were still aboard. He made his rope fast and prepared to let himself down. It was 150 feet to the deck of the ship. Martin's rope was 100 feet long. He found himself at the bottom end of it and nowhere left to go but up. With aching arms and scrabbling boots he made it back up the precipice and hustled down the other side of the Point to the lifeboat station, where he further offered his services. Mean-while the Bonita and Fort Point stations and about fifty fish-ing boats had gone to the scene. All lives were saved but that of one man who had jumped into the *Eureka's* lifeboat, then gone back for something.

Assistant lightkeeper Martin later learned that the *Eureka* had carried a carload of gasoline and two tons of dynamite in her hold. All in all, he was glad his rope had been 50 feet too short.

Early on a rough February morning in 1960 the Bonita lookout saw a tanker in trouble over near Seal Rocks and the

Cliff House. She was a big girl. For the type of cargo she carried, she was the biggest in the world. She was the *Angelo Petri*, a wine tankship, and if she seemed to be behaving tipsily, she could be forgiven for it: in her stainless steel innards were 1,750,000 gallons of California sherry, port, muscatel, burgundy and vermouth.

With this gay load she bored into a howling wind, trying to walk like a lady and not quite making it. High waves caused her to zig and lurch as she turned into the south channel. The fascinated guardsman on watch at Bonita called his chief. Chief Hogenmiller hurried to the lookout room under the light. He was in time to see an enormous wave climb the starboard side of the *Petri* and plunge into her funnel.

For the *Petri*, that did it. Everything was short-circuited. Power was lost. Communications were wrecked. The $7,000,-000 ship began to drift. The Coast Guard, notified, hurried a helicopter to the scene. Fourteen of the forty-one people aboard were lifted off. The rest elected to remain. The *Petri* drifted south in close sight of the city beach, her anchors dragging. For an hour or two it looked as if the well-tanked lady was going to land amid the bear pits and monkey cages of Fleishhacker Zoo. Finally, with only ten feet of water under her keel, one anchor took hold. Three tugs and two cutters worked all day to get her out to deep water. By evening they succeeded. After spending the next night in the lee of the lightship twelve miles out, the bleary *Petri* in her state of heavy hangover was towed back into the bay for repairs.

Not a life had been lost. The "wine dark sea" of Homer was still only a poetic fancy. But if the *Petri*'s seams had opened in that pounding surf, a considerable wine punch would have been served.

The south post of the Gate is another story. It is high and rugged too, but besides holding the sea away from the town

behind it, its function is mainly to furnish pleasure and relaxa-
tion and a site for meditation. It arouses poetry in the most
unpoetic breast. A woman climbed aboard a Geary Street bus
and asked the colored driver in this writer's hearing. "How
far do you go?" He answered, "As far as the land lasts, lady."
It was an answer that the ever-westering covered wagon of
1849, the overland mail stagecoach of 1858 would have com-
prehended perfectly.

Up the long ocean beach from southward and over the
brush and boulders leading to Point Lobos and Land's End
came Captain Rivera on that original land journey to the entrance of the Gate, and to Lobos and Land's End go the
painters, sunset lovers, marriage proposers and picnickers today. A Captain Foster built an unpretentious "Seal Rocks
House" on a terrace of the seaward slope in 1858, at the end
of rough, sandy Point Lobos Road. People thronged there,
fascinated by the cozy restaurant tables pushed up to the
farthest-west windows of the continent; fascinated by the
barking sea lions just outside, and the boiling surf and
the ships treading the watery path to and from Panama and
Cape Horn. When the resort burned in '61, another went up
and it was named the "Cliff House." Still another succeeded to
the site: a gorgeous, bediamonded stomacher for the bodice
of the great stony hill. It had soaring stories, steep roofs, tur-
rets, cupolas, bay windows and little dining rooms with
couches, and doors on which waiters knocked though seldom
tarried for answer before bolting in. A lady could lose her
virtue between salad and soup, between white wine and red,
and probably often did; and San Franciscans were edified to
reflect that though Paris also might have such goings-on, the
romancers there had only River Seine to look upon, while
Cliff Housers had the whole dreamy, violent, thousand-hued
Pacific Ocean. In bonanza-silver days a mining engineer and
former tobacconist named Adolf Sutro, who had developed a
mighty vision of tunneling and draining the whole Comstock

Lode, and had done it and amassed a fortune, held ownership of both Cliff House and the bastion above, which he named Sutro Heights. He crowned the latter with mansion and barns and coachhouses that also were mansions, and gardens and terraces and cement statuary; and below, he built a public baths, huge and many-pooled and ornate, and even equipped with a museum that contained the stuffed hide of Old Ben, biggest sea lion of the Rocks.

One day the schooner *Parallel* blundered ashore with a cargo of dynamite, and up went schooner and one end of the Cliff House. And on Christmas night, 1904, when the restaurant and hotel were packed with revelers, the ornate edifice went up like a pyre. Restored, it burned again. In 1907, a plainer, less frisky Cliff House was set up there where seals and diners could eye each other through the broad windows. This one still stands. Up on Sutro Heights, Sutro's mansion and barns have vanished, and the cement balustrades and goddesses are crumbling, but it still is a Victorian spot for saunterers.

Immediately south, Golden Gate Park touches the strand. Here rests another relic. The little sloop *Gjöa*, which bore Amundsen and party from east to west for first transit of the Northwest Passage—the long-sought Strait of Anian—takes the weather on a forever quiet berthing of concrete. The explorer felt that a spot close to the entrance of the Golden Gate was a picturesque last anchorage for his intrepid longboat.

Sutro Heights, Cliff House, Point Lobos and Land's End form a cluster of look-offs from which one may readily see the rock sails of the Farallones on the horizon. If the hour is right, the result of a visit may well be a frenzied daub, a bareback gallop on Pegasus or at least a decision to live more worthily in a universe that offers so much.

I've seen the sun in boiling red go down beyond the Fort and light those isles, whose distant sails seem galleys of a sort, forever sailing ever fixed, those ships that missed the port.

I've watched the crest of Tamalpais against the sunset throw her tawny hills in shadow, and her pines turn black below; while, standing out to sea, those sails dripped silver in the glow. I've waited till the stars came out, and from a distant dune beheld a path of tossing light upon the water strewn; and ever stood those galleons across the broken moon. Perhaps from some dim yesteryear a proper wind shall play, a proper helmsman snatch the wheel while yet's a course to lay, and ships that missed the port shall come to anchor in the Bay.

14 : DISASTERS IN THE GATE

THE Golden Gate is a laughing siren when the sun is in her hair, but a taloned hag when fog shuts down. Many ships have gone to their deaths in the Gate and its approaches, nearly always because of dense mist that skippers and pilots thought they could beat but couldn't. Every point and reef has its roster of *Emmas, Josephines, Western Shores, Sea Nymphs, Warrior Queens, Edens, Arispas, Labourches* and *Tonquins.*

March 5, 1853, a sunny Saturday, found the steamer *Tennessee,* a big three-masted sidewheel steamship, approaching the end of a 21-day journey from Panama. She was Pacific Mail's proudest, 1350 tons, and had been shuttling between Gate and Isthmus for almost three years. Her 551 passengers were excited, for the Gate and the port of gold were only 100 miles away. Fog closed in during that final night. Captain Knight kept his course by dead reckoning, slipping steadily along under an easy head of steam. At 1 A.M. Sunday he thought he made out the darker grey overloom of the North and South Heads. Very cautiously now he crept forward, the paddles just turning. With daybreak, a rock lifted through the mist. This, surely, was Mile Rock. The narrows of the Gate, then, must be only two miles ahead. The lookout was warned to watch like a cat. The lead was

89

kept going. Twenty-six fathoms—sixteen. Unhappy Captain Knight! If his charts were right, and his position correct, he should have had 100 fathoms under him at this moment. The lead went to 7 fathoms, to 6.

It was 9 A.M. A ledge of black rocks pushed angrily through the water. Not ahead. Astern!

The big paddles were reversed instantly. They smashed the sea into foam. Too late. There was no space for backing or turning. Ahead was a short strip of sandy beach. The *Tennessee* was in a horseshoe cove, its tips about 200 yards apart. The skipper ordered her ahead and pointed for the strand. The *Tennessee* rode the breakers like a surfboard, struck and swung broadside.

It was a providential landing in a place of bold bluffs and smashing waves. The "South Head" Captain Knight thought he had sighted proved to be a nameless upthrust nearly four miles to the northwest. It was thereafter forever known as Tennessee Point. The haven he found became Tennessee Cove. It is about two miles beyond Point Bonita. There was little human habitation in that vicinity in 1853; there is little today. But passengers were got ashore. Mail and baggage followed. A member of the ship's company trudged over the hills to Sausalito, rowed a boat to San Francisco, and spread the word. Two steamers worked all the next day to pull the vessel off. Embedded in three feet of sand, she wouldn't budge. On the second night a sea rose, the vessel was pounded, her engine connections broke, her back snapped, and a lugubrious scribe for the *Alta* reported, "Her officers and crew feel as if they were attending the obsequies of a dear and valued friend . . . many a tear as salt as the brine that surrounds her shattered hull has coursed unbidden from manly eyes as they have gazed on the last resting place of the gallant *Tennessee*."

No lives were lost. Today a motor road winds atop the bluffs behind Tennessee Cove and fishermen scramble down the rocks to cast for bass. A hiker toured the beach a half-century later and noticed the *Tennessee*'s boiler still in the sand, partly buried and deeply rusted.

Almost duplicating the fate of the Pacific Mailer in date, place and cause was the doom of an opposition craft, the *S. S. Lewis* of the Vanderbilt or Nicaraguan line. The *S. S. Lewis* (the initials were part of her name) was a propeller-driven steamship of 1800 tons which had first put in at the Gate in 1852, bringing 653 passengers stacked in bunks three-high. In the spring of '53, with 385 passengers including 49 women and 24 children, she encountered thick fog off the Gate and at 5 A.M. of April 19 she struck something hard and obstinate. Her master thought he'd hit Mile Rock and tried to back off. Scarcely had her screw made a dozen turns when her stern took a crashing thump. Fog partly lifted. Captain Sparrow saw, a cable length ahead, a beach where no beach should be. He aimed for it, struck another ledge, and stayed there. He was on Duxbury reef, just under the point of the same name and seven and a half miles northwest of the cove that had enmeshed the *Tennessee*. Dawn of that day saw the passengers rowed ashore and the bedraggled, frightened women and children escorted to a Mr. Plumbe's sawmill. The purser obtained a horse and Paul Revere for a rowboat at Sausalito. Over the Gate, fog descended again. Before rescue tugs could get to the *S. S. Lewis*, the sea was littered with mattresses, benches, spars and loose lumber. The upper works, torn off, disintegrated in the breakers. "So perished the *S. S. Lewis*," sighed the *Alta*'s scribe, by this time an expert at melancholy, "and thus has she sunk in the embrace of ocean in a single night. Looking upon her wreck, one would almost imagine it to be the remains lost in the latter part of the last century."

At 3:00 P.M. on October 13, 1860, the new steamer *Granada* of the Atlantic & Pacific line anchored off the Gate. She was 90 days out from New York via Magellan; and Commander Howes, finding himself in a veil of mist, was of no mind to end his successful voyage with a crack-up in an unfamiliar passageway. A pilot schooner made him out and hailed him. A Mr. James Daly assured the captain that he could take the fine new vessel straight in. Captain Howes considered. It was, after all, bleak and wet out there. The voyage, while uneventful, had been a long one. The pleasures of the seaport town, just over the intervening hills, were already world-famous— outdone, some authorities maintained, only by Cairo, Marseilles and Paris. The passengers would be more than delighted to set foot on land as quickly as possible. "We therefore," reported the master later, "weighed anchor and proceeded, made the Hole in the Wall [sometimes called Hole in the Rock, an early landmark] and soon after sighted and made our departure from Mile Rock. The pilot then ordered the ship to be hooked on at full speed." Mr. James Daly too, it would seem, was eager to be in port by nightfall for the brilliant promenade up Kearny Street, the seven-course menus, the theaters. "Ten minutes after the above order, breakers were discovered ahead, the engine was immediately stopped and backed, but too late to be of any service as we were going at great speed. We struck head on, and in a few minutes were broadside on the rock"—of Fort Point and its red-brick fortress and many guns.

In that same place, the sailing ship *Euterpe* had gone ashore a few months before. A crewman of the *Granada* swam ashore with a handline attached to a hawser. Military people helped pull the hawser, and over it the *Granada*'s passengers finished their 16,000-mile journey hand over hand. The *Granada* swiftly pounded herself to pieces, and an indignant public wondered: did agents of Commodore Vanderbilt, foeman of Atlantic & Pacific and all other opposition lines, send Mr. Daly out to lead this new rival to her doom? Nobody knew. But the Commodore, it was pointed out, always played for keeps.

The Gate too played for keeps. In 1854 the clipper *San*

Francisco, a fine new ship from New York with cargo valued at $400,000, was beating through the entrance when she struck rocks on the north side. This was nearly the spot where the English ship *Jenny Lind*, outward bound, had wrecked herself a few months before. The seaport town across the Gate had not yet cleaned out its undesirables with a Vigilante rope. As soon as word came of the clipper's plight, plunderers were at the scene by every small craft that would float. Some two hundred of them, "nearly all armed with the usual weapons, five or six-shooters and bowie knives . . . stood their ground and continued to take and rob as they pleased"— until a storm blew up, when some of the pirate boats capsized and drowned a dozen on the spot or swept them out to sea. Soon after her cargo was removed, the clipper went to pieces.

April of the same year saw the windjammer *Golden Fleece* dash herself upon Fort Point while leaving harbor. The roll grew lengthy, adding *Louise Morgan, Francis, Governor, Clark, Prince Alfred, Oxford*, and many more. Sometimes lives were lost, often a treasure went down that had been hard-wrung from the Sierra hills, and always a ship with valiant plans came to an abrupt end of its voyaging.

So the roster of the lost continued to grow. Sometimes it was the fog. Sometimes the captain. Sometimes the crew. And more than once, the ship.

Gold in the Yukon sent everything splashing to sea that twine and rusty bolts would hold together, and some vessels that would not. The *Helen W. Almy* had been lying on the Oakland mudflats when the Klondike hit the news. She was pulled off and swept out for passengers, twenty-seven of whom came aboard. Her skipper, W. J. Hogan, had a reputation for bravery if not for caution. He accepted the job of getting her to Copper River, where she would land her paying guests and become a floating hotel. Though when he looked his crew of thirteen over, he had qualms. He admitted as much to the captain of the tug *Sea Witch*, which pulled him out the Gate. A stiff March wind was blowing, that day in '98. The tug cast him loose outside the Gate and he stood out to sea.

The wind, it soon became apparent, was working up into a gale. The crew, which had been spending its Yukon gold ashore before it got any, was five thumbs to a fist and all left-handed. The bark began to leak. Captain Hogan, from the evidence or the surmises of the tug skipper who later found the *Almy*, tried to put back into port. Working up to near-hurricane violence, the winds and seas denied that refuge to him. Two days later and twenty miles south, the bark was found flat on her side, all sails set. Not a soul was aboard. Not one of the forty bodies was ever found. By wind-power or steam, many another inadequate craft put out from coastal ports for the North in that mad year and never got there.

Heavy loss of life, which had been absent in most of the Gate wrecks prior to the *Almy*, now was ready to ride the winds and fogs in earnest.

On the afternoon of February 21, 1901, the Pacific Mail steamer *Rio de Janeiro* on her regular homing run from China sighted the Farallones and made her cautious way for the harbor mouth. Fog was leaden on the water. Captain William Ward, playing safe, anchored off Point Bonita and waited for morning. At 4:30 A.M. of the twenty-second, the heavy blanket lifted and Pilot Fred Jordan advised going in. Captain Ward studied the situation. Lights on both shores could be seen distinctly. Stars were bright overhead. Going in was obviously the thing to do—enter the Gate and anchor off Alcatraz for the quarantine officer, who would be followed by the immigration and customs men. Anchor was lifted and half-speed ordered.

The Gate was only playing. It swept those stars out of the sky; lights and shores went suddenly invisible. Only a mile from where the *Rio de Janeiro* had hauled up her hook, all was dense fog again.

Captain Ward had gone back to his cabin for his overcoat. Hearing a commotion, he returned hurriedly to the bridge.

At this moment the lookout for the Fort Point Life Saving Station, in a tower on the hillside behind the fortress, could see nothing but fog. Nor did he hear anything. Farther down the shore to eastward, at the life-saving station, Captain Hodson and his crew slumbered sweetly. Their rest would continue for the next two hours.

On sentry-go between the lookout tower and the fortress, a private of Battery E, Third Artillery, paced his cold pathway and thought whatever beautiful thoughts soldiers on sentry duty think, when there's not much to guard and the country's at peace. He'd be here for three more hours. The rifle was heavy.

On board the *Rio*, freight clerk C. F. Englehardt was awake and looked at his watch. It was five o'clock. Something thumped. Two more thumps. Maybe a tug or a fishing boat. The freight clerk dressed deliberately, putting on his entire uniform and lacing his shoes. While still in his room he heard the captain shouting orders to lower the boats, followed by "Women and children first!" Englehardt dove out on deck. The *Rio* was settling by the head. But it was in slow motion. There was no panic. Not yet. Englehardt went down to the parcel room and got his dispatch bag. There was some inconvenience; the lights had gone out. He went back to his room and got the oil lamp that hung there. In a nearby room, the purser was up and dressing. Just then the ship gave a violent lurch.

Up on the nearby south shore, the soldier on sentry-go became aware of something amiss in the fog below. He left his post and ran up hill to the lookout tower. He pounded, shouted. The man inside did not deign to be disturbed. Maybe it was nothing important, after all. The soldier had no desire to be caught off post by his corporal. He went back on beat. He was well up the hill, and all kinds of rocks and brick walls were between him and the confused sounds below. All of Battery E was asleep in barracks down there; if they weren't interested, neither was he.

On the *Rio*, events had just three minutes in which to happen, and they were happening. Carpenter Frank Cramp got a boat lowered. Other boats had been lowered and loaded with varying degrees of success. Cramp's was the last to get away. A man swung down from a starboard davit and let himself slide down the side of the ship. He landed in the boat. Another followed and splashed into the water. He was fished out. Three women were pulled out through a porthole and dumped into the boat. One didn't want to come; she was dragged by main force in spite of unco-operative bosom and hips. The boat pulled away just in time to avoid a vortex. The ship careened. The boom of its mizzenmast crashed onto one boat, cutting it in two.

Pilot Jordan was safe in one of the boats, but Captain Ward, when last seen, was on the deck directing disembarkation. The last person off of the eighty who were saved was freight clerk Englehardt. One hundred and thirty-one persons perished.

The *Rio de Janeiro* was a staunch, steady ship; she had been through a dozen typhoons. But she did not have watertight bulkheads. She was the victim of a tule or inland fog, which had crept out the Golden Gate after the sea fog lifted, just in time to blind the vessel and give strong currents the opportunity to throw her out of the channel's center.

For years afterward, waterfront men speculated over what had become of the ship that had gone down with the Gate's heaviest loss of life, and without so much as a blast of her whistle. Insurance men wondered; there had been a $600,000 cargo aboard, including $300,000 worth of opium. Legends grew with the years, assigning to her strongboxes a fortune in gold amounting to millions. Tom Crowley, the salvage expert, sent a diver down and dragged up her wheelhouse, but that was about all that was ever found of her except a floating tin box containing her papers.

Wreck of the *Tennessee*

15 : GALLANT RESCUES—
A FEW OF MANY

GEORGE D. COBB, assistant keeper of the Bonita light at the turn of the century, was on watch one midwinter noon during a high southeast gale. The day was sunny but very cold. Sea was thundering against the cliffs below his tower. The wind gauge read 50 miles an hour. George looked down and saw a sailboat in process of capsizing a hundred yards out and 125 feet below. Two men emerged from the waves and managed to grasp their overturned craft; a third started swimming. There was no time to summon help from the lifeboat station in the cove. Cobb was down the long wooden staircase in leaps. He managed to lower the two-man lighthouse boat, put off through a dinning surge, and row to the upset hull. In the face of that wind, two expert oarsmen would have had difficulty pulling the heavy boat; George did it all alone. The men clinging to the sailboat were benumbed and almost unconscious; plucking them off and into his boat was a work of skill and nerve. Cobb managed it, while exposed to the full fury of the wind, on one hand, and danger of dashing upon rocks on the other. Then he headed for the third man, who was clinging to a retaining wall along the shore rocks. Again the assistant lightkeeper found the physical resources to close in, snatch his man and head off. Like the others, this man was

98

badly battered and almost out. Cobb got back to the tiny
wharf, secured and hoisted his boat, and lifted the men one
by one up that hundred-foot staircase. The Treasury rightly
gave George a silver medal for gallantry. He should have had
two or three.

Across the Gate's entrance at Point Lobos, a sport fisherman managed to fall twenty feet off some rocks one autumn
day in 1901. He plummeted into booming surf, was dashed
about until weakened, and thereupon set off upon some unusual sightseeing while his companions raced for help.

The adventure John Slater was embarked on was something for Aladdin. Instead of perishing, he was swept by the
waves into a cavern under the cliff. It was about railroad-
tunnel size and extended back for some fifty feet. There was
air space above the water, and pallid daylight lit up a fan-
tastic display of shells, anemones and other sea life clinging
to wave-polished rock. They twinkled like jewelry. Slater was
more concerned with finding a handhold somewhere, which
he finally did.

Meanwhile word had been got to Surfman Albert Bernston
of the Golden Gate Life-Saving Station. The surfman grabbed
up a life buoy with attached line and ran to the edge of the
bluff. He was lowered by willing bystanders until he reached
the mouth of the grotto. There he threw the buoy in and
yelled to Slater to grasp it. The fisherman was too exhausted
to dare let go with one hand from his slippery clutch. Bernston hauled the buoy back, passed the line to some comrades
who had got down the bluff by a roundabout way, and
donned the buoy himself. He swam in, lashed Slater to the
buoy, and took the rescued man's place at that slippery handhold while Slater was hauled out. Time passed. Bernston's
clinging fingers grew nerveless. Tide was coming in. He wondered how high it would rise. To force his way through its
forceful bore was beyond him. He was beginning to hear

pretty mermaids singing when, by grace of the persistence of well-wishers at the sea end of his cavern, the buoy on its line came floating back to him. The Treasury Department sent Al Bernston a silver medal.

On November 23, 1914, the steam schooner *Hanalei* got off her course during fog and ran onto a reef off Point Bolinas, fourteen miles north of the Golden Gate. The vessel had sixty-six people on board including fourteen women and children. Exclaimed the Coast Guard later in its annual report to the Secretary of the Treasury, "It is doubtful if in the annals of shipwreck any. . . within the scope of the Coast Guard establishment was attended by so many dramatic incidents and spectacular features, or one where those whose lives were in peril were subjected to so long a period of mental distress while waiting for their vessel to break up under them, or compelled to face a more terrifying ordeal after that event took place."

The 600-ton steamer had left Eureka the day before with passengers and a cargo of railroad ties and shingles. When she neared Point Reyes, weather was foggy but lighthouse and buildings could be recognized. After proceeding southward far enough to round Duxbury Point, as he thought, Captain J. J. Carey ordered the course changed to haul for Duxbury whistling buoy. However, he was long in his reckoning. At a half-hour after midnight, breakers were seen too late. He rammed hard and fast. He thought he was on Duxbury but was miles north of it.

When wireless calls for help reached the various life-saving stations, power boats immediately set out and the revenue cutter *McCulloch* also hurried to the supposed scene. They arrived at 3:30 A.M. No *Hanalei*. Keeper Joe Nutter of Bonita station, who knew there was no beach at Duxbury, hadn't brought his Lyle gun and other beach rescue gear. The power boats searched the dismal coast in darkness and dense fog by running inside the line of breakers—a deadly dangerous feat. Three miles of it, and they found the stricken craft. She lay listed at 45°, exposing her deck to the full force of heavy swells. Passengers and crew were huddled in the lee of her deck housing.

There followed some very brave but unsuccessful boatmanship. Both power boats tried to get close. Twice they were almost smashed under and their motors were drowned. One boat capsized. She was built to right herself and did so, but flung off keeper John Clark of Fort Point station, and surfman Stoll. Stoll managed to reach the wreck. Clark shouted to his men to row beyond the breakers and get the motor started again, and he set out to swim for shore. He battled breakers, jagged rocks and adverse currents for two and a half hours, was thrice swept out to sea and once entirely around the *Hanalei*, and was finally dragged ashore unconscious.

At life-saving headquarters in San Francisco, officers waited anxiously for news. At the office of the *Examiner*, the staff hung closely about the telephone of city editor E. D. "Cobbie" Coblentz. Cobbie was an old waterfront reporter himself and he had an idea. He called keeper Nelson of the station near the Cliff House. If Cobbie furnished the truck, would Nelson and his men get over there with beach rescue gear? Nelson would. He and his crew of seven and a batch of reporters crossed the Gate by ferry and started the wild ride over the heights. Reported the life-saving service which became Coast Guard in the year following, "The road traverses a mountain range, densely forested in parts, and is notable throughout the State as one of the narrowest and most crooked roads in existence." The progress of the expedition in places was at a foot pace. It was sometimes necessary to back uphill. On downgrades the crew wished they were in surfboats; they were almost hurled from the truck.

Arriving at the scene at 2 A.M., hours before the power

boats got there, Nelson immediately began operations which ultimately saved 29 lives. Six lines were shot at the wreck. None were secured by the people aboard the *Hanalei*. At 3:30, crash of timbers indicated that the vessel was breaking up. Nelson shifted operations to the top of the bluff and fired shots across pieces of wreckage where people were clinging. For 200 yards off the beach, and for a mile on either side, the water was covered with tossing, grinding material. Joining hands in a living chain, rescuers rushed into the water wherever a human form was seen struggling. They held to their work until daybreak, hauling in every soul that could be reached. Of the 30 pulled to the beach, only one was lost.

At dawn the power boat *Majestic* was maneuvered by Bonita station keeper Joe Nutter through the dangerous reefs, over which a tremendous sea was breaking. Quantities of oil on the water made this possible. Objects scarcely resembling human beings floated covered with oil, some dead and the rest so exhausted that they were unable to signal. In growing light and a fog that had grown still more impenetrable, the life savers picked up everyone. Surfman Maxwell leaped overboard and supported two struggling survivors until the boat could reach them. Thirteen were thus picked up and conveyed to the *McCulloch*. Their clothing was in tatters, their faces and bodies covered with wounds. They were carried to the cabin and stripped, noses and throats freed of oil, their limbs chafed, and dry underclothing provided. The *McCulloch* took them to Meiggs Wharf, where a multitude of spectators were gathered to witness the forlorn arrival.

Keepers Clark and Nutter and surfman Mike Maxwell were awarded gold medals for their night's work. Cobbie's *Examiner* had a scoop. And his reporters had a late breakfast and went back to work.

The U. S. Military Sea Transport Service Hospital Ship

Benevolence, of 15,450 tons displacement, was by any standard a beautiful vessel and one with an angelic mission to perform. Brand-new and agleam in white paint, she went out the Gate for her trial run on August 25, 1950, and set homeward from her short cruise at midafternoon. At that moment the freighter *Mary Luckenbach,* of 8,162 gross tons, was outbound through the main ship channel en route for Philadelphia.

August is a month for fog, and this day was no exception. Both vessels sounded the regulation signals. But both were proceeding at excessive speeds. The *Mary* passed under the Golden Gate Bridge, finding visibility of 300 to 400 yards. Twenty-three minutes later she heard a whistle dead ahead. In seconds, the bow wave of the oncoming *Benevolence* was sighted. "Hard right" order was given to the *Mary's* helmsman, and four whistle blasts were sounded. But there was a crash. *Mary* ordered "Hard left rudder" and passed astern of the craft she had encountered. Twelve minutes later, still swathed in fog, she let go her anchor. She didn't know what she'd hit. Ninety-eight minutes after the impact, she learned of its seriousness by the arrival of a Coast Guard rescue vessel with some *Benevolence* survivors on board. The *Mary Luckenbach* then lowered a lifeboat that picked up about 35 persons, besides towing two life rafts with 50 more.

Many strange facts emerged from the inquiry into this disaster which claimed 23 lives, although 504 were saved. Among the reported oddities were:

The *Mary Luckenbach* had radar but it wasn't in working order.

The *Benevolence* had radar in working order but didn't pick up the *Mary Luckenbach.*

The *Mary* did not send a "CQ" in plain language to determine the identity or condition of the vessel she had struck.

An effort to send an SOS by radio from the *Benevolence*

was made but it was later discovered that the antenna had been disconnected.

The *Mary* notified her San Francisco office before notifying the Coast Guard, though claiming that both were notified within one minute of impact.

The Coast Guard's Rescue Coördination Center received an emergency message at 5:21, twenty-six minutes after the impact. It had rescue operations going at 5:22. The *Benevolence* took twenty-seven minutes to sink.

As visibility by this time was extremely short, and the survivors scattered all over the water, rescue was not easy. But every type of craft was soon present—Army, Navy, fishing boats and yachts.

The splendid *Benevolence* lay in a dozen fathoms of water four miles west of the Golden Gate Bridge, 1¾ miles off Point Lobos, on the southern boundary of the channel. Her career had been brief, but long enough to snuff out more than a score of lives and change many others. Including, in the second category, that of John Napoli, commercial fisherman. And thereby arises one of the great, gallant sagas of the Gate.

John Napoli, native of San Francisco, son of a Sicilian fisherman, was in his one-man fishboat *Flora* that day. He'd ranged thirty miles out and had had a full sixteen-hour day, and there was more than a quarter of a ton of salmon aboard —enough to net him the money he still owed for a recent overhaul of the *Flora*—when he turned homeward. At five o'clock he arrived at the lightship and took bearings for the channel. Twenty minutes more of traveling, and he heard whistle blasts of a large ship in distress.

John slowed the *Flora* down. A black object bobbed in the water just ahead. He warned the boats behind him, turned right, and pulled the object aboard. It was a half-drowned man, cut and bleeding, in a Navy uniform. A Coast Guard boat passed close by. It was invisible but the guard yelled that people were in the water all around. John pulled another man out and aboard his *Flora*. The fog miraculously thinned and he saw a big freighter one hundred feet in front of him and hundreds of people in the water, kept afloat by life preservers. He said to himself, "Now, John, get to work." Overboard went the fish, as fast as he could tumble them. And fast as he could grab and tug, he hauled people up and out.

John was a short man. He had to kneel and lean out to reach down for them. Every hoist was a two-man job that he somehow managed alone. It was a two-and-a-half-foot lift. Fortunately the water was between tides. He cruised over to the *Mary Luckenbach,* some of whose seamen slid down his mast to help. More slow cruising, the sighting of someone in the water, the tossing of a rope. "God give me strength to pull these people in," he prayed aloud. A voice spoke up behind him. "God will give you strength." John said afterward, "I almost jumped outa da boat." The voice came from Chaplain Reardon of the *Benevolence,* one of the people John had pulled in. The good chaplain was too spent to help John more than spiritually, but it was enough. John went on hoisting, hauling. He pulled one person from the water by unexpectedly convenient handles. She was a Navy nurse.

Boats were all over the scene by then, but John worked till nightfall. His last act was to throw a towline to a raft that had sixteen persons aboard. He had more than a load in the *Flora* at the moment.

John Napoli that day had pulled people out of the water until he lost all count. In two trips he put half of them on the *Mary Luckenbach* and the other half on an Army tug which arrived on the scene.

The next day John couldn't stoop or, if he did, couldn't straighten. He had wrecked his back. He went to the hospital, came out unable to fish any more, sold his crab traps at a sharp sacrifice. He asked the Luckenbach people for reimbursement for the fish he had thrown overboard. They told him to see their lawyer. Destitute, he filed a claim with the Coast Guard for 550 pounds of salmon at 30 cents a pound, 2 pair of woolen pants, 4 shirts, 4 blankets, $700 damage to a bent propeller strut, $20 for a sprung bow post and $37.50 for hauling up his vessel in a shipyard. The Coast Guard did what they could for this man who had saved 30 persons by his own remembering—70, by the count of others; but John, after more bouts at the hospital, conceded that he could fish no more. He sold the *Flora,* also at a stiff loss.

Eleven years later, Congress awarded John Napoli $25,000 for his heroic efforts in behalf of the Navy ship. After working at odd jobs, John had become a shipping clerk with General Steamship Corporation. "First," he said when news of the Congressional action was brought to him, "I square up everything. I owe a lot of bills yet, medical on myself and on a funeral for my wife. Then the rest in a trust fund where nobody can touch it. Not even myself, except maybe $50 a month for a while. With my job, I oughta get along."

John Napoli often comes down to Fisherman's Wharf to see old cronies and swap tales, and smell the good sea smells. But one sad thing he has to tell, when pressed about it. Only one of those thirty—or seventy—people ever wrote a line of thanks to him, ever phoned or even dropped around to say howdy.

16 : FATEFUL DEPARTURES

FORTY-FOUR years to a day before Japanese bombs fell upon Pearl Harbor, an officer of the United States Navy sailed out the Golden Gate as a passenger on a transpacific liner. In his pocket were orders from John D. Long, Secretary of the Navy, that were to have considerable impact. They read:

. . . [You] will proceed to San Francisco, Cal., and thence to Yokohama, Japan, taking passage in the steamer of the Pacific Mail Steamship Company sailing from San Francisco on December 7th next. Upon your arrival at Yokohama you will report to Rear Admiral Frederick V. McNair, U.S.N., the Commander-in-Chief of the Asiatic Station, on board the U.S.F.S. Flagship OLYMPIA, for duty as Commander-in-Chief of that Station, as the relief of that officer.

Commodore George Dewey, as the *Gaelic* slipped out the Golden Gate that appointed day, did not have the sweep of history before him as we now have it in hindsight, but he well may have sensed something of it. For strong impulses were guiding the United States into ultimate collision with Spain in Cuba, and the Navy was taking a long view of what that might entail. By the time he caught up with the *Olympia* at Nagasaki on December 31, plans were teeming in his head. He found awaiting him a highly improbable squadron

107

of fighting ships with which to affect coming events. Besides the *Olympia,* of 5870 tons displacement, he had the small cruiser *Boston,* the gunboat *Petrel* and the paddlewheel steamer *Monacacy.* Four months and one day later, with these plus some increments and by dint of a great deal of gunnery practice, he steamed into Manila Bay and blew the four-hundred-year Spanish empire out of Pacific waters.

That battle, which was practically bloodless from the American standpoint, gave responsibility for the Philippines to the United States for the next half-century. And it ultimately brought Japanese bombs raining down not only on Oahu but on American forces in Manila.

The coincidence of the two December 7th's was paralleled by another. In 1942, Dewey's commemorative monument in San Francisco's Union Square had just been temporarily removed for the excavation of an underground public garage, when Japan erased all of Dewey's work at Manila. When the garage was finished and grassed over and the monument restored, United States Naval and Army forces almost immediately knocked Japan out of the Philippines.

As stated, all just coincidence.

Three and a half months after passenger George Dewey sailed out the Gate on the unwarlike *Gaelic,* another fateful departure took place. The battleship *Oregon,* having loaded fuel and ammunition at San Francisco, steamed out the Gate at 8 A.M. on March 19, 1898, for an epochal voyage and a rendezvous with destiny.

The *Oregon* was a product of the local Union Iron Works, launched in 1894. She was a superb fighting unit for her times, equipped with 13-inch guns among other killer armament. Her skipper, Captain Charles Edgar Clark, was a one-man navy in himself.

The United States and Spain were not yet at war. But events in Cuba were tending that way. The battleship *Maine* had mysteriously blown up. A Spanish fleet was said to be approaching. The whole Atlantic coast of America was in panic. The *Oregon's* four 13-inchers, her 16-gun main battery and her 10,288 tons of steel and general truculence would be a comforting thing in conjunction with the rest of America's Atlantic fleet.

So, loaded with coal and painted a grim grey, the doughty, broad, squat *Oregon* moved out between the Heads with a 15,000-mile voyage before her and Key West her destination. And, communications being what they were, she promptly became lost to the world. Sixteen days later, she put in at Callao, Peru, to replenish her coal. She had made 4,112 sea miles at an average of nearly 11 knots. At Callao she picked up a small consort, the U.S. gunboat *Marietta*.

On April 16, the pair put in at chilly Tamar, Patagonia. On this run, they had made 2,550 sea miles at just under 12 knots. They approached the reef-strewn entrance to Magellan Straits after nightfall in a high gale. With anchors down and engines ready, they rode 'er out. Captain Clark addressed his men. After telling them about the fleet that might try to whip the socks off them, he said of course it was his duty to the Government to get the ship around on the other side and steer clear of the Spaniards if possible. But in case he did meet the fleet he was sure Spain's fighting efficiency on the sea would be diminished. So all hands gave him three rousing cheers.

Not yet knowing that war had been declared, the *Oregon* bustled into Rio de Janeiro, coaled, and continued on. She picked up the cruiser *Buffalo*. Both companions proving too slow, she shed them, reached Barbados May 17, and arrived at Key West May 26. Three days later she steamed for Santiago as part of Sampson's fleet. In the battle of July 3, she moved in with a tremendous rush, sharing the brunt with the *Texas, Brooklyn* and *Iowa*, and throwing more metal than any four Spanish ships.

Not since the U.S.S. *Constitution,* "Old Ironsides," had one man o' war constituted itself a force ready to fight a whole navy, if need be; and until its year of glory no warship ever had made such a long voyage under such dire pressure, or at such speed. When the *Oregon* again steamed through the Golden Gate, she received a welcome that rocked the hills. Two decades later, when a new American fleet on tour sailed in through the Gate, the little *Oregon* was pulled off the scrap heap and recommissioned as a proud flagship for that one day. Then she passed into limbo; Time was one adversary she couldn't lick.

The First World War was half a month old. The United States was neutral and would remain so for two and a half years. In the Pacific, as in the Atlantic, the German and British navies were sparring. Off the Golden Gate, the protected cruiser *Leipzig* of the Imperial German Navy had been loitering for a week. A commerce raider with 10,000 tons of British shipping already bagged, she was short of coal and in sore need of the legal 24-hour refuge and assistance of a neutral port.

At 12:30 A.M. of August 17, 1914, she slipped in through the Gate. Running lights out and others dimmed, she anchored between Black Point and Alcatraz and sounded four short whistle-blasts to make her presence known to port officials. With daylight, her decks stripped for war, she took on enough coal for 3500 miles of steaming. Her Captain Haun and his officers were genial fellows. They had many friends ashore, and they made more. Resplendent in gold braid, the captain called on Mayor Rolph and left his valuables with him.

Exactly at 12:30 A.M. next day, the *Leipzig* stole out without lights as she had come in, to rendezvous secretly with Admiral Graf von Spee's armored cruisers *Scharnhorst* and *Gneisenau* and light cruisers *Nürnberg* and *Dresden* off Easter Island. Wrote "Pop" Hamilton in Hearst's *Examiner,*

"Yesterday her officers and men were putting in their effects at the custom house to have those effects sent home—a watch, a portrait, a lock of hair . . . and they knew that they were going out to die. But the captain of the *Leipzig* says 'I will fight the enemy wherever I may find him.' " Added Phil Francis, purple-pen editorialist, "The *Leipzig* came in from the blue water for a day and laughter rang on its bare steel decks. And then in the dark, under the legions of kindly stars, it slipped away. In some far offing, ambushed in the long plunge of the open sea, the death they court may be awaiting those laughing sailors. There is something about the way they went to meet it that thrills up to the skies."

On November 1, Rear Admiral Sir Christopher Cradock with a slow pre-dreadnaught British battleship and four cruisers picked up the radio voice of the *Leipzig*. She was off Coronal, a small town on Chile's west coast, and her voice was pure bait. Cradock tore thither, thinking to bag the pestiferous commerce raider. Von Spee's guns promptly lifted him from the water. Two armored cruisers, the *Good Hope* and *Monmouth*, were obliterated. The *Leipzig* actually charged at flank speed through the wreckage of the *Good Hope* without recognizing it.

After this heady victory, the Germans edged around South America. On December 8, Spee sent two of his cruisers to examine Port Stanley in the Falkland Islands and smash its radio tower. To their horror they discovered the tripod masts of the two heavy cruisers *Invincible* and *Inflexible,* which were lurking there with six other British cruisers. The Germans hightailed, the British pursued. *Nürnberg, Gneisenau, Scharnhorst, Dresden* and a collier went down. Two British cruisers that had escaped from Coronal caught and sank the *Leipzig.* Its "laughing sailors" had kept their promised appointment.

The United States battleships at Pearl Harbor had taken an almost mortal blow. Japan in one concerted set of operations had pushed the boundaries of empire almost to Alaska, Midway, Australia. What dramatic counter-blow could be struck to lift American morale and bring home to the Japanese homeland the stern reality of war? Could Tokyo be bombed? By carrier bombers, no. They lacked the range to get inside the 300-mile sweep of Japan's shore-based aircraft. By American Army bombers? Absurd! Where would they take off from?

Well, could the B-25, a land-based bomber, take off from a carrier? Possibly, thought Hap Arnold, commanding general of the Army Air Force. Perhaps, agreed Captain Don Duncan, Admiral King's air operations officer, who was given the problem for study. Why not? exclaimed Lt. Col. Jimmy Doolittle, and he took on the task of training the selected fliers on a strip of ground in Florida, marked out like the deck of a ship.

The carrier *Hornet* steamed out under the Golden Gate Bridge in the deathly wartime secrecy of the spring of '42, accompanied by two cruisers, four destroyers and an oiler. Not even Captain Marc Mitscher had known, until a few days before he sailed, why his Navy planes had been ordered below and those sixteen landlubberly B-25's, or Mitchells, derricked to his flight deck. Only six other officers of the entire Navy or Army knew why that crazy cargo was aboard. But Jimmy Doolittle's 70 officers and 130 enlisted men—pilots, crewmen and aircraft service men—certainly suspected.

One day outside the Gate, Captain Mitscher broke his sealed orders and read them to his crew. The *Hornet* was going to carry the war to the Japanese homeland.

The Pacific Ocean is wide, very wide. The *Hornet* crossed it fast. She picked up Halsey's task force, refueled at sea, and with the carrier *Enterprise* for company she made the final lunge. The plan was to toss those bombers into the air when just outside Japanese shore-based plane range. On April 18, while still 700 miles east of Inubee Saki light on line with

Tokyo, the *Hornet* was discovered by picket boats. There was nothing to do but fling the planes into the air at once. There'd be no coming back to the *Hornet*, but maybe the fliers could go on to China and find friends. Admiral Halsey radioed from the *Enterprise*, "Good luck and God bless you."

No B-25 bomber had ever lifted off a carrier's deck before. The deck was so crowded that some of the bombers' wings extended over the side. The deck gave them an incredibly short run and only a 60-mile-per-hour takeoff; their rated need was 90. One by one they lifted off. Some barely made it, but all did.

Not one bomber was lost over Japan, but some crewmen were captured on the mainland, following the raid. Three were executed and one died in prison. One crew ultimately showed up in Persia, making its hard way home.

The sixty-four 500-pound bombs dropped on Japan in that nervy raid broke forever the Nipponese sweet sense of security and suggested that more, much more, was coming.

For the next three years and four months the Golden Gate was a four-mile-long, mile-wide cannon or mortar heaving shells and bombards across the ocean; heaving tankers, freighters, troopships. Behind the Gate, the Bay was one vast arsenal and clanging workshop. Until Midway, Guadalcanal, Philippine Sea, Iwo Jima, Okinawa. . . .

The heavy cruiser *Indianapolis* was known to her sailors as a happy ship, but naval authorities had always questioned her stability of design. She was, in fact, not to have a happy ending. Moreover, she had been roughly handled by a Kamikaze in the Okinawa campaign. Hastily repaired at Mare Island, she was off for the wars again. Destiny appointed her to leave the Golden Gate on a July night in 1945, heavily blacked out, on what was surely the most fateful sea errand in all history.

The *Indianapolis*, unescorted, made a high-speed run to

Tinian Island in the Marshalls, where she arrived on July 26, discharged some military cargo, took on other stores, and proceeded for Leyte via Guam. Her orders were to report at Leyte for two weeks' training before joining the forces off Okinawa again.

Among the material she deposited at Tinian were some guarded cases whose contents were wholly unknown to her Captain McVay and everyone else aboard the warship, except Captain William S. Parsons, a Navy ordnance specialist, and an assistant. The innocuous cases landed, the *Indianapolis* steamed on for nearby Guam, and two days after clearing that island she passed between a full moon and a Japanese submarine, and went down with 350 to 400 gallant men.

That was the end of the *Indianapolis*. But not yet the end for the package she had left on Tinian. From the time he landed there, Captain Parsons and his assistant had been busy assembling something. General Le May, in charge of strategic bombing, divided his minutes between watching Captain Parsons at his inscrutable work, and inspecting the weather. The night of August 5 looked promising. A B-29 bomber was wheeled into position and the *Indianapolis'* recent bit of cargo was delicately placed aboard. Col. Paul Tibbets took the *Enola Gay's* controls. Parsons and his assistant swung aboard to make some last-instant adjustments. With two observation planes for company, the *Enola Gay* lifted off at 0245 of August 6 and winged for Japan. When over Iwo Jima she started her Everest-like climb to 30,000 feet. Her reconnaissance planes reported, at about nine, "Clear over Hiroshima." At 0911, Col. Tibbets passed the controls over to his bombardier, Major Tom Ferebee. At 0915 the Major toggled out the gift the *Indianapolis* had brought from overseas. The plane was at 31,600 feet.

Below, on a parade ground, a section of the Japanese Second Army was doing calisthenics. It was included in the 31,-

379 people who died, along with the 20,000 who were injured and the 171,000 rendered homeless.

The *Enola Gay* was back at Tinian in time for late lunch.

The *Indianapolis* had been at the bottom of the sea for a week.

Japan's war lords got out their silk hats and morning coats and prepared for a visit of surrender to the nearest U.S. flagship.

And the world began coping with the Atomic Age.

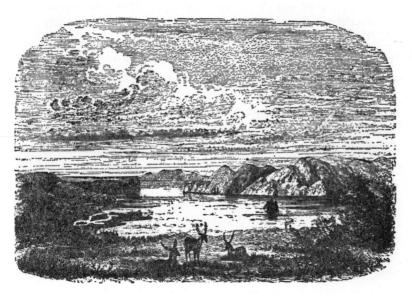

The Golden Gate

17 : GUNS OF THE GATE

No OUTPOST of empire was ever more listlessly armed for
defense than the Presidio of San Francisco under Spain and
her Mexican successors.

American occupation changed that somnolent attitude.
The situation in the Pacific, the posture of other powers, was
far from clear. The Golden Gate appeared to be ideal for attack and ideal to defend. Especially appealing to military engineers, as to later bridge builders, was the narrow throat of
the Gate where a long rocky point reached from the south,
with the stubby point of an immense escarpment opposite
and only a mile away. Surveyors and stakemen appeared one
day, followed by diggers and masons, and a strong fortress
started rising. Its foundations were close to water level; its
location was directly below the Mexican earthworks. A local
citizen named E. J. "Lucky" Baldwin took the contract for
making hundreds of thousands of good red bricks. With the
nest egg thus acquired, he went on to become one of California's colorful plunger-millionaires, best remembered for
acquiring and naming the site of Santa Anita racetrack.

Congress had appropriated $1,038,000 for the Gate's new
strong point. It was modeled on the Fort Sumter pattern then
fashionable, but was more robust: it had three tiers of mov-
able guns instead of Sumter's two, and a fourth tier of bar-

bettes—fixed guns—mounted on its rim. Officially named Fort Winfield Scott, popularly called Fort Point from its location, it was begun in 1854 and completed in 1860, and there it has stood for more than a hundred years. It never fired a gun in wrath but its mere presence in earlier days may have been a sufficient deterrent. Waves beat about its footings on three sides and in squalls sometimes dash clear up to the now empty casemates.

For eight decades the stout brick building was the dominant man-made structure offered by any view of the Gate. So embedded was it in local affections that when the Bridge was planned, to spring directly from that site, an outcry arose to Save The Fort. So the Fort was saved. The Bridge swoops right over it and cuddles the warm red bricks in a cozy embrace of steel girders. But try, today, to find the Fort. So overwhelmed is it by the immensity of the Bridge that one Army engineer who travels that lofty route every day, but is an import from Louisiana, confessed to this writer after a year of frequent crossings that he had never seen or heard of Fort Point's fort.

But the capacious walls and galleries are worth touring. It was definitely built to distinguish itself in the battle which never came. The iron entrance gate was originally flanked by two Spanish guns, unmounted, bearing the arms of Charles III. They'd been cast in 1760 and were believed to have once been part of the armament of a Spanish frigate. Those ornamental guns and all others now are gone, but in its day the American armament within the entrance gate was strictly for business.

Inside the walls, one comes on a large court open to the sky. The walls that surround it are arched and tunneled. The ground-floor tunnels were for ammunition and supplies. Above were officers' quarters, then barracks for enlisted men. There was room for a regiment, and the Third U.S. Coast Artillery moved in. Around the walls, about 100 guns were in position. (Ultimate plans called for 164.) In the courtyard, furnaces stood ready to heat the shot for them. The ordnance in favor was a style called columbiads. These were heavy cast-iron smoothbore cannon capable of throwing both shells and shot. The bottom tier were 10-inchers. Second and third tiers were 10's and 8's. The wall summits were also graced with bombards, and plans were drawn up for the coves and cliffs directly across the water. And from Alcatraz, batteries with a total of 47 guns aimed directly at the Gate.

Californians at the Civil War's onset were a long way from the rest of the Union, connected only by wagon, stagecoach, ship and pony express. Rumors thrived. Confederate raiders and privateers, largely imaginary, were reported everywhere. The attitude of England was suspect. The land batteries of the Gate were supported by only one armed vessel, the little revenue cutter *Active*. Earthworks were built for miles behind Fort Point; Black Point (Fort Mason) was fortified; scores of guns were emplanted across the Gate; Angel Island received fifty and Goat Island too was readied to make a bang if necessary. A battery was placed at the southeast base of Telegraph Hill, giving name to a street.

In '63 the British warship *Sutlej* stood into the Gate and didn't salute. A shot across her bows from Alcatraz corrected her manners. In '64 rumor spread that an "Anglo-China fleet" of six vessels was headed Gateward, in company with the Confederate raider *Alabama*. But the *Alabama* was already a ghost, having met the guns of the *Kearsarge* off Cherbourg, France.

In '65 the raider *Shenandoah* made a sensational capture of twenty-nine whaleships in the Arctic and Pacific. Many of these were based within the Gate. When the whaler *Milo* came in with word that Captain James Waddell and the *Shenandoah* were right behind, anxiety reached a peak. But Waddell encountered the English bark *Barracouta* thirteen days out from the Gate and learned from her that the war was over.

Eleven years later, as part of the exercises celebrating the centennial of both the United States and the Presidio of San Francisco, a great sham battle was held on the Presidio's hills and plains. In conjunction, there was a lively naval display. Much powder was burned, and a gala time was had; but military eyes watched closely, and military minds came to a regretful decision. All those guns, many of which were of 1812 pattern, were obsolete. The ironclad, as typified by the *Merrimac* and *Monitor,* could smash its way past all the Gate's many-score smoothbores.

As the new century opened, rifled guns had taken over the defense of the Gate. They were on two types of carriages, disappearing and barbette. From the water, the 10- and 12-inch disappearing guns were wholly invisible until they rose to peep and fire. The recoil knocked them back and down into a cradle of two arms and two air cylinders, and there they remained until a large wheel on the side of the carriage was cranked to raise them again. The snouts of the barbettes, however, were always above the parapet.

The personnel for either type included a gun pointer, two men to trundle powder and shell from the magazine hoist, two ramrod men to drive home the shells and silken bags of powder; breechblock operator, lanyard man, and swabber to clean out Old Betsy after firing. Another crew was required in the magazine and plotting rooms, both underground.

In 1901 the modernized defenses of the Gate were augmented by another post, on the heights above Land's End. Known as Fort Miley, this was headquarters for the Pacific Coast Artillery District. Fort Funston later was created on the ocean front three miles south of the Cliff House. Here, into bluffs and dunes rising two hundred feet, a tremendous gun emplacement was dug in 1939 known as Battery Davis.

During the war with Japan, guns of enormous caliber trained straight west.

On the whole, the public took the defenses of the Gate with respect but also with light-heartedness. When the National Guard practiced with Fort Miley's 12-inchers, it was open house for wives and sweethearts. Six pretty girls were once seen decorating one of the gun emplacements and they really decorated it; the boys had lined them up on the parapet on their tiptoes, mouths open, eyes tight closed, fingers wedged in ears. When this human frieze was nicely arranged, the artillerymen methodically proceeded to clean the gun, load it, train it, and check and recheck their mathematics. If a damsel's eyelid fluttered, she was whooped at. Finally all was ready. A tug out at sea towed a canvas target across the field of fire. Bang!

To the guardsmen's own amazed unbelief, they had shot the kingpost right out of the target.

"Up on your toes again, girls," said the elated captain, "while we do it a second time."

Bang! But that time the boys of Battery B missed the target completely and a metal ring, separating from the shell, almost hit the tug, which cut its towline and ran for its life.

On the frowning bluffs of Forts Baker and Barry across the channel—heights which no ship-borne guns could hope to touch—were installations known only to the Coast Artillery and a few jack-rabbits. Their remoteness and mystery made them super-formidable. During World War II, the sound of heavy guns being moved over the highways during the nights, to further strengthen these defenses after Pearl Harbor, added to this secure feeling. Unwarrantedly, perhaps. A 16-inch naval piece was trundled up the coastal roads and across the Bridge, dollied sharp right off Highway 101, then angled left into the low, narrow half-mile tunnel leading to the north-shore military reservation. And there, like a sword halfway into a rusty scabbard, the huge gun stuck.

"The war just about had to stop," recalled one citizen soldier, "while we considered that situation. But did we fail? No, siree. It took fifty tons of vaseline, but we got the gun through."

Just in time, it might be said, to find the mighty weapon already obsolete. The rifles of monumental size atop the Gate's cliffs could shoot twenty and more miles out to sea, but a carrier could stand hundreds of miles off and pound the futile shore guns into steel filings.

The guns of the Gate at this writing are of another description altogether. They are the planes of Hamilton, Travis and other fields, and the Nike-Ajax and Nike-Hercules combat-ready surface-to-air missiles of the U.S. Army Air Defense Command.

Nike-Ajax was the nation's first combat-ready, surface-to-air guided missile. Twenty feet long and a foot in diameter, it whooshes at supersonic speed for individual targets to a range of 25 miles and the altitude of any known bomber. It can kill any target which its radars can "see." Nike-Hercules, its younger but bigger brother, with a range of 75 miles and an altitude capability of anything that is required from 1,000 to 150,000 feet, can search out whole groups of targets and has demonstrated itself against objects moving faster than 2100 miles per hour.

The only thing today that seems to travel faster than a rocket missile is the art of missilery itself, which leaves written words obsolete almost as they fall from the typewriter.

18 : ON THE BEACH

THERE was a man who entered the Golden Gate in Gold-Rush times and found himself uniquely fitted to lead that strident orchestra of events. He'd been born in 1826 on an Ohio farm. He'd spent his youth on the Mississippi River as a steamboat-man. His name was William C. Ralston. He was twenty-three when the gold fever hit the little nation of 29 states and 23 million people. He sailed from New Orleans for the Isthmus of Panama and got a job there under three steamboat captains whom he'd known on the Mississippi. They had a forwarding, banking, and steamship agency business on both sides of the Isthmus and put him in charge at Panama on the Pacific side.

They operated a steamship, the *New Orleans*. She was a sidewheeler, built of wood, uncompartmented, a prey to every hazard of rock, wind and fire, but she hauled freight and people. In '52 she lacked a captain. Twenty-six-year-old Ralston couldn't disappoint his 200 waiting passengers. What did the Pacific Ocean have that the Mississippi River didn't have, except size? As a matter of fact, it had a lot. It had the stormy Gulf of Tehuantepec. It had a 4,000 mile coast to the Gate without a lighthouse. It had reefs and mists. But Mississippi captains and pilots were a confident breed. Ralston offered to skipper the *New Orleans*, and those passengers

122

—made brave by a desire to get onward—cheered him for his nerve. He made it, in eighteen days.

At the Gate, he fell in love. He fell in love with a rowdy, raw jerry-built town. He took the *New Orleans* back to Panama but his heart remained in the north. In four years he returned, to stay.

Between 1856 and 1875 he revolutionized the appearance and fortunes of that town. He started a bank. Only two in the nation, both in New York, had equal or larger capital. His bank's capital was all paid up, in gold. It soon dominated the growing city. It spread out, dominating the Comstock Lode of Nevada. California had produced $400 million of placer gold in the 'fifties. The Comstock, beginning to fountain silver and gold when the California placers played out, revealed bonanza after bonanza in the depths of the earth. Much of the wealth rushed down to Ralston's bank. It made him a very great man. Six foot two, two hundred pounds, massive of head, Ralston walked the streets and knew everybody. His country home was regal and he entertained all important visitors to the West.

He put industrial and mercantile foundations under his town. He financed mills, factories, steamboat lines, drydocks, vineyards, wineries, canneries, irrigation projects, commercial firms, railroads. He built a notable theater. He decided to build a great hotel. It would be the biggest most luxurious in the world. Where Chicago's largest hotel had 58,000 square feet and New York's 36,000, San Francisco's would have 96,250. It would have fireplaces in every room, 438 bathtubs, quarters for 1200 guests. Why, a carriage would be able to drive right into it! He bought a city block of land. Up it went, that edifice, story on story, tier on tier of bay windows, mile on mile of steam pipe and water pipe and parquetry and carpet. A partner protested, "If he needed a plank, he bought a whole forest. If he got into anything, there was no end to it. He never beat a retreat until he struck the ocean." The remark was prophetic.

Ralston by this time saw his little frontier city not as it was but as it should be. He saw it as Pericles saw Athens, as Lorenzo de' Medici saw Florence. He saw it a destined world leader of culture, of music, of elegance, of art, of graciousness and glory. There must be opera, symphonies, galleries, great drama, great letters. Meanwhile his Palace Hotel was being completed. In went silverware by the ton, fine crockery by the shipload. From New England came 900 specially made spittoons, from Old England 960 splendid toilet seats— whether Chippendale or Sheraton is unrecorded. The whole $5 million glittering jewel for his bedazzled sweetheart was about to be pinned to her in a civic gala when Comstock shares took a wild sag, there was panic, the creeping depression from the East struck the Coast, everybody dashed for his money, the bank paid out more than it took in, the doors closed, and William Chapman Ralston was fired.

He always had loved the Gate. Daily he had gone swimming in it. This day he went thither as usual for reinvigoration. He traveled by horsecar to a public bath at the foot of Hyde Street, hired a cubicle and suit and towel, and plunged in.

He was seen to be in difficulties. A boy went out in a boat and brought him in. He died on the sand. No water was found in his lungs. The death of his dreams, the shock of his downfall, had perhaps been too much for the athletic heart.

He was forty-nine years old. The range of his achievements gave only a suggestion of what his soaring civic imagination might have wrought with a little more time.

They took him up from the beach where he'd been cast. Fifty thousand people attended his funeral. He'd busted a lot of them, temporarily, but that was forgiven. He was the most popular citizen the town had ever had.

Five weeks later the bank reopened. (It's running still, and a hundred times larger.) On the same day, the Palace Hotel also opened for business. It was the marvel of its time, and to this date a score of world cities have Palace Hotels modeled after Ralston's glittering outpost caravansary.

The number of tall, blond, rawboned, somewhat unreasonable men who have poured down the mountain slopes of Scandinavia and put to sea before the mast is almost as great as the number of short-tailed, furry-footed lemmings who annually rush for those same shores and into the deep. Thank God for the angry men of Norway and Sweden! They get drunk, they play knuckle-headed, they argue, they are blasphemous, they would rather be stubborn than right, and they fight, but give them a ship and a rag of a sail or a coal shovel and they'll take you to Niflheim, Valhalla, Asgard and all the outyards of earth. And maybe back again. Particularly if that s.o.b. they left under a table in a whiskey mill on the Embarcadero still thinks a Finn can lick a Norwegian, or a Norwegian a Swede.

One of these irascible men hit the cleft between Points Bonita and Lobos in the British ship *New York* in 1880. His age was twenty-six. He was born in Christiania, Norway. He'd just rounded the Horn. He had been to sea ten years and under every flag; he had even sailed America's Great Lakes. He was tall, bony, prow-beaked, deep-set of eyes, high of cheekbones, high of voice, and exactly as rich as all other sailormen of his day, which meant that he didn't have a cent. Or if any of his pay still was due him, it would be in the pocket of a boardinghouse crimp by nightfall, and he would be tossed on board an outgoing ship and left to find out, tomorrow, where he was going. To Shanghai or Sydney or Puget Sound or Curaçao.

This one's name was Andy Furuseth.

There were some things odd about him. He was quiet,

good-natured, with a dry sense of humor. He could take his grog or leave it. He wasn't too interested in the ladies of Barbary Coast and Morton Alley, whose mission was to make a sailor's shore stay ineffable. Worst of all, he read books. John Walker, his boardinghouse keeper in Finn's Alley, looked at some of the tomes. Tolstoy, Emerson and a book about a fellow named Spartacus, who had led a revolt of the slaves in ancient Rome.

Andy made voyages to Puget Sound for coal, to the Columbia River for salmon. He slept on a plank, ate moldy food, ducked the fists of bucko mates, shoveled coal, hauled rope. Always he came back to the Gate, where he read more books, developed a slow burn under his good-natured exterior, and joined a faltering, stumbling little seamen's union. Since he had read a book, or been seen carrying one, they made him secretary.

They sent him to an AFL convention at Birmingham, Alabama. Bills for aiding seamen were discussed there. The most kicked-around class on the face of the earth, whose lot hadn't improved since Dana's *Two Years Before the Mast*, these cheated, robbed, often-clubbed, bewildered men wanted a leader. Andy was shy. He didn't offer himself for the job. But he went out, rang San Francisco doorbells and helped elect a friendly congressman, and in 1892 he astonished the great Pacific Mail Steamship Company by forcing it to quit evading the Chinese exclusion laws and staff a new ship with white men. In that same year his little Coast Seamen's Union guided the founding of the International Seamen's Union. Andy was planning big.

By this time Andy Furuseth, raging up and down the boardinghouse rows of San Francisco and the halls of Washington, was that most terrible of obsessed, single-minded humans, a Viking with a cause. His *Coast Seaman's Journal* had compiled a devastating "Red Record." It was factual. It told of ninety-four cases of sailors who'd been beaten, maimed or killed on shipboard in a specific period. More than half of fifteen cases of plain murder had taken place without a conviction. He had countless cases of disasters at sea which could have been avoided if reasonable safety measures had been taken. Gone now was the good nature, the dry humor. Andy Furuseth had become a human lightning bolt, a hammer of Thor. Where he struck, chunks flew. Politicians fled before him. Socialists, Reds fled even faster. Shipowners sought hatchways and fell down ladders. With the aid of his great friend Sam Gompers of the AFL, and the sponsorship of Bob LaFollette of Wisconsin, he forced through Congress in 1915 the bill that liberated American seamen from grinding abuse. Woodrow Wilson signed it, and the Pacific Mail left the overseas traffic lanes forever.

Andy died in 1938. He was eighty-four. By that time the Reds were after him with hatchets, breathing hard. But he'd won his victory. American seamen at last had decent quarters, clean food, protection for their wages, a fair shake ashore. From the hour he'd landed on the beach beside the Golden Gate in 1880 he'd been fighting. In '41, on Labor Day, the men he'd done so much for placed a bronze bust of hawk-faced Andy on a granite shaft in front of the Ferry Building on the Embarcadero. Thin hair flying, beak outthrust, the planes of his thin cheeks resembling a clipper's bows, indomitable Andy looked exactly like a windblown, spray-cleaving figurehead of a Cape Horner. The granite shaft had a quotation from him that pretty well summed up the whole Andrew Furuseth: "You can put me in jail. But you cannot give me narrower quarters than as a seaman I have always had. You cannot give me worse food than I have always eaten. You cannot make me lonelier than I have always been."

Men who follow the sea have since lifted Andy to a kind of sainthood. That would puzzle him. Better leave him, as the monument does, a very human figure at the prow of a driving ship. Parting the waters and leading the way.

This one didn't come by way of the Gate. But he lived a short while beside it. He sauntered, brooded, wrestled with himself. A monument was afterward erected to him in Portsmouth Square.

He was a grandson and a son of lighthouse builders. He was trained for the law, a matter of laughable amazement to him to the end of his brief days. He was a wanderer, a dreamer, an advance Conrad with Scots burr and mild tongue, a belated Melville with enmity for no one, not even a whale.

Robert Louis Stevenson was born in Edinburgh of wellfixed parents. His rambles through Europe were predictably bohemian, orthodoxly romantic. He was lanky, thin, predisposed to weak lungs, more in need of mothering than mistressing. In France he had met a lady who was another man's wife. When Fanny Osborne went home to Oakland, California, and the cottage of her husband, "Louis," age 29, followed by steerage and then by emigrant train. In 1879, an overland emigrant train was practically a string of cattle cars. His flat purse was due to parental disapproval. He wandered in pursuit of Fanny Osborne in the Monterey Peninsula and then took lodgings on San Francisco's Bush Street, where he wrote verse and newspaper pieces and from which he went out to ten-cent breakfasts and two-bit dinners, and wore his soles thin and his body thinner climbing newspaper stairs to peddle manuscripts at one-third of a cent a word. He sold only a very few. He was sick much of the time, half-starved the rest of it.

In the Telegraph Hill home of his friend Charles Warren Stoddard, another romanticist and penman, he picked up Stoddard's own *South Sea Idylls*, also Herman Melville's *Typee* and *Omoo*. Sensing the excitement of coming discovery, he borrowed them. Promptly they tore at his heart-strings.

Fanny Osborne slipped her marriage hawser to Sam Osborne and she and her Louis were united in a church on Post Street close to Mason which, running northward, climbed his familiar Nob Hill and plunged down to Meiggs Wharf and the Gate.

His parents managed to relent. He and Fanny went home to his Scotland, to other scenes. In 1888 they returned to the town by the Gate. By that time publishers were fighting for his manuscripts, waving $5,000 checks. Louis and Fanny chartered a white-winged schooner, the *Casco*. They were bound for Stoddard's and Melville's South Seas—Honolulu, Tahiti, the Marquesas—wherever coral and coco palms called. As they passed beyond the Heads he wrote:

> The broad sun
>   The bright day:
> White sails
>   On the blue bay:—
> The far-farers
>   Draw away.
>
> Light the fires
>   And close the door
> To the old homes,
>   To the loved shore,
> The far-farers
>   Return no more.

He died at Apia in Samoa at age 44 and is buried on a mountaintop there. He'd given the world *Treasure Island, A Child's Garden of Verses, The Strange Case of Dr. Jekyll and Mr. Hyde, Kidnapped, The Master of Ballantrae, The Wrecker, The Ebb Tide* and a budget of graceful jottings that left the scene a little more luminous where he had passed.

The little monument that was reared to him in Portsmouth Square had a bronze ship that looked more like Cabrillo's caravel than R. L. S.'s schooner, but it swelled its sails right bravely.

In the notebooks he filled while sitting in bed, fever-wracked, in Mrs. Mary Carson's lodging house eight blocks up the hill, that winter in 1880, he'd penned:

> Where all the deep-sea galleons ride
> That come to bring the corn,
> Where falls the fog at eventide
> And blows the breeze at morn,
> It's there that I was sick and sad,
> Alone and poor and cold,
> In yon distressful city
> Beside the Gates of Gold.

19 : SOUTH SEA PERFUME

THE soft winds from Hawaii and islands south have blown through the Gate long enough to bewitch a considerable gaggle of novelists and maybe even a few of the G.I.'s and Marines who steamed for Polynesia in 1942-45. More than a hundred years before, New England shipmasters knew all about those dulcet bowers of the sea—a whole lot more than they told their wives. The whalemen who came through the Gate a generation or two before the Gold Rush, and stocked up with wood and water in Latitude 38° North, had wild gardenia fragrance still in their nostrils. Herman Melville, the *Moby Dick* man, spent three months in and about Tahiti as a roving sailor and when he brought out *Omoo, a Romance of the South Seas*, in 1847, he didn't make the stay-at-homes any less restless by reporting:

"Such enchantment breathes on the whole, that it seems a fairy world. . . . The ineffable repose and beauty of the landscape is such, that every object strikes like something from a dream."

That belt of the seascape from Capricorn to Cancer caused many a ship to make a long tack in search of a wind not only navigable but scented, and sailormen welcomed the change from chasing whales to chasing girls.

For the Gold-Rush men, Hawaii was a spot already civilized enough by the missionaries to have ankle-length garments, schools and a printing press, and to furnish potatoes and other foodstuffs to the mainland. Later, Tahiti, Samoa and the rest offered pearl for shirt buttons, copra for soap and exotic whole coconuts for breaking and grating over cake. Still and all, for many a year the southern waters below Hawaii were chiefly places where mariners got blown to. And despite the tales of languor, free love and free bananas, life could be rough.

For instance, the clipper ship *Wild Wave*. She sailed out the Golden Gate in 1858 for Valparaiso with ten passengers, mixed cargo, and Capt. Josiah Knowles' own $18,000 in gold. Twenty-four days out of port, at 1 A.M., the lookout reported sudden breakers where the chart recorded no such hazard. *Wild Wave* piled on a coral reef. This was Oeno, an uninhabited two-mile atoll and lagoon directly on Capricorn and southeast of Tuamotu Archipelago. Captain Knowles lost his fine 1500-ton ship but landed all souls safely. Nearest land believed inhabited was a hundred miles away—Pitcairn Island, the refuge of the famous *Bounty* mutineers. Knowles and six men took one of the ship's boats and sailed to Pitcairn for help. In landing there, the boat was smashed by surf. They found the island deserted; the British Government had taken off its occupants. We pick up the captain's diary at this point; bracketed portions are our own:

> Thursday, April 1, 1858.—We decided today to build a boat and sail for Tahiti [1500 miles], as we almost despaired of being found here.
> April 2.—Our stock of tools 6 axes, 2 hatchets, 3 planes, 2 chisels, a hammer and a spike gimlet. [But no saw.]
> Sun. Apr. 24.—Two of us planing and hewing plank for our boat. Our clothing all but used up. . . . We must soon take to goat skins after the style of Robinson Crusoe. We have been barefoot a long time.
> Apr. 29.—In the afternoon laid the keel of our boat.

May 7.—Making sails today from rags of every hue and fabric we could find. [Also a red, white and blue ensign from a church pulpit cloth, an old shirt and what was left of a pair of dungarees. This ensign is today in the Maritime Museum beside the Gate.]

May 12.—Burned houses to get nails but hardly got enough of them.

May 26.—Morning picked oakum awhile, then went out after breadfruits. Long shall I remember this, my 28th birthday.

May 29.—Devoted the day to making a charcoal pit; we shall need a good deal of fuel when we start off.

June 2.—Began work on a rope walk, it being necessary to make ropes to use in rigging our boat.

Fri. July 23.—Dug up my money, [that $18,000 in gold] which had been all this time directly under the boat while building. Soon after noon weighed anchor and started off to sea. Our men who proposed remaining on the island . . . left us with three cheers.

Fri. July 30.—One week after leaving Pitcairn Island and have done well. Made over 100 miles each day.

Tues. Aug. 2.—Close to the Island of Ohitahoo, one of the Marquesas. The natives anxious for us to anchor, but I was quite anxious to get away as they were a savage looking set.

Wed. Aug. 4—In the morning saw the Island of Nukahiva. [In Marquesas.] We rounded the point of the harbor, and to our great joy and surprise there lay at anchor an American Man-of-War. [The *Vandalia*.] So great was our joy that we were unable to speak for some time. [Knowles sold the crude schooner to missionaries for $250. The *Vandalia* took the plucky seamen on board and rescued the balance of the party from Oeno and Pitcairn islands, returning all safely to the Golden Gate.]

Sept. 29.—Arrived in San Francisco. . . . My old boatman [whitehaller] looked at me in perfect amazement and exclaimed, "My God, is that you, Captain Knowles?"

Fri. Oct. 30. Boston—Found my wife in a feeble state of health, but the baby well and hearty. The meeting with my family was quite affecting. Everyone had long since given me up as lost. I was indeed glad to be at home and at rest.

Doughty Captain Knowles later skippered the McKay-built *Glory of the Seas*, made a passage from New York to the Gate in ninety-six days, and retired from the sea in 1880 to be a co-founder of the Pacific Steam Whaling Company and one of San Francisco's most respected shipping merchants.

For these voyagers, uninhabited islands and a lucky escape. But for others, the enchantment persisted. Charles Warren Stoddard, the incurable romantic, wrote in *Overland Monthly* and *Atlantic* his *South Sea Idylls*, which were made into a book in 1873. "A green oasis blossomed before us—a garden in perfect bloom, girdled about with creaming waves; within its coral cincture pendulous boughs trailed in the glassy waters; from its hidden bowers spiced airs stole down upon us; above all the triumphant palm-trees clashed their melodious branches like a chorus with cymbals; yet from the very gates of paradise a changeful current swept us onward, and the happy isle was buried in night and distance."

As if that weren't enough, he further rhapsodized: "I can see you, my beloved, sleeping, naked, in the twilight of the west. The winds kiss you with pure and fragrant lips. The sensuous waves invite you to their embrace. . . . Return, O troubled soul! . . ."

But skippers were practical men, and if they trusted their troubled souls or those of their seamen to such Edens stuffed with Eves, mangoes and yams, it was because they had no alternative. For example, the iron ship *Ada Iredale*. She was sailing from Scotland for the Golden Gate in 1876, when her cargo of coal was discovered afire after passing Cape Horn and she was hastily abandoned. The crew reached island safety, but the ship tossed about in the Pacific for over a year, slowly smoldering. Mariners occasionally sighted her and re-marked her white figurehead of a lady with hand to breast, peering out over the ocean with the soles of her feet presumably mighty hot. The floating oven was bought in at an auction in Papeete by Captain I. E. Thayer, who had come down from the Gate to acquire her. He nudged her ashore on a coral atoll, careened her, extinguished her deep-gnawing blaze, and relaunched and refitted her under the most primitive conditions imaginable. And with islanders for his crew, Captain Thayer sailed her back to the Gate. She was re-rigged and renamed *Annie Johnson* and off she went again for the South Seas or wherever a cargo offered, her figurehead still scanning the waves, and she was one of the last windships to stay in business. She didn't give up until 1929.

Thayer did another and similar wrecker's job in much the same waters. It was for the four-masted bark *Pyrenees*, bound from Tacoma for Leith, Scotland, with wheat and barley. On the long reach southward her cargo got damp and caught fire from spontaneous combustion. Her skipper immediately headed for Pitcairn Island but couldn't find a sandy place to beach her. On the island this time was a descendant of the *Bounty* mutineers, Governor McCoy. He came out and volunteered to pilot her personally to the nearest sandspit, which was on Manga Reva atoll in the Tuamotos, three hundred miles away. The metal ship, practically a red-hot stove, made it through the reefs and was abandoned, and her crew was picked up by a trading schooner and taken to Tahiti.

When the story got to the Gate, Captain Thayer was off like a veteran fire horse. But this time he took some experienced salvage hands and went to Papeete by steamer. He hired there an army of Polynesians and chartered a schooner and made for Manga Reva. They extinguished what fire was left, and they sailed that deckless, burnt-out hulk nine hundred miles to Papeete, laid temporary decks on her, and proceeded for the Gate, which they entered on July 27, 1902, just twenty-three years after Thayer had brought in the *Iredale*.

After being thoroughly repaired, *Pyrenees* sailed again but under a new name, *Manga Reva.*

Sometimes the fairyland waters of Polynesia were made red by mutiny. The *Hesper,* one of eleven barks that were built on the Pacific Coast, sailed from the Gate in 1892; and the men in the fo'c'sle, tiring of the hard life of a windjammer and bemused by the green, beguiling islets they were passing, decided to seize the ship. A seaman named St. Clair led the uprising and told the men the captain had chests of gold in his cabin—an added incentive. They slew the mate on watch with a cleaver from the galley. The mutineers then woke the other mate and told him it was his turn on deck. As he was usually awakened by an officer, this mate became suspicious. He went to the sleeping captain, shook him and said so. Arming themselves, the pair went on deck. The mutineers still had only that cleaver. A sharp tussle and they were in irons. They were handed over to the French authorities at Papeete and were returned to the Gate on the packet *Tropic Bird.* St. Clair swung for it at San Quentin.

But the flood of purple prose about the coral islands and the nut-brown maids continued to pour. Mark Twain had done his bit in letters from Hawaii to the *Sacramento Union.* Pierre Loti dallied with Queen Pomare's court at Tahiti and tattled about it.

The lure even put one important early-day Coast shipbuilding firm out of business. The Dickie Brothers, John and James, had built forty vessels on San Francisco Bay before a Señor Montalvo arrived from Mexico with credentials from his government and $300,000 for the construction of a gunboat. The Dickies built it. And under cover of darkness Señor Montalvo sailed away without paying for the vessel, and was presumed to be headed for the Perfumed Isles; in fact, was thought to be taking a full cargo of beauty and sin along with him. In vain the Dickies waited for reimbursement for the gunboat *Democrata.* John finally took a hired job as superintendent for the Union Iron Works, and Jim went to the Fulton Iron Works.

A treasurer of Wells Fargo, the big western banking and express house of decades back, had a cashier at San Francisco who grew tired of the stand-up desks and heavy ledgers and made off, South Seas-bound, with the company cash. In after years a preacher at Chico, California, heard the Circean summons and started for those coral heavens—further fortifying himself for romance, however, by taking along a locomotive engineer's wife. And many a yachtload of intrepid lotus eaters and pirate-treasure diggers set off, and still do, some with sails that don't last five hundred miles. In my own day and circle an intrepid lady of delicacy and refinement, tiring of bridge and cocktails, bought herself passage first to Honolulu, then to Tahiti, then on a paying-guest yacht out of Papeete for the Tuomotus, that cloudlike archipelago of coral islands. She was shipwrecked on a reef but bravely stuck it out all night, submerged to waist and neck, and waded ashore at dawn still clutching an umbrella.

To get at least part of this South Sea hanker and cargo-hauling on a basis competitive with the windships, Pacific Mail put the steamer *Costa Rica* on regular run to Honolulu in '73. She was wrecked in the Golden Gate on her fifth round-trip. But sugar production was booming in the Hawaiian group and in '76 the United States made a deal with the little island kingdom: sugar to come in free of tariff, and the U.S. to have naval use of Pearl Harbor. This reciprocal treaty and rising American influence in those islands led to the annexation of Hawaii as a U.S. territory in '98. From '78 until 1915 when it pulled down its houseflag from transpacific voyaging, Pacific Mail made Honolulu a regular port of steamer call. One of its steamships, the *Moses Taylor*, was known as "Rolling Moses" and went no farther than between the two ports; others went to Japan and China. The jauntiest of its vessels was the *China*, a yachtlike steamer with four masts that originally were used for auxiliary sail. Her arrivals and departures were of great moment in Honolulu and always brought out the royal band.

When Claus Spreckels of Hanover arrived at the Gate in 1856 and went into the grocery business, he noticed that beer and sugar were his retail staples and decided to manufacture both. The brewery in time was displaced by his burgeoning sugar refinery, and when he won a large chunk of the island of Maui from King Kalakaua in a poker game, several things happened to the linkage between the Gate and Diamond Head, and also between the Gate and certain garden isles below the equator. Claus's son John D. started a sugar-carrying fleet with a small brig and presently had a fleet of nine vessels. In the late '80's the Spreckels' Oceanic Steamship Company began serving the Society Islands with its original *Mariposa*, first of three of that name. Service from the Gate had previously been given by a German company, the Oceanic Commercial Society of Hamburg, with the iron steamer *Raiatea*. Her round trips of four or five a year were made in twenty-one to twenty-six days each way, about sailing ship time, and came to an end in 1887, the third year, when *Raiatea* burned at sea, singeing her captain's beard and killing by fright a passenger who was pulled through a 12-inch porthole. The Spreckels-owned Oceanic Line steamers continued onward to New Zealand and Australia. Sometimes they gave up the Tahiti calls, but later came under Matson management and today the steamer travel between Golden Gate and the Tahitian and Samoan ports, Papeete and Pago Pago, is more enthusiastic than ever.

Captain William Matson began linking the Golden Gate and Hawaii with a lei of ships in the '90's. A boy of ten and an orphan, he had left Sweden on a sailing vessel and at fourteen was a handy boy on the Cape Horner *Bridgewater*, which brought him to the Gate and Hawaii in '82. For twenty years he carried sugar out of Hilo on vessels of ever increasing size, leaving Honolulu mainland service to the island-owned Planters Line. Then he was serving Honolulu too, with some important steamships and many important "firsts" on the Pacific—first electric lights, first refrigeration, first steel sugar-carrier, first steam turbine. Bill Matson was two inches short of six feet, with barrel chest, broad shoulders and springy step. He was the nattiest dresser in San Francisco, kept a stable of fast trotters and clattered briskly about the Embarcadero in a shiny buggy. When he died in 1917 he left a small empire of fine, fast ships that hauled 99,332 doughboys to France in World War I and more than 700,000 military personnel in World War II. Matson Line for long has been serving Hawaii, Fiji, Tahiti, Samoa, New Zealand and Australia.

One more personality belongs in this roster of ship operators to the Perfumed Isles, though in his case it was only to Hawaii and then on around the world via the Far East. Captain Robert Dollar broke into shipping as a timberman. Born in Falkirk, Scotland, in 1844 of a lumbering and seafaring family, he was doughtily educated by a one-armed schoolmaster who knew how to lay the rod on with that remaining hand. Dollar left school at twelve and when his family emigrated to Canada he put in his youth getting timber out of the lake, ice and river country between Hudson's Bay and Lake Superior. His practice at arithmetic was done around loggers' campfires at night on slabs of birch bark. By 1883, Michigan had a Dollarville and Robert Dollar was its sachem. As a timber shipper, chiefly to the British Isles, he got around. In one year, by water, rail and horses, 31,000 miles. He'd got out ten to fifteen million board feet of pine a year. When the area began to play out, he moved to the west coast and set up beside the Gate. He wrested timber from the woods to northward and shipped it down by steam schooner, and from the little *Newsboy* his fleet advanced until it amounted to some very large steamships, girdling the globe on regular schedule. When he began sending his ships through the Suez Canal he found that they had to stand in line and wait their turn. He noticed that a ship flying the Egyptian flag always bypassed and went through without waiting. On inquiry he discovered that this ship carried the Egyptian mail. So, when the next annual bids were called for he bid one dollar and got the contract. After that his ships didn't have to wait and he saved money on time and standby fuel. There was no nonsense about gruff, shrewd Captain Dollar. When some of his officials wanted a skipper fired for being occasionally rude to passengers, the white-bearded shipping-line head demanded, "Does he always take his ship to where he's sent?" "Yes." "Does he always bring it back?" "Yes." "Then keep him."

Today that enterprise is known as the American President Line. It too helps to tie Telegraph Hill with Diamond Head by a bridge of ships. But the course of the *Presidents* is around-Pacific or else globe-girdling. When they return to the Gate they smell of Japan, Hong Kong, Singapore, Ceylon, Bombay, the Red Sea and the Mediterranean; the scent of Hawaiian frangipani and pineapple is part of quite a blend.

20 : THE LUMBER FLEET

OVER on Hawaii a huge tree would sometimes come floating, and it promptly became the king's: a mighty war canoe requiring half a tribe to paddle—though how a tree could grow so big and where it came from, none could guess. Lying there on the beach, its thickness was twice the height of a man!

Spanish explorers, moving by land, came upon a forest of such stems south of Monterey Bay and from then on in pockets northward. Father Pálou, nearing the larger bay to northward in 1774, wrote: "In a valley which was very full of these trees, I saw an extremely large one which had its heart burned out, forming a cave, and one of the soldiers, mounting his horse, rode into it, saying, 'Now I have a house in case it rains.'"

Before his *San Carlos* sailed for its triumphal entry of the Golden Gate, Shipmaster Ayala had his carpenters construct his famous smallboat on Carmelo River. It was made from a single trunk of redwood.

But the redwoods really whacked in on the skulls of modern man when, in 1848, some prospectors at Rich Bar, now Crescent City, had to strike south afoot and walked through woods that shored up the sky. Here were single trees big enough to provide lumber for half-a-dozen houses, and there were thousands and thousands of them. The stand, they reported, was fully 30 miles wide and 300 miles long. Henry Meiggs was one who capitalized on that information. He crossed the Gate with companions and a portable sawmill, and in 1852 was making future San Francisco dwellings out of the enormous trees on Big River 120 miles north. And on and on the timber cruisers pressed, until they found that the redwoods never ceased until Oregon was reached; and beyond that were the endless fir and pine of Oregon, Washington, Idaho and British Columbia—for a thousand continuous miles, the greatest forest on earth.

It took some doing to fell the redwoods, those daddies of all trees. Men drove "springpoles" into the bark to stand on, sixteen feet above the ground and at the top of the butt, and up there they went to work with axes. Logs forty feet long were then rolled by jackscrews to the river bank and floated down to tidewater. At that point, the "redwood fleet" was born.

It soon numbered dozens of schooners, and there came to be more than fifty ports of call. Most of them were "outside" ports, or exposed loading places, consisting of a headland or the mouth of a creek, with a mill on the bluff and a wooden chute or loading wire extending out to just beyond the surf. Under these chutes or wires the little ships would slip, snatch their cargo from the skies—often the timber from one tree was a whole cargo—and then get the hell out of there between shifts of tide and weather.

Eventually a donkey engine was tried in one of the schooners and it gave skipper and crew just a shade more control over their precarious fate. In that hour the "steam schooner" was created. The first formally designed steam schooner was built on the south shore of the Gate in the North Beach yard of Charles G. White and was launched as the *Surprise* in 1884. Presently a hundred little steamers were flaunting coal smoke into the dogholes of the Mendocino and Humboldt coasts, taking pianos and coffee and sugar and whiskey in and bringing timbers, planks, rafters, shingles, railroad ties and grape stakes out, and making the chugging run for it back to the Gate. The little "work horses" of the Gate even took on the Alaska adventure, the 830-ton steam schooner *Excelsior* getting off on July 28, 1897, for Skagway with gold seekers packed to her rails—a reminiscence, in reverse, of the gold hunters' arrivals by sea in '49 and '50.

On that frequently foggy and always rocky west coast, where lighthouses still are few, the steamer's whistle was used to get a telltale echo off the shore cliffs. The shipmasters were unlettered men, but they had nerves of iron, and with a whistle, a compass and a box of Copenhagen snuff, what more in the way of navigation instruments did a competent seaman need?

Some steam schooners carried passengers. The *Sea Foam,* Captain Hendricksen, which operated from the Gate to Point Arena and back with accommodation stops here and there, carried a dozen. Cabins opened onto the deck. Bunks were three-high. A bride and groom might find an interested stranger in the top-side bunk but it was all a jolly part of steam schooner life. A lady of my family went north in the *Sea Foam* to visit a young bride at Gualala, near Point Arena, and I saw this unsuspicious passenger off. She pointed with amusement to a sign in her cabin, "Passengers will please remove shoes before retiring." She asked, "What kind of passengers can those be?" After loading sheep, crates of lettuce, farm wagons and a sewing machine down the hatch, the *Sea Foam* sailed, and I later learned that this lady just did make her berth as the vessel hit the bar, and all night long neither got her shoes off nor her gloves, her veil nor her hat. Nor was she able to close that door, which was hooked open. The night was stormy. Crewmen lurched by in the dark. There were end-of-the-world sounds when the propeller came up out of the water and raced. The landing facilities at Gualala were strictly on the order of a wire lumber sling, or a breeches buoy, so this chastened passenger went on to Point Arena, where the "harbor" was a trestle between a bluff and a rock.

The merry little *Sea Foam* tightroped the creaming surf between the Golden Gate and points north for twenty-seven years, until on a wild February in 1931 her skipper took her into Point Arena, found he had underestimated the waves, tried to back out, and was heaved upon the beach. There the *Sea Foam* broke up.

For eighty years the lumber schooners from the redwood, cedar and fir ports at the north were a familiar sight in the Gate, arriving and departing daily and even in bunches. Though sometimes the arrivings were unconventional. The *Svea* one time showed up keel uppermost; she had collided with a stubborn contender for the right of way and been arse-overed for it, but had happily picked up a tow. The *Dirigo*, caught in a January gale off Cape Blanco, opened her seams, lost her fires, jettisoned her cargo, saw her rudder carried away, and was rescued and towed in through the Gate by the comradely steam schooner *Shasta*. The *Esther Johnson*, last wooden steam schooner to be built, turned the corner into the Gate and met a riptide which lifted 50,000 feet of lumber off her deck and spread it from the Cliff House to Point Reyes Head. During a January storm in 1901, the steam schooner *Pomona* ran down the sailing schooner *Fearless* off Bolinas Point and sliced her almost in two. The *Fearless* felt she already had had enough trouble, for she'd previously lost her deckload. A towboat brought her in.

The heyday of the steam schooner fleet and its hundred or so operators was following the great quake and fire of '06 when San Francisco and several other California towns had to rebuild. There were over 150 steam schooners homing for the Gate in 1913, including a couple dozen of steel. The wooden vessels rarely exceeded 200 feet in length but the steel craft went to 240 feet and could totter under a million and a half board feet of lumber. In the mid-twenties there

still were over 100 lumber steamers still on the doghole
run.

Ashore behind the "dogholes," jackscrews for rolling logs
down to streambanks gave way to strings of bullocks and
corduroyed, greased skidroads. Up Eureka way a man named
Dolbeer applied the donkey engine to log-yarding by ground-
line, which was followed by the spectacular highline, and the
bull teams shed their yokes for good. By 1880 the mills on
and near the Gate were dressing a million board feet of that
redwood a week. (A board foot is 144 cubic inches, whether
made up into bridge beams, boards or lath.) In early times,
in the redwood country, all the saws available were too short
to bring down the big stems, so poleaxes, then doublebit axes,
were used. When the saw did finally bite into the 16-inch
bark, it was a pair of 12-footers wrought into one 22-foot
blade. When a tree dropped, shaking the ground for half a
mile around, handsaw buckers went to work—silent, lean,
solitary men far in the depths of the woods—and they worked
the trunks down to logs. In 1923 the power saw showed up.
Since then, fallers and buckers here and there have grown
plumper about the waistline. More recently the boom tractor
has waddled upon the scene. And as timber was thinned out
around the coves and headlands where the first mills were,
the logging operations pushed inland until they were over the
coastal ridges entirely, and dependent upon other forms of
transportation.

The ocean was a broad highway leading along the Coast
and its usefulness as a chute southward for the redwoods, firs,
pines, and cedars of the north coast could not be conceived
as ever ending. But shipping men forgot to glance inshore.
There, up interior valleys, steel rails and blacktop highways
were extending. And at the narrows of the Gate a structure
was going up which would put the whole north country at
the end of a city street. On May 28, 1937, a "ribbon" was cut.
It was a string of three big logs laid end to end. Three cham-

pion "buckers" and their partners were there, each pair with an immense crosscut saw. At a signal, saws started on those logs of redwood, fir and pine, steel flashed, sawdust flew, and chunks thudded almost simultaneously and were rolled aside. The Golden Gate Bridge was open.

Today almost all of the once-busy "dogholes" and seaside communities that lived by and for the lumber business are ghostly places. An occasional fisherman stops for bait, a motorist for a Sunday meal, or a sea gull for a ride on a rusting cable, and those timbers that perch on a rock off-shore may be the rotted relic of what was once the terminus of a lumber chute, or the deckhouse of a steam schooner that tempted fate too narrowly. More than one hundred of the lumber vessels, sail and steam, had died on Mendocino County's coast alone.

And for the wooden steam schooners over in an Eastbay mudflat, which had been huddling there with fires drawn since the Depression while waiting for better times, there would be no more rattle in the winches, steam in the whistle, coffee in the tall black pot, nor bucko-mate's bawl. The fleet was in for keeps. The tide was out.

The truck had won.

21 : INTO THE SUNSET

IT MAY be that the first American ship ever to visit the Golden Gate was a New England whaler. Certainly the far-ranging whaleships of New Bedford were using the Gate very early. A visiting trader found seven American whaling schooners and barks taking on wood and water in the vicinity of present Sausalito in 1826. But Hawaii long was the chief Pacific rendezvous for the harpoon men. There they wintered; and there, after hunting all the succeeding summer in Arctic and South Seas waters, they returned to transship their plunder to New England-bound vessels and to winter again amid the leis and hulas. A true whaler was expected to stay away from home for a good three years.

When the Gold Rush brought ships to the Gate by hundreds, the whaleship captains had reason to shun that port. They would have lost their crews.

But with the later 1850's, whaleships were built and serviced inside the Gate in increasing numbers. A sperm-oil and spermacetti works had been established. The American whaling fleet in the Pacific in the last year of the Civil War numbered about ninety. Escaping the Confederate raider *Shenandoah,* twenty limped back to the Gate in the fall of the year and about twice that number regained Honolulu.

Ten years later, New England's whalemen had begun seri-

147

ously to move their capital west. The bark *Gay Head,* New Bedford-built and based, shifted to the Gate in '77. J. C. Beetle, builder of whaleboats, left the Massachusetts port for Alameda soon afterward. They were members of what became a long parade.

Between the mid-eighties and 1905, San Francisco was the chief whaling port of the world. The humpbacked or flat-decked unfragrant vessels wintered in Oakland Creek and set forth in spring to range from Antarctic to Arctic, sometimes chasing grey whales along the very coast of California and into the Gate itself.

When steamers were first proposed to supplant windships in the Moby Dick trade, the thought was derided. The commotion of propellers would practically give the big beasts wings in place of flukes, and nothing but thunderbolts would ever catch them. But steamers were tried. They chugged out the Gate one spring, five owned by San Franciscans and one by an unconvinced New Bedforder, and they were a signal success.

Two important enterprises, the Pacific Steam Whaling Company and the Arctic Oil Works, thereupon set up shop behind the Gate. In the Potrero district a large area sprouted with what looked like cactus plants. They were clumps of whalebone, acres and acres of them, drying in the sun and wind with a harsh rattle. The bone, tough, thin, flat and pliant, was shipped east to confine women's ribs in what were advertised as "Armorside," "Rustproof" and "French Military Figure" corsets, "bias cut, full-gored, high-busted, straight-front, never break down at the sides."

Fifty whaleships homed through the Gate in '93, bearing oil for various commercial purposes and much bone that would soon have the fair sex further full-gored and straight-fronted. For the Gate, this was the peak year of the whale-ship. Already, bolder vessels had begun to winter at Point

Barrow in the distant Arctic. Fifteen—three sail and twelve steam—wintered there in '94.

Whalebone remained in brisk demand and sometimes reached $5 a pound as the ladies continued to gasp and struggle for the Lillian Russell balloon-style bust and the Lily Langtry allegedly attainable 18-inch waist. Then flexible steel replaced whalebone, being "absolutely unbreakable over the hips." Also, some of the girls had taken to the bicycle and were beginning to claim the right to breathe. And kerosene, coal gas and electricity had long since replaced whale oil for illumination. The whale-chasing industry, on the whole, was headed about the way of the makers of beaver hats.

Yet today two whaling firms, perhaps the only ones in the United States, operate from the Golden Gate with modern factory-style steamships that roam the Pacific in search of prey. These efficient vessels haul their kills on board and render them then and there into a number of useful commodities, from whale-oil soap to dog meat.

But the picturesque whaleship fleets that wintered in Oakland Creek, and sailed or steamed out the Gate along about Groundhog Day, are vanished along with the Armorside and the Full-Gore, High-Bust, Straight-Front. Forever? Only the gals can say.

One day in the early 'sixties the brig *Timandra* was sent out the Gate with an assorted cargo for the northeast Asiatic coast. On her way back she was becalmed in the Sea of Okhotsk. While waiting for a capful of wind, her sailors tossed some fishing lines overboard. They hauled in so much codfish that they started an industry. Seven ships went out the Gate for those new grounds in 1865, and seven cargoes came back. The next season saw eighteen vessels off for the far fisheries. From then on the Okhotsk and Bering Seas and Alaskan waters were regularly fished for the Gate market.

Fishing, then salting and canning bases were established in Alaska.

The Alaska Packers Association took hold of a good part of the Alaska salmon-canning business at the turn of the century and to it goes the glory of placing on the seas the last large fleet of American sail. Its vessels, including many a proud full-rigger, were renamed *Star* of this and that. One of these, the British bark *Willscott*, had logged a typically doughty sea career before she joined the Packers. Typhooned and dismasted off the Japan coast, she set forth across the Pacific with a jury rig to her stumps of masts and made it to the Golden Gate in sixty-one days. Rerigged at San Francisco and changing ownership, she raised the Hawaiian flag and sailed until dismasted again. In 1901 she joined the Packer fleet and became *Star of Iceland*.

This *Star* fleet wintered in Oakland Creek, where Fortman Basin on the Alameda shore was a close-packed thicket of mast and spars. As a boy I lived nearby and never saw those tall sticks without feeling, smelling and hearing the winds of far places in the well-tarred rigging. With approaching spring the ships were readied to a mighty trundling, scraping and painting and were away with their cannery hands and fishermen, to return in the fall. As years took their toll of the windjammers of older vintage, trouble to get some of them off the shore was considerable. The *Llewellyn J. Morse*, which had missed being renamed when the stars were being handed around, was one such lazybones. Three tugs, lashed together, couldn't yank her off the sack. Even a fourth tug, hastily sent for, couldn't budge her, so finally a dredger came and ingloriously dug her out. The *Morse* reached the fishing grounds a trifle late.

The movement of the final fleet of windjammers by towboat across the bay and out the Gate, and the shaking of their white wings to the breeze, was a sight to bring pangs to the hearts of old salts who witnessed it. Each fall the starry windships raced home—of course—and many a season's pay changed hands on the result.

Alaska Packers bought their first steamer in 1925. After 1930, no more sailing ships were sent north. In 1941 their last square-rigger, *Star of Finland*, ex-*Kaiulani*, departed the Gate for South Africa with a cargo of lumber, and on into limbo.

Alaska Packers still carry on most valiantly and successfully between the Gate and northern waters, but with modern motive power. Alaska-based fleets now predominate.

The miners of '49 and '50 couldn't get across the valleys of California and up to the diggings fast enough. But the broad level sweeps of natural grasses which lay in their path caught some discerning eyes. Here and there land was taken up and wheat was planted. The result was startling. "Why, it just jumps out of the ground!" "It comes up before the plowing bullocks can get out of the way!"

In the spring of 1855 the bark *Greenfield*, which had brought a cargo of general merchandise around the Horn, partially loaded for the return trip with 4,750 bags of California wheat. The *Charmer* followed her long watery furrow with a full cargo of sacked wheat, 1,400 tons, at a freight bill of $28 a ton. Here was a sudden bonanza of return cargo for the ships which had been coming out laden and going home empty. It also was bonanza for the pioneer farmers, who never had seen such staggering crops and who cried to each other, in strict error, "Why, this soil will never even have to be fertilized!"

The great wheat ranches that came into being were phenomenal. One had 100,000 acres broken to the plow. By 1868 little San Francisco of 75,000 people was one of the great wheat-shipping ports of the world. In that year the clipper ship *Ontario* brought to the Gate a cargo of 7,000 bars of railroad iron and 700 kegs of spikes for the Central Pacific

Railroad that was building over the high Sierra, and her voyage just about marked the end of the clipper-ship era. She went home with sacked flour and wheat. Four years later the Gate saw its first steamerload of wheat off for Europe. Its carrier was the British-owned *Quang Se,* previously a tea trader between China and the Coast. She set off for Britain with several thousand barrels of flour and eleven tons of wheat in her hold. This was but a sifterful. A bumper crop in 1880 put steamships really in the wheat-for-Europe business. One that slogged out the Gate was the *Escambia,* which ran into unfavorable weather and capsized on the bar and immediately disappeared. Only four people were saved.

In the sixteen years beginning with 1872, more than four thousand vessels—six million tons of registered tonnage—cleared the Gate with flour and grain. Five to ten vessels a week set out. The path was around the Horn and the chief destination was Liverpool and it was a race all over again, but in reverse direction from Gold-Rush days. Voyages took from 100 to 200 days. For a time many of the ships were old clippers with shortened masts, their planks a bit waterlogged and their joints rheumaticky. By 1880, forty million bushels of wheat were being raised annually in the broad valleys behind the Gate. "Bushel" was a term of measure only; the familiar bushel basket of the East had never come west and the chief container was the burlap sack. These bulky packages came down from interior river ports on barges and steamboats and were hoisted up and chuted down into the holds of ships and layered into place by barefoot stevedores. The men were barefoot because boots would cut the sacks. Bulk shipment was out of the question because any shifting of loose wheat, on the long rough voyage around half the world, would be liable to lay the ship on her beam-ends. As the sacks weighed up to 140 pounds and were borne into place on men's backs, it was wearing work and one man was kept busy running to the nearest saloon to replenish the always-present bucket of beer.

The grain trade climbed whoopingly during the 'eighties. Its customers were the bread-eaters of Europe, for the United States east of the Rockies had both wheat and railroads. The vessels that took it away were mostly "limejuicers," the proportions being about twenty-five British to fifteen American and seven French, Norwegian, German and Italian and others. The yelling among the brokers in San Francisco's "wheat pit" in the Merchants Exchange Building could be heard for a block.

But in about 1890, the grain trade out the Gate began to decline, although barley outlasted wheat. Reckless soil depletion and diversification into orchard and truck crops cut heavily into California grain production. By 1910 the wheat-exporting era was virtually over. The tall ships, barks and schooners and the tramp coal-burners swung out to sea in quest of other cargoes or some quiet mudflat to rest their bones upon, and the grain sheds on the Seawall at the southeast corner of the Gate went vacant. Wreckers came one day and pulled them down. Today, sleek, white Matson liners, with bands playing and confetti flying, fill their steel hulls there with passengers for Hawaii and the South Seas.

One member of the old grain fleet stands silently nearby. She is the *Balclutha,* of which more later.

22 : THE FISHING FLEET

THE town alongside the Golden Gate has many pleasant traditions. One, that should be lettered in silver and framed in gold, concerns its love of opera. Whether one incident of lost date occurred in the Grand Opera House on Mission Street or at the Tivoli on Mason depends upon the historian. At all events, opera was scheduled and a sell-out house assured. And the chorus went on strike. It suspected that it would be the last group paid, so determined to be the first. But the box office had already been garnisheed by other creditors. The impasse was complete.

Then someone had an idea. He went to North Beach, saw Achille Paladini the wholesale fish dealer, and fervently asked that the cultural reputation of San Francisco be preserved. Paladini took it up with the Crab Boat Owners' Association, who were at the moment in session. (They always were when not fishing. At the card tables in the Association's hall next to the Hicks Marine Gas Engine boatshop.) Response was immediate. Forty Genoese, Neapolitan, Pisan and other fishermen, in wide-topped sea boots, baggy pants, twisted belt-sashes and striped jerseys, variously topped with felt hats, berets and dented derbies, clumped for the Union Street cable car, transferred to Kearny, got off where required, and without a moment's rehearsal or hesitation clomped on stage

154

and gave forth with a will the appropriate background to Alfredo's tenor, Violetta's soprano, Germont's baritone and Flora's mezzo, while the audience, recognizing a good try when it heard one, went crazy. The fishermen's voices may have sounded like the bellow of seamanly communication from boat to boat through a southwest gale, but they knew their *Traviata*. Then, their adopted city's honor saved, back to North Beach they trooped.

The story deserves to be true. Nothing better illustrates the close bond of Italy with Golden Gate, of Fisherman's Wharf with all San Francisco, of lyric larynx with lusty lung-power or of loyal heart with civic need. The fishing fleet is a physical part and extension of the town just as Golden Gate and Farallon Islands are, and the fishermen know it, though many of them are out on the water so much that their language is still straight out of Italy. Even after being here sixty years.

The first comers, back in Gold-Rush times, were from Genoa. They still predominate. They painted their boats a pale green and they were a pretty close-knit community, though some Dalmatians also came in. Today they are from all parts of Italy and from the Azores, Finland, Norway and other countries, or are second- and third-generation Americans; but from the elders you still can have Verdi any time you want it, as they mend their nets.

For almost half a century the Gate was creased by feluccas, or adaptations of the long, narrow, forward-raking dispatch and fishing boats long used on the Mediterranean. Their triangular or "lateen" sails were held wide by long tapering yards slung to the mast at about a quarter of the distance from the lower end. The men from Genoa who brought this design to the Coast soon learned to hang block and tackle to the mast for sail-handling; they preserved the sharp, plumb sterns and steadying keels, but reduced length to between 26 and 36 feet. One man or two, oars were also used. The fisherman went out early and he came in late and a familiar sight was the becalmed boat proceeding home, its rower standing to his oars against the sunset and pushing them as he faced forward. Because of his efforts, cod, sardines, crabs, salmon and more than one hundred other types of commercial seafood reached Fisherman's Wharf daily except Sundays and saints' days, and so they do—but by gasoline power—to this hour.

Other vessels of the market fleet were "cats," the original crab boats, 15- to 18-footers that were used inside the Heads; it was the feluccas that ventured out. The "Columbia River salmon boat" also put in its appearance, a stout craft that looked as if it ought to go after whales. And Chinese, who were attracted chiefly by shrimp, had some junks built locally to Cantonese specifications and away they went for certain Gate and bay coves they knew about, the crazy-looking but extremely seaworthy vessels being powered by wind in the squarish sails that were stiffened and sectioned by horizontal spars. Then, in later days, the "Monterey hull" came along: double-enders, clipper-bowed, their beams nearly one-third their length. They were boats that invited any sea to try to capsize them, and they were particularly adapted for the marine gas engine which began appearing shortly after the turn of the century. They are the ruling boat today.

Early-day quarters of the fishing fleet were at Meiggs Wharf. Then, during a seawall-building and filling-in period, the fleet was berthed off the east face of Telegraph Hill, at the foot of Union Street. Here the feluccas, in their off hours, floated in two rows facing. Wharf-long nets stretched out on the planks for mending and drying, hoop-framed crab nets were stacked about, and housewives stepped and tripped over them while bargaining. Later the industry moved back around the hill and quartered off Meiggs Wharf again, close to where it is now. In those days, fishermen worked hard and earned maybe a dollar a day. Or worked harder and made less. In more modern times, at least until very recently, the first-rate fisherman, the one who owns a two-man boat of 50 feet or longer, drives a car to work that takes a lot of room to park.

Back in 1867, Achille Paladini, who'd been fighting in Garibaldi's forces, arrived in the Golden Gate on a Cape Horner. He had traveled something less than first cabin, more likely fo'c'sle. For a time he quartermastered on a steamer to Portland. Then he acquired an old sailboat and some nets. He was from Ancona on the Adriatic and the sea was in his blood. For a time he fished for the market on the upper bay. By 1871 he was a merchant, hawking fish from a pair of baskets on the streets of San Francisco. He advanced from baskets on the curb to a stall in the Washington Street Market. Soon he had his own small building.

He married. His seven children came to include four strong sons. He was up every day at 3 A.M., pulling the sons from bed by their heels. At 4 A.M. he and the boys, sleeves uprolled, aprons at waist, were ready for the day's business. When their school opened at nine, the boys had already put in a fair chore of work.

A. Paladini of Ancona prospered. He was a stocky five foot six, weighing 200 pounds. His customers came to be the best restaurants in town. To keep the seafood coming, he staked his countrymen to a boat or two until he had an interest in a considerable part of the fleet. Any decent man, preferably Italian, who knew fish and fishing could get a grubstake from Achille Paladini. The sea was wide. The fish were many. San Francisco had some of the best chefs in the world, and customers with notable appetites. Achille Paladini catered to those appetites and he knew those chefs.

He was slow to render a bill. When he did, it was a good-sized one. By the custom of the times, it was paid in gold. At the Palace Hotel, Paladini would lay $100 of it in shining pieces on the bar and order drinks for the kitchen staff from dishwasher to chiefest tall white hat. Much of the rest he would frugally put into choice real estate.

His wholesale and retail market at 540 Clay Street was redolent of finny merchandise and daily hosings. It had a cash register and, beside it, a tank for live fish. Coins that were paid for fish sometimes landed not in the cash register but in the fish tank. "You're being robbed," friends would tell him. "Yes, but they always leave plenty for me," Paladini would answer. He personally cleaned the fish tank, regularly. What coins came out of it went into more fishboats, more real estate.

That market was an unusual place. Besides sons Alexander, Attilio, Hugo and Walter, who were as wide and thick-armed as he was, it had a pet rooster and a pet seal. The rooster, a Rhode Island Red, was enormous, and he strutted the district with authority. When he disappeared, heartbroken Achille offered $100 reward for his safe return. The rooster didn't come back; he was probably already somebody's chicken *cacciatore*. The seal, which had been brought up from the sea as a baby in somebody's net, also had the run of the shop and was given to flopping down Clay Street on sightseeing tours. Since nobody had a recipe for seal pan roast, he grew to large size and honored old age.

Achille Paladini also had a mule, whose wisdom was great. He could find his way back and forth between the business and the family home on Filbert Street without a hand at the reins. He covered himself with glory one time at the Butchers' Picnic by winning the trotting race from a full field of the offsprings of nobler parentage. His passing, though sad, was characteristic of the town he graced. He was struck and demolished by a Clay Street cable car.

A. Paladini was in a fiercely competitive calling, but he more than held his own. In this, he had the undying loyalty of the fishing fleet. In addition to setting the feet of many a fisherman on the way to prosperity, or anyway a living, he carried much of the industry on his broad back. He canned the Coast's first tuna. He built a smoke house, which still stands and functions, on little Gold Street near his market. He opened one of the first cold-storage plants for the harvests of the sea. By 1915 he had five fishing tugs, two trucks, and seventy-five employees. The great citywide fire of '06 had moved him simply to say, "Boys, let's start over again." He passed on in 1921, in his eightieth year. His sons, about a third of a ton of them, and a ton or two of grandsons and great-grandsons operate the business still.

The greatest thing that ever happened to the Gate fishing fleet, except six-bit salmon, thirty-cents-a-pound crabs and Prohibition, was the gasoline engine. It was followed by something almost as time- and muscle-saving, the "gurdy" or engine-powered reel. The gas engine came at the first of the century, the gurdy fifty years later. For market-fishing off the turbulent Gate, a number of engines were devised. Then men who knew and had worked on the Union, Frisco-Standard, Atlas, Imperial and Enterprise got together and developed, with Frank Hicks, the locally designed and produced Hicks Marine Gas Engine. It was as simple and easy to fix as the power plant of a Model-T Ford and it did for the craft of the Gate what Henry had done for the buckboard and the buggy. Frank Hicks offered one-, two-, three- and four-lungers that would turn a propeller once every time the motor popped. His shop was right at Fisherman's Cove. Every time a muscle-sore fisherman came in after the wind had failed, Hicks had a customer. By about the time of World War I, Hicks, who'd started in 1907, had sent fishboats dependent upon sails and oars into the limbo of Roman galley and clipper ship. Hicks built his engines on the pier until the early '20's, when Yuba Manufacturing Company took over his designs and made the engines at Benicia. They continued for another twenty years, finally succumbing to the high-speed motors of the present era. Some folks do say that Prohibition, making it possible for a man with a fast Hall Scott-engined boat to come in with a good load of Scotch under his albacore, helped to chase Hicks into obsolescence. Today Hicks' old shop and sales outfit, Boicelli-Boss, sells Chrysler marine engines in quantity at the foot of Jones Street.

Fishermen's Cove, in the three-lagoon preserve that extends from Taylor Street three blocks to Hyde, is an extremely small setting for such a booming and active business. In former days there was color galore to the scene, but the arriving fish were only to be looked at and smelled, or purchased off the boat; there was no place at hand to eat them except a few stand-up coffee and chowder counters patronized by the fishers themselves. Shortly before the bombs fell on Pearl Harbor, a North Beach citizen named Tom Castagnola got the idea—perhaps fish-chef Joe Sanguinetti tied him—that was to transform the Cove into a gourmet's paradise. He opened the first big-menued restaurant close to Pier 45 and it started a parade that now includes a dozen names, all famous, all mouth-watering; that brought the sidewalk crab cauldrons; and that brought gimcrack souvenir stands. Back of a long right-angled row of succulent-smelling restaurants lie two of the crowded lagoons where boats rub elbows and masts lean over and gossip. Farther along, behind Andy's Lookout (a surviving chowder counter for fishermen) stretches another lagoon, and this one is seldom seen by townsfolk; it is all business. Receiving sheds embrace it, engine repair shops and shops for radiotelephones, automatic pilots, direction finders, depth recorders and radar stand by, and old-time fishermen, squat and thick-chested, sit about on stacks of crab pots and puff pipes and discuss the world gravely.

The people who run the fishboats, the restaurants and the sidewalk markets work in tight family units. From wiggling in the sea to served hot on a plate, the fish has been dragged up, borne in, cleaned, cooked, and presented to the customer with lemon by papa and the boys, mama and the girls. The Cove provides jobs for more than a thousand people. From November through May, crabs are in season and they mustn't be less than seven inches across not counting the legs. From June through October the boats double in salmon, or other toothsome offerings of the sea. And the boats that do bottom fishing spread their big *paranzella* nets and scoop up flounder, sand dab, sole and rock cod, and sometimes small sharks or maybe a part of a ship that went down long ago. The boats bring in a billion pounds of seafood a year through the Gate. That's a lot of crab legs *Tofanelli*, crab legs *Mornay*, boiled halibut *Scandia*, boiled fish-of-your-choice *Sicilia*, *Neptune* pan roast or rattle-shell *cioppino*, going down with a small ocean of wine and sopped up with a deal of sour garlic bread. It's all gift of the sea, gift of the Gate.

Of late the crab catch off the Gate and environs is falling off materially—from nearly five million pounds a year to an alarming two million. Permanently? Nobody knows. That the gift of the sea may continue, the fishermen once a year dress in their best and move in solemn procession from twin-spired Saints Peter and Paul Church behind the effigy of Santa Maria del Lume, gentle St. Mary of the Light, down to the Wharf. There a priest blesses the fleet. And at 2 A.M. next day the fishermen are up and off, or by sun-up are sitting cross-legged on the planks mending their nets with long wooden needles, or are painting their boats, repairing their engines, and occasionally bursting into song. Verdi? Verdi. Or perhaps bebop. It's a hundred years now, for some of them, since great-grandpa came over from Genoa, and a man can like something from a juke-box along with his opera.

Fish change their locales. Catches and prices go up, go down. Sails give way to gas. What does not change for the people of Fisherman's Wharf is the fog, the wind, the storms, the creaking gulls, and the swishing, surging, heaving, keel-slamming tides and currents of the Gate.

23 : FERRIES ACROSS THE GATE

WHEN Kit Carson was ordered by Frémont to embark in a ship's oared smallboat in 1846 for crossing the Gate to spike the Mexican cannon, he is reported to have said to his chief, "I'd ruther chase grizzly b'ar in the mountings than ride in this thang"—but he and his captain forthwith inaugurated a travel route that eventually grew to proportions.

Scheduled ferries came in the 1870's. There were two lines. One steamed from Sausalito to San Francisco, the other from Tiburon. Neither, strictly speaking, crossed the Gate itself, but moved cautiously around its eastern end. They took its lusty blows of wind and water and they were belted likewise by river currents from the interior. For eighty years the single- and double-enders, the paddle-wheelers, coal-burners, oil-burners and Diesel-electrics made it—with a record for safety scarcely to be equaled. And with a variety of delights not elsewhere to be found on the bay, for they packaged a full thirty-minute trip in which eyes could meet, dates be made and romance ripen; in which large meals could be eaten at leisure, including pie; in which an overhanging mountain could be eyed in detail, perhaps with a view to challenging it; in which great ships could be studied as they swept by on stately errands to and from the far ports of earth.

All this was begun by a little bouncy-ball called the *Prin-*
162

cess, in 1868. She was owned by the Sausalito Land & Ferry Company and she plied for five roundtrips a day between the foot of Princess Street in Sausalito, which is just around the north inside corner of the Gate, and Meiggs Wharf at close to the southern corner. It was a journey of four miles. Every buyer of a Sausalito town lot got a pass on the ferry. Sometimes a little yacht, the *Diana*, stood in for the *Princess*.

A rival operation started soon after from a cove called Tiburon, two and a half miles, a supplementary bay and a fat peninsula northeast of Sausalito. Peter Donahue, a foundry-man grown millionaire from building government ships, steamboats and street railroads and operating steamers to Sacramento, fostered the Tiburon enterprise. Donahue countered *Princess* with his own single-ender, the *Antelope*, which he brought over from the Sacramento run. Back of Tiburon, reaching northward, he had a short standard-gauge railroad, the San Francisco & North Pacific.

In 1875 the Sausalito Land & Ferry Company sold out to another railroad aspirant, the North Pacific Coast, which laid narrow-gauge rails across two counties to the Russian River. This owner replaced *Princess* with a larger single-ender, the *Petaluma*. She was no spring chicken, having been hatched in 1857, but she had a lunch room and a bar and she introduced strict sailing schedules if not always prompt arrivals. Two more boats followed, built in the East and brought around the Horn in sections on the decks of windjammers. The *San Rafael* went into service in 1877 and the *Saucelito*—an erroneous and temporary spelling—soon afterward. Both were wooden side-wheelers, 205 feet long and 32 beam, stuffed with red plush and walnut and grand staircases and with the "Eureka" goddess, grizzly bear and other elements of the great seal of California painted on their paddleboxes. The *Saucelito* burned at her dock, taking her misspelling with her. The *San Rafael* continued for another eighteen years.

The Donahue line countered with *Tiburon*, a coal-smoke

hurler of no mean capacity. The Sausalito and Tiburon rivals just loved to race—until both vessels tried to get into their San Francisco slips one day at one and the same time, like two people in one doorway. The *Tiburon* lifted jackstaffs and lifeboats out of the *San Rafael* with one stiff poke. On the opening day of 1893 the unruly *Tiburon* burned on the water while waiting for belated New Year's Eve revelers.

Petaluma and *San Rafael,* and later a new *Sausalito* with capacity for 2,000 passengers, and a steel-hulled *Tamalpais,* built by the people who had built the battleship *Oregon,* carried on through the decades ferrying people, eggs, vegetables, occupied coffins, horses and buggies, and other assorted freight. In 1907 the two Marin ferry lines and the rails behind them passed to the dual ownership of Southern Pacific and Santa Fe.

It was an ever-varied performance, that run across the head of the Gate. I recall with personal satisfaction the mortal adventure of one piece of freight. It was a drum-cylinder flat-bed press of antiquity and balkiness which had done long and aberrant duty with a newspaper in Alameda on the east shore of the bay. Pressman Jack Parrott had battled with it for years. One day the owner bought a new rapid-fire beauty, and the old press was sold to a purchaser in San Rafael and Jack Parrott was sent along to set it up and show the new owner how to fight it.

The press was shipped by transbay ferry to San Francisco. There it was shoved aboard the *Tamalpais,* north-shore-bound. It was blocked up at the stern of the main deck and wedged fore, aft and sideways. Bells rang. Paddles churned. The *Tamalpais* was off. Ferry Tower and Telegraph Hill receded. Alcatraz slid by. The *Tamalpais* hit the chop of the Gate. The ferryboat rose. The ferryboat fell. The press soared over its chocks. The boat passed from under it. Jack Parrott stared at the hole in the water, which closed rapidly. He took off his hat. "Not in my wildest dreams!" he murmured.

"I used to pray for this. But not in my wildest dreams did I think it ever would happen!" But, gorgeously, it had.

As the auto age advanced, southbound cars lined up for miles on Sunday and holiday evenings, to inch forward whenever an arriving boat would empty and refill. It became common for motorists to leave their cars in the streets and come back for them on the following Monday.

In 1920 an opposition line, the Golden Gate Ferry Company, organized to grab that business. It operated between Sausalito and the foot of Hyde Street. It started with one boat, which had the engine and boilers of a former U.S. destroyer, the *Farragut,* as innards. In 1922 appeared the *Golden Gate,* later rebuilt and renamed the *Golden City,* a Diesel-electric. She lasted but two days under that name before she was rammed and sunk on a night of light travel and heavy fog. No lives were lost. Her destruction didn't halt the new company, which flowered like poppies after a spring rain. Its boats all were painted a gay yellow and gladdened by the names *Golden West, Golden Dawn, Golden Era, Golden Bear, Golden Coast, Golden Shore* and *Golden Age.* Everything but Golden Yolk and Golden Goose. Southern Pacific found way to make bedfellow with the lively concern and for a time practically every car that crossed the bay in any direction was guest, or hostage, of Southern Pacific Golden Gate Ferries, Ltd. Then, as swiftly as barriers could be lifted or silken cords cut, the gasoline-powered golden bonanza was over. Two great bridges offered paved highways instead.

Away went the ferryboats, to Seattle and Coronado, to British Columbia and Uruguay. *Golden Bear,* in tow of a Puget Sound tug, had a hard time getting to her new location. In a heavy sea, bolts broke loose; the exhaust system failed; the crew nearly died of monoxide; and the two hawsers parted. After a wild night's struggle the tug got hold of her again, yanked her to the nearest port, and left her there. She became a Coos Bay cement barge and later an integral part of a British Columbia breakwater.

In the Pacific Northwest, four others of the Golden fleet were given more modest paint—white—and different handles. *Golden State* became *Kehloken. Golden Age* became *Klahanie. Golden Shore* turned up as *Elwha. Golden Poppy* flourished as well as she could as *Chetzemolka*. Thus toned down, they regard their reflections today in Puget Sound.

This leaves the finish of a memorable Gate ferryboat still to be accounted for. The *San Rafael* has been gone for two-thirds of a century, but in 1901 she still was a part of the pageant of the Gate. She was the 6:10 boat one Saturday evening, waiting at the Lombard Street wharf while 260 passengers boarded her for Sausalito. They were a happy throng. Many had been to hear Madame Sembrich in *The Barber of Seville* at the Grand Opera House, a matinee performance. Others were the usual commuters in a hurry to get home for dinner. The week-end hikers who swarmed across the Gate in spring, summer and fall were lacking, for this was the last day of November. Captain Jack MacKenzie, standing on the hurricane deck of the *San Rafael*, watched his charges press aboard and wanted to call down that there was no need to shove. He wasn't going to leave on time this trip. The densest fog in his memory was on the water and he wanted to give it time to lift.

But it didn't lift, though it wasn't more than 50 feet thick. After delaying twelve minutes, he signaled the engines and backed the single-ender out, swung her, and headed north. He was uneasy, though, for even the wharf lights couldn't be seen. He proceeded at greatly reduced speed, steering by compass and tide calculation, and keeping his fog whistle sounding.

At 7:15, when the *San Rafael* was halfway between North Point and Alcatraz, something loomed through the mist. It was the *Sausalito*, southbound. Both vessels reversed engines.

Too late. Captain Bill Tribble delivered the bow of his vessel straight into the *San Rafael's* restaurant, killing a cook and creating pandemonium. After moments, the two skippers got their crews in hand and the two steamboats were lashed together. A gangplank was laid across. Most passengers of the *San Rafael* used it, though many flung themselves into the icy water and were hauled aboard the *Sausalito* by ropes. Fireman Gielow of the *Sausalito* leaped aboard the struck vessel, forced his way down into the boiler room by wading and diving, and shut off the steam. He came out half-drowned, but with explosion averted.

There were other heroes. Engineer Gormand of the *San Rafael* was having a day off and was riding as a passenger, but he took charge of a lifeboat and pulled many loads from the water. A bartender named Gus hoisted women and children to safety. The tug *Sea King* bustled up. "Where are we?" yelled Captain MacKenzie. "Off the Presidio light and heading out to sea!" The current was swift. All lights had gone out. A Mrs. Waller of Sausalito had her small children Ruth and Cyrus with her. She hung on to Ruth but a sudden lurch shot three-year-old Cyrus from her arms. She never found him in the darkness.

Twenty minutes after the crash, with all known passengers but three safe on rescuing vessels, the *San Rafael* went down in eighty fathoms. Jack London used her fate in his novel *The Sea Wolf*.

The Golden Gate Bridge, begun in 1931, opened in 1937. For the Gate ferries, that was three blasts of a whistle and good-bye. It had taken able skippers to thread that course back and forth across ever-changing currents, through every degree of visibility and invisibility. They'd learned to steer by compass, lights, bells, echoes, sounds, smells and just plain instinct. Some of the jobs as masters, mates, engineers and deckhands had been passed along in certain families for three generations. Those officers and crewmen had steamed, each year, far enough to circumnavigate the world, and all of it across that one slender chop of dangerous water. They left a remarkable record—only three passengers lost to those swirling waters in two-thirds of a century.

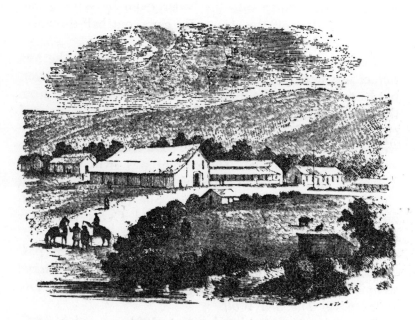

Mission of San Francisco

24 : LITTLE BOATS, ALL
BUSINESS

THERE was the *Goliah*. A wooden sidewheel steamer, she reached the Gate in 1851 by the long way around; and for nearly half a century she was tug, towboat and salvage boat, pulling this vessel off the rocks and rescuing the passengers of that. At almost every wreck and stranding from Point Arena to Point Arguello, a gull flight of 250 miles, the *Goliah* was swiftly found standing by. The *Thomas Hunt* was frequently helping her. The seagoing tugs that came later made her furious paddles look futile, but *Goliah* was the best, biggest and most powerful that the Coast had to offer for many a day, and a more welcome if more ungainly prow never hove over the horizon.

There was the *McCulloch*. She was built at Philadelphia in 1897, she was of steel and wood interestingly commingled, she was 219 feet long and she displaced 1,400 tons, but she also displaced a lot of history. At the outbreak of the Spanish-American War she was enroute via Suez to the Golden Gate as a revenue cutter when, at Singapore, she was ordered to join Dewey's forces at Manila. There she distinguished herself in the Battle of Manila Bay, though one shell would have upended her if it had found her; after-

169

ward she raced to Hong Kong with news of the American victory so that it could be dispatched to the world.

There was the *Fanny*, trim windjammer of 84 tons, 71 feet long, built by Dan Kelly at East Boston in 1850 and commanded by his brother Bill. She arrived in the Gate on February 18, 1851. Bill had put her through the Straits of Magellan like a thread through the eye of a needle, no mean feat for a bit of wood and canvas. She became the pilot boat off the Gate and served for years, prototype of a multitude of her kind—the all-business little boats that no great port can do without.

For decades the pilots waited for incoming ships in the *Fanny* or dainty schooner yachts just like her. They relieved each other on stated schedules. They rolled and pitched with the swells while their owners—everyone a master mariner, member of the San Francisco Bar Pilots—played pedro and swapped lies in the cheerful cabin. At the century's turn the pilot boats were the *America, Lady Mine* and *Gracie S.* All three were sleek two-masted schooners carrying full mainsail, foresail, staysail, jib, flying jib and main topsail. *America* was flagship, and Benny, a Chinese, was her cook. On a rough night in November, 1901, the *America* was cruising near the Farallones in a stiff southwest blow. The *Gracie S.* approached to relieve her and crashed into the *America* instead, carrying away main boom and mainsail. Four pilots and the crew of the *America* piled into a boat and pulled to the *Gracie S.*—to discover that they hadn't brought along Benny the Chinese. To their further horror they saw the *America* speeding off into the northeast with her broken boom hanging overside. She was moving fast. *Gracie* started in pursuit. With her single reefed mainsail and foresail, the *America* went faster. The chase lasted 80 miles and all night. Twelve hours after the start of the race, by the collective seamanship of her skipper and four pilots, *Gracie S.* caught up with and boarded the errant schooner, which by

that time was approximately off Fort Ross and more or less
headed for Kodiak. They climbed aboard and shouted for
Benny. No reply. Then they found him. He'd been asleep in
his bunk all night and he still was asleep. He got up with a
grumble: "All light, all light. Cookee bleakfast light away.
Whassa mally you?"

But in the end, as most craft on the sea must do, the
pilots' sailing schooners gave way to coal, then petroleum.
In the late fall of 1961 Captain Dick Smith, skipper of the
twin-screw pilot motorship *Golden Gate*, brought his vessel home to Pier 7 and retired after thirty years on her
bridge, during which he had sailed her 34,320 miles and
never had been more than eleven miles out to sea. Eleven
miles out to station where inbound ships could "take a pilot"
and outbound vessels could drop one; where fogs and sun
and starlight alternated; where seas could be glassy, or
whipped up into rages by winds of 75 miles per hour.
Steaming in circles in rough seas, laying-to in calm, Captain
Dick had put in a tour that could have taken him once and
a half around the earth.

And then, for the sake of this record, there was the first
whitehall boat, which probably never had a name, but which
also was to be followed by a mighty fleet of its kind—the
unruly boats that met the ships out at sea, captured their
crews for the boardinghouse keepers, landed their passengers, helped shanghai the new crews when it was time to
sail, and after a wild half-century gave way to motor
launches and a more stately tempo, if one did not look too
far beneath the surface.

Tugs, pilot boats and whitehalls—what a part they have
played!

The whitehall boats, those nervy, quarrelsome sea-taxis
which, like fishboats, ever were companions of the pilot
boats, were also vessels of distinction in their way. The first

of them in the Gate were from the yard of a boatbuilder named Emerson at Elizabeth, New Jersey. They were 18 feet long, 4 feet 8 inches wide and 22 or 24 inches deep, with centerboard and demountable mast. Though a single pair of oars was the power of extra recourse, the redoubtable little craft, with 12-foot mast and 18-foot boom, could throw a lot of canvas to the wind—mainsail and jib, and spinnaker also when running before the wind; and these were the most deadly-rival, business-bound boats that ever kicked a wave. For they bred a race of men who belonged more to water than to land, who hated peace with a mortal hate, and who hated each other with a fury that lasted at white heat until a stalked ship had been hooked and bagged, whereupon a spirit of loving brotherhood settled down to last anywhere between several hours and five minutes.

Into this catfight of oar-swinging boatmen waded one David Crowley in or about 1872. He'd come around the Horn as a sailor. Dave Crowley had been busy since he'd left Ireland's County Cork at age 16. He'd been a windjammer seaman and a quartermaster on the U.S. Navy sloop *Saratoga* in the Civil War, which had given and taken good blows; he had attended Lincoln's funeral. When the three-masted schooner *Galatea* brought him into the Gate, Dave Crowley picked up a job as keeper on the lightship *Caleb Curtis*, three miles outside the bar, where he learned something new about weather. Two years of that, and he bought himself one of the whitehalls, which by that time were being turned out in quantity by local boatbuilders John Twigg and Dan O'Connell. The idea was to lay-to near the lightship and, when a ship approached, to sail, row, steer and battle with such skill that one made himself the first to throw a shackle into the chain plates of the oncoming ship and ride 'er in. By tradition, the first man aboard got the desired business—stevedoring, sailor-boarding, meat and grocery supplying, chandlery, or the taking of men ashore. As the ships came rushing in at up to 12 knots an hour and never thought of slowing for a whitehall, the art of maneuvering into the lee and grabbing on was an art delicate, precise and wetly hazardous.

The whitehalls usually had two men to a boat, one highly proficient at the oars and the other at the sails. They also had an iron pole 10 or 12 feet long, equipped with a curve for latching on, and 60 feet of line. Dave Crowley, as runner for the Golden Shore Meat Market, became the peer of them all at snagging the passing ships, so much so that he was known as "Hook-on Crowley." His business came to include soliciting for a seaman's boardinghouse keeper named Wilson on Pacific Street, that hotbed of crimping and shanghaiing which made San Francisco's Barbary Coast a legend. Dave married a widow who lived on the brow of Telegraph Hill. She had a year-and-a-half-old son. Dave adopted him and named him Tom Crowley.

Tom cut his teeth on the oars of a whitehall boat. He grew up to be a giant of about five foot five, his weight 140 pounds wringing wet, and "giant" is used advisedly, for it became rather widely accepted that you could either take matters as Tom advised or have the hell knocked out of you. Where he got his dynamite was a mystery, but he had it. And a sharp set of brains.

Tom showed he meant business at the age of eighteen when his stepfather Dave, who usually won the whitehall boat races in the Fourth of July regattas, decided to make sure this time around and got himself a fine new boat. Tom guilelessly asked if he could run the old one. Sure, said Dave. Tom black-leaded her to the smoothness of a ripe, oiled olive, cut some new canvas for her and had it sewed up, and showed up for the race. It was from the foot of Union Street, the old Fisherman's Wharf, out to Blossom Rock buoy southeast of Alcatraz, then to a marker off Meiggs, on into the eye of the wind off Black Point, and the finish back at

Meiggs. The city put up a prize for that annual contest, and it was $100. A man on the Front would shanghai his grand-father and send him to China for $100, and throw in a couple of uncles. Tom Crowley, spinnaker flying on the home leg before the wind and the old whitehall keel just about four inches off the water, led the way in and lifted his old man's crown as King of the Gate. And that he remained.

In the 'nineties, fishing ships returning from Alaska used to bring in furs which their seamen had obtained from the Indians for a few beads and mirrors. In '97, when gold was discovered on the Klondike and a rush developed, those headed for Skagway and Dawson were ready to pay any price for such furs and wear them back to the land of their origin. Tom Crowley saw opportunity there. He met the Alaska ships, bought their furs for his own account, and re-sold them to the gold seekers. With his first $500 profit, he bought one of the new-fangled benzine launches which other whitehallers were jeering at, but which Tom took seriously. A few years later, with his brothers for partners, he had most of the launches on the bay, and the whitehall boats had all but vanished. When great events occurred like the visit of the U.S. battleship fleet to the Gate in '08, Crowley made thousands a day as a water taximan, and he knew just how to reinvest it.

In 1917 he bought a tugboat business, the Red Stack fleet, and became the Crowley Launch & Tugboat Co. He branched out into shipping of all kinds. But he never gave up his launches. When a better one was built, he acquired it, and the supplanted launch was sold off to reappear at Nome, in Magellan Straits or at Papeete. But wherever a ship anchored in Gate or bay, a swift Crowley launch put out for it, followed by as many more as business suggested. In the 1930's the world's biggest warship, the British battle cruiser *Hood*, came in through the Gate on a visit and an-chored in Battleship Row. Open house was held for the

citizenry and they visited by thousands, almost as if aware
that the mighty *Hood* would someday be sunk with practically one shot by the stalking *Bismarck*. On this day, snug
within the Gate, Admiral Field stood on his bridge, lost in
admiration. To a newspaper reporter he remarked, "That's
a wonderful skyline. That's a beautiful city. This is a magnificent harbor. These things I'd expected. But what I can't
get over is the prominence of this fellow Crowley."

That bantam with the fighting heart was the biggest man
on the San Francisco waterfront.

Thirty-five years later, at the age of 85—taking nothing
from the late Captain William Matson, the late Captain
Robert Dollar, or the very much present Harry Bridges—he
still is.

25 : SOME SALTY PERSONALITIES

SHORTLY after the turn of the century, an ungainly vessel waddled out the Golden Gate, crossed the Potato Patch, and made the turn around Duxbury Reef for the north channel. It was the suction dredge *Portland*, a type of "ship" that is more at home in sloughs and bayous, where it "walks" by means of spuds or stilts that it alternately lifts and drops, and spews mud through a long flexible pipe to some point ashore. Now it was in tow. Almost as wide as it was long, it took everything the sea had to offer.

Its engineer was an almost legendary figure of the waterfront face-lifting business, Gus Linderman. He'd lost his right arm by catching it in a winding gear while dredging off Mare Island. "Bring a pinch bar and a sack!" Gus had yelled, and when men came running to open the gears and wrap the torn arm in the sack, Gus superintended matters. He was rushed to a hospital and his arm was amputated. In a few days he was practicing at learning to write with the remaining hand. He was also reading up on steam engines.

Before the accident, he had simply been a deckhand and roustabout. Once out of the hospital, he got a job on a little steam tug. He shoveled the coal as fireman and juggled the levers as engineer, doing both with one hand. Then, in 1904, he took the burly dredge *Portland* up the coast. He
176

went on up the career ladder to become Puget Sound Bridge & Dredging Company's general superintendent and refashioned the Tacoma and Seattle waterfronts.

A tough spirit was in the engineroom of the ungainly *Portland* that day in '04 when she chugged out the Gate.

Edward A. von Schmidt was the son of the Russian-born engineer, Alexis von Schmidt, who blew the top off Blossom Rock, close under Alcatraz Island, in the world's first underwater use of dynamite; surveyed the California-Nevada boundary; and built and operated the first hydraulic dredge in history, in the 1870's, on the shoals of San Francisco Bay. Young Ed spent much of his youth in the Hawaiian Islands, where he developed great skill at boating and swimming, together with a bronzed hide and a disinclination to wear clothes. His notion of full dress, even when going ashore and well inland, was a breechclout and a sheath knife. In the early 1880's this was considered a little informal.

In San Francisco Bay waters he worked and slept on a dredge, where his bed was a 2-inch plank. The rest of the crew were Russian Finns who were practically wild men. Among these, Ed von Schmidt and his knife kept order. When one of the annual Fourth of July regattas approached, Ed looked over his bunch of mud-sucker Finns and decided that they weren't dredgermen, they were yachtsmen. They agreed with him joyfully. All hands turned to and shaped up a small square-rigger with an enormous amount of keel.

They performed this work in secret at Mare Island. When they had sail to their liking and enough keel to support it, down they boomed from San Pablo Bay, Von Schmidt at the helm and most of his crew sitting out on a plank thrust overside to balance the wind pressure. Nothing could be found in the regatta's regulations to rule them out and nothing had any such spread of canvas. The dredgermen swept the field. But along with their honors went a ducking, for as the victorious craft passed in the lee of a tall ship at the finish, all the wind went out of its canvas and dumped the Finns.

Ed von Schmidt became a bar pilot later and brought many ships in through the Gate. His end was starkly tragic. He went home one night, slew his wife with that sheath knife, and finished himself off with another blow. It was the second son Colonel von Schmidt lost by violence. His first, Walter, had been swept overboard from a ship.

Andrew F. Mahoney was a shoe drummer. A big, handsome Irishman and a lucky one, he won $15,000 with a Little Louisiana lottery ticket, looked around for something to do with it, and heard of Oliver J. Olson, who had started a lumber-hauling business by buying 1/64 of a new steam schooner, followed by a second one in the same proportion. Lots of lumber was pouring in through the Golden Gate following the '06 fire and "Shoestring" Oliver was making money. Fine! decided Andy Mahoney. The firm became Olson & Mahoney. Andy promptly exercised his muscles as a shipping tycoon by having the Olson & Mahoney hulls painted a spirited green. Oliver Olson emitted a shrill Scandinavian yell and battle impended. Then somebody talked Olson into having a big white O painted on each side of the stacks, meaning Oliver on the port side and Olson on the starboard, with no room for an M anywhere. Strained peace returned.

Andy Mahoney felt that his chief gift to the shipping business was an Irishman's luck, and in a measure it was. When the firm sold its *Virginia Olson* to E. K. Wood Lumber Company, and the steamer moved away from her dock under the new ownership, within fifteen minutes she smashed into the steam schooner *Claremont* and was sunk. "See?" said Andy Mahoney.

Later Andy went into a shipping partnership with Tom Crowley. But the politicians made Mahoney a police commissioner, his old acquaintances presented him with a diamond-studded police star, and that ruined Andy for the shipping business. He had no more concern for the waterfront. He was just having too grand a time making personal arrests for traffic violations, right and left.

San Francisco had a murder that transcended most; for pieces of the victim were found all over town—a hand here, a foot there, a whole leg somewhere else. But who was the unfortunate victim? It was a jigsaw puzzle with too many parts missing. Al Williams, the *Examiner's* man at Meiggs Wharf, one day phoned Jack Barrett, his city editor, "I've got his head in a sack. I'm coming in with it." While Barrett shrieked, Al caught a conveyance. The head was identified as having belonged to one Tortorici, who must have had an enemy.

But Jack wasn't at his desk when Al arrived with the trophy. He was at the Old Crow saloon on Market Street, running his office by remote control. Al's feelings were real hurt.

He came through the Golden Gate in the British ship *Reindeer* in 1864, a youth from Germany, where his people made tower clocks. He found a job with Charles P. Pace, a scholarly gentleman who wore stocks and frock coat and a plug hat and repaired ship chronometers and sold sextants. In time the youth from Bockenem near Hanover, Germany, bought out Old Man Pace and the shop at Battery and Washington Streets and for the next half-century he occupied a high stool in front of a chronometer-maker's bench, forty inches by twenty. He grew an imperial, his hair whitened. He serviced half the ship chronometers that came in through the Gate.

Before the Great Fire, the Louis Weule Company was at Battery and California. After the fire, for another thirty years, it was at No. 6 California Street. It was a place where chronometers and clocks ticked like crazy. "Old" Louie tended quietly to business. It hurt him when his adopted America and his native Germany became locked in war in 1917. In convictions and citizenship he was wholly American. But the Germany he remembered had been a pleasant land. He had some cards printed. When anyone tried to talk war to him, he took a card from his pocket and silently presented it. It read, "I do not care to discuss the war." If the other party persisted, he quietly handed a second card: "Please respect my sentiments."

The clocks and chronometers ticked on.

Ship captains came in and assaulted the bowed back jovially. Louis Weule, watchmaker's loop screwed into his eye, would accept the wallop with a wince and would try to keep some tiny spring or screw from leaping out of his tweezers; would slowly turn to see who it was this time; and would get down from his stool and fetch the bottle of "chronometer oil," Kümmel, smelly of caraway and anise, that was kept for these reunions.

They came from long voyages, those shipmasters. They'd left Louis sitting there on his stool and they knew, returning, they'd find him on his stool, repairing ships' instruments—himself, and the instruments, utterly dependable.

One day a chronometer came in to him by messenger and its walnut case interested him by its workmanship. The old craftsman in Louis Weule knew joinery when he saw it. This handsome dovetailing was perfection. Now who, he wondered, could have made that box? I'd like to meet that man.

Inside, the chronometer rested on a velvet pad. The pad was faded. It was a piece of once-purple corduroy. I used to have a pair of pants made of material like that, thought the old man.

He took out the chronometer. The pad. He opened the latter. "Those *were* my pants!"

They'd been around the world a lot of times since he put that fragment there, in that case his hands had built.

He made the chronometer shipshape again, oiled it, scratched his secret mark on it, and the date, and put it back in the box on its velvet pad.

One morning in 1927, the old gentleman did not come down to the shop and mount his stool. His eye loop, his pincers and tiny screwdrivers remained in an orderly row, undisturbed.

He was not there, in World War II, to be asked what his opinions of the war might have been. Instead they named a freighter after him. The Liberty ship *Louis Weule* steamed out the Gate and ran its share of submarine blockade and Murmansk ice. As dependably as if its engines nestled on a velvet pad in a walnut case, and ran on Kümmel.

He had worked on so many newspapers, or claimed he had, that he was nicknamed "Hobo" Ross. The San Francisco *Bulletin* gave him a job and sent him to Meiggs Wharf to become a nautical expert. Which is where I knew him, but not very much of him. For the Marine Exchange telephone switchboard had a lovely operator and the "Hobo," much of the time, found it necessary to frequent her radiant presence. He gave all the signs of a man planning to propose. The gentle operator would have none of it. Not with "Hobo." She wanted a man with a future.

So Harold Ross went on to become editor of the Army's newspaper *Stars and Stripes* in World War I and then to found *The New Yorker*; to hire and put to work such ultimate notables as Alexander Woolcott, Peter Arno, Dorothy Parker and James Thurber.

Norman Nelson more or less fell into the sea, as Norwegian boys do at an early age, for the shores of Vikingland are steep. He made his way as a seaman to the Pacific Coast, worked up and down its length, and was at Eureka on the California shore on Christmas Eve, 1888, when the steamer *Mendocino* stranded and a life-saving crew put out. Nelson went along just to be useful. He did such feats that he was offered a job; and for the next thirty-five years he was in the life-saving service, ten years at Eureka, eight at Coos Bay and seventeen at the Golden Gate Lifeboat Station, where he was credited with saving hundreds of lives.

Captain Nelson's station was close to the Cliff House. He made a specialty of patrolling the sands and watching for suicides. A calm, cheerful, pipe-smoking man, he trudged along and studied faces closely—especially the face of any woman who was near the surf line. "I got so I could spot 'em," he once said. "Most ocean suicides are women—men prefer to go out more violently. The ratio is about seven to one. A woman seeks oblivion. She comes to the ocean as to a mother. There are three types. One comes to the beach with a lunch hamper—no thought of death. The croon of the ocean fascinates her. The swish of the water, the cease-less roll of surf, is like a cat and a bird. Such women always shun publicity after they are saved, and beg to be taken home. The second type is of that frame of mind due to illness, financial trouble, a lovers' quarrel or brooding over some one's death. I pulled such a one from the surf three times. The third type is a fugitive from justice, anxious to end it all ahead of some detective and his warrant. After they're saved and given a cup of coffee, they're usually sorry it all hap-pened and glad I came along to change their minds."

Keeper Nelson intercepted about one hundred would-be suicides before they made the cold dive; dragged out an-other hundred or more who got there ahead of him; and went, by boat or swimming, after still another hundred who succeeded in eluding rescue. Otherwise his hours, for the seventeen years he patrolled the beach near the Gate's south corner, were spent rescuing fishermen from rocks and boats. He was credited with saving more lives than any other man in the U.S. Coast Guard. He retired in 1928 at about the age of 55, giving as his reason a hanker to go into the real-estate business.

Like many men of the Gate and its south shore docks, Heinie Benges was short, stocky, tough, comical and unpredictable. He was born two blocks from Meiggs Wharf; and if he ever got any farther than that from his site of nativity, it was by boat. With one scintillating series of middle-aged exceptions.

In youth he became a whitehall boat "boy," taking sailors and runners to vessels out in the channel, and next he was an agent for a ship chandler. He was well able to hold his own in the rough-and-tumble of rowing out through rowdy water to incoming ships and boarding them. A famous professional oarsman, Oscar Lewis, came to town and posted $500 with a saloonkeeper, challenging anyone on the wharves to match it and row against him. Heinie didn't have $500 but he raked up $30 and Lewis agreed to row him for that. Heinie beat him by several lengths. In his mature and what might laughingly be called his thoughtful years, when I knew him, he had the resounding title of port captain in charge of news services for the Marine Exchange, his "office" at Meiggs Wharf. In other words, he was lookout for Exchange subscribers—merchants, newspapers, hotels, ship chandlers and suppliers and all others interested in being informed of arriving ships. He knew every vessel that came into port. In foggy weather he knew them by their whistles. A trail of smoke on a clear day off Point Bonita and Heinie would name the craft before a landsman could distinguish her smoke stacks. He was a prodigious hunter under the wharves for "floaters," for which he got $10 each from the coroner.

Heinie was no beauty by any standards, but he had something. And some like 'em briny and Heinie was fully that. Once a month or so, a long black car with driver in a visored cap would draw up adjacent to the wharf and Heinie, perceiving, would drop his hand at pedro, yell to Eddie Mc-Carthy to take over his Marine Exchange post, and climb into the car—it was a limousine, complete with glass vase for posy—and be driven away. Three days later Heinie would be back, smelling of brandy and champagne and his shirt pocket stuffed with excellent cigars. Where he'd been he never explained.

Heinie died at age 43 on Christmas day, 1915, of pneumonia. Three bar pilots, two ship captains and a delegation of Pacific Coast Baseball League players were his pallbearers.

At the lookout post of Meiggs Wharf, Heinie Benges was followed by Captain Edward F. McCarthy, who'd been his assistant since 1907 and was destined to continue on the job for a total of fifty years. Eddie McCarthy was a self-appointed life saver. The number of people he dragged from the bay was never counted. One of his last acts was to leap in and drag a sixty-year-old woman ashore. Then, at the end of a day's work in 1957, Captain Eddie started down the wharf for home, had a fainting spell or heart attack, and fell in and was drowned. The only person who probably would have seen it and pulled him out in time, had he been on duty, was the Captain Edward McCarthy who at that moment was the victim.

The handsomest hunk of man and the physically most magnificent who ever roamed the Gate and its environs was Captain Henry Clarence Peterson, born at Howard and Steuart streets in the heart of the sailors' boardinghouse district in 1863. His sire was a whitehall boatman, and a white-haller Harry became.

It was the hard school that produced Crowleys, Benges, Finnets, Beans, Haydens, Fitzgeralds and scores of other hard-fisted citizens, and Henry Peterson, horse-strong and deer-graceful, started boatmanship very young, with a shortened pair of oars. But it wasn't sheer business, it was the sport of oar-swinging that took root in him. He trained by rowing from the foot of Folsom street around Goat Island and back every morning, and developed a graceful twist of the wrist that took him to the heights. While in his teens he rowed against eight other professional entries from all the Coast and beat the lot. After that he went out and beat the world. He joined a rowing club and learned the ways of the sliding seat. He took on the champion of Australia at single sculling and beat him on the Oakland Estuary before 60,000 spectators. In 1900 he was America's representative in an international contest at London and he swept the Thames. Returning to the town by the Gate, he started a launch and barge service, added tugs and lighters, and became a big-scale operator, selling out in 1917 to Tom Crowley.

Henry Peterson was considered not only the Adonis of the Gate and its landside docks, but its sweetest-tempered denizen. Tall, thick, rugged, and aglint with athletic prestige, he was a Hercules that nobody ever was known to scuffle with. They just said "Yes, Henry." Especially when he remarked, "The sun seems to be over the yardarm." "Yes, Henry," they'd chime, and troop behind him into a bar on the Embarcadero, where he was the buyer by divine right.

He dropped from sight after selling out, and became a gentleman farmer down the Peninsula, where appendicitis knocked him from life's sliding seat at the age of seventy-one.

And there was Izzy Gomez.

He was a man from Portugal, wide as a full moon **and**

dark as an eclipse, who'd run away from home at the age of fifteen, sailed on a square-rigger, been shipwrecked off the shore of Spain, made it in another bottom to the U.S., and hoboed across the country, arriving at Gateside as a mere slip of a boy weighing 250 pounds.

The town by the Gate was his goal. A street called Pacific, stemming from the Embarcadero and skirting Telegraph Hill, became his habitat. He almost turned Salvation Army drum-pounder. Instead, he opened a short-order lunchroom. His problem was that he gave away his food to whoever asked for it. As he was directly in the area of sailors' boardinghouses, dance halls with tinny pianos and floosies with notorious hearts of gold, generous to themselves in the extreme where Izzy's food was concerned, he had plenty of clients.

In 1900, at about age 24, he fell in love with a dark-eyed charmer of 18 and then astonished her and himself by falling still harder in love with her mother, who was a widow and 44. To the day of his death he and the lady he'd rescued from widowhood remained married sweethearts, a period of 45 years.

During Prohibition, Izzy opened a "soft drink" establishment above a suspicion-lulling soda-bottling works at 848 Pacific. A dangling lantern marked its grey, battered door and a narrow, rickety stair led upward. Here Izzy's circle followed. Only now there were more of them: not only sailors and floosies, but writers and artists from the town's bohemia, and people who found an enjoyable shudder in the ghostly nearness of the district's bygone Whale Whiskers Kelly's, Bucket of Blood, Shanghai Brown's, Mother O'Brien's and Mrs. Hare's Firemen's Boarding House. Izzy prospered in spite of interruptions by Prohibition agents. Whenever he went to the county jail for a few days, he made friends with jailers and everybody else in the place by doing the cooking, his specialty being a dish he called "Lobster Newburg chez Gomez à la Bastille."

The artists did his walls for him at No. 848. There were snakes, pink elephants and a slogan, "Awake, My Little Ones, and Fill the Cup Before Life's Liquor in its Cup be Dry." In spite of broken furniture, cockroaches and the dubious creaking staircase, Izzy's became a gala place. Under a great mural of himself complete with droopy mustache, paunch, watch chain in double festoon, and black hat on his head with its brim turned down all the way around, stood Izzy himself behind his bar. He was Bacchus, great-cheeked, jovial, so big-hearted that it was said, "Izzy never turned down anything in his life but the brim of his hat." Why he always wore his hat, never removing it, was his own secret. One news-hen did claim to have snatched it off and peeked, but wouldn't reveal what she'd seen. She derived quite a prestige from sharing the mystery with Izzy. In his shabby loft, Izzy held court nightly, and gave away steaks to his busted friends whenever Joe Lopez, his cook, and Dad Niemeier, his assistant bartender, would let him— or "The Countess," a striking lady with wide smile, shining cheekbones and great compelling eyes, who had also constituted herself one of the guardians of Izzy against Izzy.

Nobody came through the Golden Gate, or went out that cleft to the broad seas beyond, without a call at Izzy's.

At closing time each night he caught the last ferryboat to, of all places, the quiet town of Alameda, where he lived a private life of perfect bliss with the mother of the girl he had almost married many decades before.

In 1944, President Roosevelt cleared the slate of those Prohibition charges, and Izzy died a few months after at the Alameda Sanatorium. Every year since his passing the "Izzy Gomez Alumni Association" meets in some suitable place and toasts his memory; and, it is said, there isn't a dry glass in the house.

The grey door, the rickety stairway and curious oasis above have all been swept away by wrecking ball and bulldozer. Izzy was the last of the Barbary Coast and its odd, fierce, savage, mellow and amazing ways. In truth, he had outlived the Barbary Coast by a quarter-century. And without the Coast and now without Izzy, in the opinion of a good many shipmasters and their seamen and passengers, it was about time to close the Gate as well.

26 : THE ROCK

IT HAS been called Bird Island. It has been called White Island. It is sometimes called The Rock. To most of history it has been, and is, Alcatraz, for the pelicans the Spanish found upon it. It is an angular block that stands at the inside end of the Golden Gate like an anchored ship. It is 148 feet high, a quarter-mile long and 525 feet wide. It is one of the friendliest and at the same time surliest spots on earth. Friendly, because its original lighthouse was the first ever built on the west coast of the United States, and because a guiding, kindly light has burned there continuously ever since. Surly, because it houses in a grim masonry cage the toughest convicts in the nation—when they don't escape.

Early ships found Alcatraz inhospitable and spurned it. The stony slopes offered neither wood nor water and there was no good anchorage. But it looked to the Americans to be a fine place for harbor defense. In behalf of the United States, John C. Frémont bought it from private claimants for $5,000. In 1854 its conversion to a strongpoint began. A dock was built on the north shore and a citadel of brick was imposed up top. The two were connected by a covered way. The banks were terraced and heavy ordnance pieces were set up. They consisted of smoothbore muzzle-loaders. They were 68, 42 and 28-pounders, a thoroughly first-class assem-

189

blage for their day. By 1861, Alcatraz was a prime fortress with a 120-man garrison, massive brick guardhouse, and barracks three stories high. Three bombproofs held 10,000 pounds of powder each. There was a 50,000-gallon cistern for water, which was barged over from Sausalito, and a large furnace for heating cannonballs.

But these preparations for assault that never came were soon rendered obsolete, even as those of Fort Point. The parapets and bastions were razed and the citadel demolished. Years later, when the island became a prison for wrong-doers, certain cells deep in the rock were used for places of penitence and solitary confinement. Because they were of time-stained brick and were dark and underground, they were called "Spanish dungeons" and were reputed to date practically to Cortez, Philip II and the Inquisition. Imagination draped them with wall rings, chains, rack-and-pinion machines and iron maidens, but "Spanish" the little dens of arched brick never were. They were magazines and gun emplacements of good 1854 Yankee brick.

At the post-Civil War reconstruction, the tip of the island was leveled off for the emplacement of big mortars. Terraces were also hacked into the south and west slopes for earthwork batteries of thirty-six guns. A parade ground and spot for officers' quarters was terraced on the east.

During this period the islet was also made to serve as a military prison. For many years "U.S. ARMY DISCIPLINARY BARRACKS" was blazoned on structures visible to the ferries as they passed east of the island. Soldiers convicted on the Pacific Coast of infractions of military law were sent to the "Rock" for correction. They were allowed to strengthen their muscles working on the fortifications, and received ten cents a day for it. Something above a hundred was the usual prisoner population. Among their number were a batch of Modoc Indians convicted of participating in the murder of General Canby in the lava fields of northwest

California. For these lifers, the government wigwam and rations were a definite improvement over their former way of life, and they made few complaints.

But except for Modoc Indians the island was a dreary place, and that went for its troops who were merely stationed there. Twice a day the quartermaster steamer *Mc-Pherson* ran to and from the city a mile away. Food, newspapers, books, even drinking and cooking water had to be brought from the mainland. In winter the rain and the sea became one watery inverted bowl for the lonely island, and in summer the fogs made it spectral and as isolated as the planets. In hours of radiant sunshine, which were many, the city's windows and streets beckoned frustratingly, and on clear nights the lights and other reminders of life and laughter were maddening. Alcatraz was the U.S.A.'s Devil's Island or Chateau d'If, and it still is.

In 1934 the Federal Bureau of Prisons took the rock over from the Army and retooled it for housing a different type of criminal. A place was wanted where the more difficult escape artists and hell-raisers in federal prisons could be housed with absolute security. The iron bars were replaced with saw-proof steel. Invincible locks, electric eyes and other paraphernalia were installed. And the Dutch Louie Schultzes, Machine Gun Kellys, Creepy Karpises and Scarface Als were removed from Leavenworth, McNeil, Atlanta and other cages and spirited to The Rock.

The first "guest" to check in at the strengthened and improved jailhouse was Robert Moxon, a mail-box looter and forger, from McNeil Island. He had once been a guard on Alcatraz itself in its Army disciplinary-barracks days, so he felt right at home. With him were forty-six others, all arriving in August, 1934. Soon afterward, a couple of railroad cars left Atlanta, Georgia, with Capone's chubby face grinning from one of the windows. The scarfaced one may have thought he was going to have a civic reception at San Francisco, but the cars were shunted from the main track to Tiburon, the car-ferry port on the bay, and barged to The Rock, where Al soon found himself in a 9 by 5 cell equipped with folding bunk, blankets, washstand, toilet, shelf, three hooks, soap, cup, toothbrush, and toothpaste—and silence. The place was run with precision and sterilized cleanliness. The guards were picked men. There were no trusties. Only one phone on the island took or made outside calls, and that one was on the warden's desk. Four watchtowers guarded every foot of ground. The four hundred cons who eventually arrived were the country's toughest two per cent, and they and their successors hadn't been sentenced to Alcatraz; they had earned it. Their stay there was for an average twenty-five years.

In its first fourteen years as a maximum security federal prison, nineteen prisoners tried to escape. They tried everything schemeful man can devise. Five were shot to death or executed, twelve recaptured, and two disappeared forever. This pair, Ralph Roe and Theodore Cole, selected a foggy December day to crawl through a ground-floor machine-shop window, jimmy a gate in a 20-foot fence, and just plain vanish. Guards in a tower not far away couldn't see for the fog cover. Undoubtedly the two put off into the tide rip, and always have been considered drowned.

Floyd P. Wilson, doing life for murder during a holdup, disappeared from a work gang. Next morning he was flushed out from a hiding place beneath the foghorn. In all the world it would be difficult to imagine a more uncomfortable spot than beneath a foghorn, during a fog, on Alcatraz Island. His cell must have seemed mighty quiet when he got back to it.

Aaron W. Burgett, rather pleasant and good-natured, was a rangy gunman from St. Louis, doing 26 years for a $15.26 postoffice robbery. A string of twenty-five other holdups decorated his record. Clyde Johnson, a Memphis bank robber, had been the FBI's No. 1 public enemy in '49. One day in '58 they flashed a knife in the face of Guard Harold Miller, bound and gagged him, and laid him in thick brush at the southeast corner of the island. The eerie blast of the Alcatraz klaxon sounded the news. Coast Guard, metropolitan police and FBI men rallied. Four cutters circled the island. Sixty searchers in pairs probed every recess. Johnson was spotted standing forlornly in shallow water, a September Morn in overalls. Burgett was found two days later. He'd made a pathetic pair of waterwings out of scraps of wood and had embarked for San Francisco. He'd been dead two days.

In '46, The Rock staged its biggest battle. A crafty little Kentucky bank robber named Barney McCoy, who was washing windows, reached in through the bars and collared a guard with his T-shaped squeejee, clawed him close, almost garroted him, and grabbed his pistol, rifle and keys. He released two co-conspirators from their cells; and for three days Alcatraz was a shooting, screaming, milling, grenade-dodging, tear-gas-ducking bedlam which brought out the Marines and held thousands of distant spectators spellbound on San Francisco's hills and Golden Gate wharves. The three ringleaders failed to throw open all the cell blocks, but they hid in a three-story-high service alley in one block and by climbing water pipes and popping out at unexpected levels held the besiegers at bay for half a week. Two guards were killed and thirteen wounded. A door to the service alley was finally kicked open. A shotgun blast was sent down the dark slot. The last of the three who had tried to deliver the penitentiary was blown to kingdom come. And the whole Battle of Alcatraz, on the convicts' side, had been waged with one rifle, one pistol.

James A. Johnston, a one-time vice president of a bank, was the humane, implacable warden through all these early arrivals and set-tos. He had formerly been warden at San Quentin and he was writing a book about it. As we were friends, he showed me the galley proofs for review. Later we went down together in a San Francisco office-building elevator. I discovered afterward that my social standing had taken a leap upward. I had been seen shaking the hand of Scarface Al's boss. When the Pride of Chicago finished out his term—for income tax misbehavior—and betook himself and his paresis home, lots of people lost interest in staring across the mile and a half of water toward the Isle of the Pelicans.

But for visitors to the seaport city, Alcatraz is the No. 1 attraction, scarcely surpassed even by Chinatown, and for ten cents a telescope on Telegraph Hill will put one practically over there.

However, its reputation for invincibility against escape exploded with a bang when three inmates, on a June night in 1962, slipped through an air vent into a passage behind their cells, climbed to the cell-block roof, clambered down a pipe to the ground below, scaled a high wire fence or two despite guards and searchlights, and vanished. A week later they were officially pronounced drowned. The chagrined officials had no bodies as yet to prove it. All they had was a paddle, a waterproofed packet containing names and addresses of some shore contacts, and the dummy heads, complete with hair, that Frank L. Morris and John and Clarence Anglin, bank robbers, had left in their beds. The men had insulted Alcatraz still further by digging their way through the brickwork with tablespoons.

27 : TWO LANTERNS

FAR more important to the world than the scrofulous denizens who lead such highly antiseptic, dreary lives is that
other occupant of The Rock, its lighthouse. This is the true
lantern of the Gate. Its swinging beam, 214 feet aloft, is
housed in a shaft of airy architecture; and the long finger of
light touches, in turn, the windows of a million people. Like
a watchman in the night, it seems to cry "All's well!" That
long beam can be picked up from twenty-one miles at sea.

A bonfire on a headland, or burning tow raised on a pole,
was all that the Coast had to offer to mariners at night until
1854, when this first lighthouse was reared. It was a job of
work of the first order. The stubby wharf and the necessary
stone barges were, however, available from the fortification
task that was going forward at the same time. And mules and
men were cheap. So Alcatraz was quarried for some of its
stone where gun emplacements were needed, and the stone
was dressed and hauled higher and lifted by mule-powered
block and tackle into a hollow spire with an oil lamp and a
Fresnel lens on top, and with the keeper's quarters at the
bottom, all the ships of the seven seas in his charge.

To make his duties still more worth his meager salary, he
was given a fog bell. This was no puny affair. It was of bronze,
weighing 1,500 pounds, and it had steam machinery to op-

195

erate it. At least that was the theory. But sometimes, when fogs were at their thickest, the engine went on strike and the keeper had to whack his bell by hand. This could last for hours on end. Shapes of ships would glide through the cloud mass on the water, phantoms and wraiths and outlines seen then lost, or more often not even seen. The keeper, in his task of noise-maker, had company. Over on Angel Island was a woman keeper, and she had a fog bell that she sometimes had to bang by hand too. In 1906 she did this for a stretch of twenty-one continuous hours. It would be pleasant to think that man and woman, Alcatraz and Angel, worked out a romantic code whereby they said something to each other besides "Bam!" but there's no evidence of it. Just the plain hard task of keeping ships off the rocks—and not always succeeding, at that.

The original light tower lasted until 1910. In its fifty-six years it guided at least a couple hundred thousand ships and small craft beyond count into the shelter of the Bay. For Alcatraz is not a part of the Gate as such; it is a mile or more inside, though squarely facing the front and center of that busy cleft. Like a pylon it directs traffic around itself to the north for the upper bay reaches, and to the south for San Francisco, Oakland and anchorages between. When the old structure was replaced by the present one, the bay acquired an architectural gem. Of octagonal shape, it looms sixty-six feet above The Rock's summit. For years its outline and that of the island and structures below bore a striking resemblance to a battleship with a thick basket mast. Additional prison buildings have gradually effaced some of that effect.

But at night, for all the bay, Alcatraz is king. Its five-second revolving flash courses a great flat circle like a benediction. And in foggy hours, the brassy howlers speak with no uncertain voice. In the days just between relinquishment of the island by the Army and its assumption by the Department of Justice, this writer was on it for a day (strictly as a visitor) and was standing a few paces in front of the north-west ear-buster, when first wisps of fog came dancing in. The keeper turned on the mighty blaster. There all but followed the longest broad jump in history. The whole Gate was achorus with howls, yells, banshee shrieks and lost souls moaning. Lime Point bull-moosed to South Tower. Pier 45 whooped to Alcatraz Southwest. Mile Rock two-noted with hoarse passion to Point Bonita. Bonita anguished of love undying for silent Lands End. Black Point implored, reproached and reviled Angel Island. And Treasure Island, Goat Island and Bay Bridge joined in. All was bawl, blare, blat, bray and boo, but the fog didn't falter. It still came boiling in.

The lantern keeper at Alcatraz is lonesome, but at least he has the couple hundred guards for neighbors as well as the forbidden three or four hundred baddies. But consider the fix of the light keepers on Mile Rock out in the Gate near its south shore. They are only half a mile from town, close enough to hear its church bells and auto horns. But they are on a needle of rock surrounded by crashing surf; and they are visited only once a week, by a Coast Guard supply boat, and official callers have to climb a dangling Jacob's ladder to reach their perch.

Mile Rock is 30 by 40 feet in area and its lighthouse fits on top of it like a white plug hat. Its attendants' front yard is an iron-railed circular balcony a few feet wide, 78 feet above the sea. Waves are known to dash completely over it. Six men at a time live there, keep watch, turn on the fog signal, cook their own meals, view the passing ship traffic, batten hatches when the storms blow, and wonder what women look like.

Mile Rock Light was erected shortly after the *Rio* went down a little east of there, at the century's beginning. Light and fog signal both are slated in good time to become automatic and remote-controlled, making human vigil as unnecessary there as it is at Point Diablo and Lime Point across the strait. But at this writing the automation is still in the future; and Keeper Joe Soto, engineman first class of the United States Coast Guard, and his five assistants live on in their stony Eveless Eden, the lonesomest lighthouse in America, because it is only a sea-biscuit throw from a lively city—which they do visit by turns, but only every few weeks.

It's almost a blessing when fog or drizzle blots out Mile Rock's tantalizing 360° sweep of nearby parks and drives and golf courses, and of ships going out and coming in.

Over on Alcatraz even the cons have at least a yard to exercise in.

Here a man has only that airy balcony. Fifty-five laps make a mile.

"The lantern keeper at Alcatraz is lonesome, but at least he has the couple hundred guards for neighbors as well as three or four hundred baddies."

"From this shelf, all is view." Point Bonita from the south.

"The function of the station is not only to light the Gate, but to holler." Point Bonita from the north.

Ansel Adams

The Golden Gate, San Francisco, before The Bridge (1932).

"So the Fort was saved. The Bridge swoops right over it."

From the opposite shore, "Windowpanes sparkle on the (city) hills." The Gate entrance is shaped like a bell. "Its bridged narrows marry the Pacific Ocean to river waters that have eloped from California's Great Central Valley."

"The nearest neighbors to the Farallon light keepers are the men aboard the red-hulled San Francisco Lightship, 12 miles shoreward."

28 : THE WEATHER MAKER

THERE are two types of fog in the Gate's vicinity. Most marked is the summer-afternoon sea fog which forms west of the Gate or sometimes right within it. It gathers against the south slopes of Mt. Tamalpais and its foothills above the Gate and rolls inland at about sixteen miles per hour. This is a hale, hearty, energizing fog, the great cosmetic and elixir. It cultivates healthy complexions, puts bounce in the step, makes a blanket welcome at night and produces a sound, refreshing sleep.

The other is the tule or ground fog, a miserable, lurking thing which exhales from rivers, marshes and damp ground during winter, and is wholly pestiferous; for it lies about in wads like cotton balls, it is apt to be almost impenetrable by headlights, it defies windshield wipers, and it causes accidents. Nothing kind can be said about a tule fog; like smog, it is utterly despicable.

But the sea fogs! Those are brave fellows, honest and lusty. Though shipmasters and airplane pilots cuss them out, they are the Golden Gate region's tossing banner, announcing that the towns below are summer-cool and fighting-fit.

The sea fogs, which are most prevalent in July, August and September, form beyond the Heads and along the coast, usually in local pockets but sometimes in a continuous belt for a thousand miles. They tend to be densest near the shore-line. The layer of cool marine air they occupy is up to about 1,500 feet thick. Globules of moisture form about nuclear centers of condensation, and the result is visible, palpable clouds that roll like breakers and charge like cavalry; you who stand beside the Gate or drive across its Bridge—or, better, walk—see them coming, feel them pass, and tingle from the experience. How much moisture passes you? Alexander McAdie, who spent years as chief of the regional weather bureau, decided that not less than a million tons of water were carried inward each hour between Points Lobos and Bonita when the fog was thick. If it could be condensed as rain, it would deliver one inch in a seven-hour stretch.

What brings those fog winds inland? Topography, and low pressure at the interior. California's Central Valley, thirty miles inland, is a great oval pan with high sides and one narrow pouring lip. Its enclosing mountains are clamped between two rival weather factories, ocean on the west and deserts—real, convincing, summer-blistering and almost endless—on the east and southeast. Along about May, Central Valley and those deserts beyond it begin to warm up.

If the Valley's westside mountains were as high and unbroken as its eastern and southeastern, it would simply contain its increasing temperature and that would be that. But it possesses that pouring spout, where its two merging rivers rush out. Actually, this is a double gap. The rivers flow through Carquinez Strait, an almost sea-level gash in the Coast Range, before they reach the Bay and then the Golden Gate. This pair of in-line water gaps not only let the rivers out, but the winds of ocean in as interior heated air rises.

And the ocean has winds to deliver. The prevailing west wind of summer has brought its moisture across the cold surface of the current that is moving southward from the Gulf of Alaska, causing condensation just as warm breath does on a cold pane of glass. That's the fine cool ocean fog.

The winds that bear it find the Coast Range something of an obstacle. But they bump through the Gate with ease. The fog sweeps inland until it is absorbed by the dry air of that great central valley or heating pan.

During the hours of greatest heat inland, the Gate is at its busiest as a funnel for wind and water-vapor. The rollers, eddies and tumbling cascades of the fog are exhilarating to watch. They billow through at a pace about four times faster than a man can walk. They split on Alcatraz into two main streams. One heads for Carquinez Strait, the other for the bay's southward reach. The fog forms a layer over the bay from a hundred feet to a quarter-mile thick. Sometimes the summer cooling system doesn't work, and the razzing that jangles Weather Bureau phones comes in joyful quantity from points inland and south. But usually it does work, producing average Bay Area highs in July of around 64 degrees, in September (the warmest month) 68 degrees. Visitors of attenuated blood damn it heartily and wish they had brought their woolies.

The varying altitudes of the Coast Range crests and pinnacles cause some of the unique effects which motorists can encounter approaching or leaving Golden Gate Bridge. It may be cool, foggy and 58 degrees at the toll plaza on the southern end and, up on Tamalpais a few miles north, clear weather and 85 degrees. Seen from up there, the fog thumps against the lower part of the mountain and lets a bridge tower, an islet or a city skyscraper pop through. Other vagaries of wind movement may leave the water and bridge deck clear but hang fog around the waist of one tower—and leave its summit red and naked. The layman merely knows that when he starts out to cross the Gate, whether with his overcoat or without it, he will have guessed wrong.

So much for fog. (Of thunder and lightning, there is practically none.) But how many *sunny* hours pour their gold down on Gateside? About 2,869, or 60 per cent of the annual daylight, Professor McAdie determined. This compares surprisingly well with the sunniness of other American localities: 2,729 at New York, 2,763 at Boston, 2,423 at Chicago, 2,263 at St. Louis. Absence of summer rainfall over the Gate makes this balance possible.

McAdie's figures were obtained in downtown San Francisco, not in the Gate itself. Fog rules the latter 18 to 22 per cent of the time. But four-fifths of the time, all's clear. Any shipmaster from Ferrelo and Drake onward would snort at this statistic, and demand to know why he never experienced any of those 80 per cent of sunny or starlit hours, but they are there. And though the fog signal at Point Bonita has howled for as many as 1,996 hours in a single year, 1,534 would be more the average and this does not necessarily mean that shapes of ships in those hours could not be seen. Sometimes the thing officially called "fog" is a merest scarf. Bonita starts howling *before* the fog is thick. But often enough it is the real thing—an army of ghostly sky-riders; a charging, trampling herd of formless wraiths rushing, swirling, caroming, sliding, lurching; silent, leaderless, headed nowhere in particular, but seemingly bound on very important business.

29 : A POET AND HIS BRIDGE

THERE were awesome counts against it.

There was doubt of its immediate need. But the little man with the far-seeing eye beheld the oncoming sweep of population.

There were winds and currents and depths and earthquake faults. There was a gap, shore to shore, such as man had never spanned. The little man smiled.

There was the prospect of clawing a great scar across the very breast of beauty. It will not be a scar—it will be a necklace, pledged the man of dreams. Listen to me, he urged. Consider my record, and trust me. This is the greatest thing I shall ever do. It will be worthy of its setting.

Joseph Baerman Strauss, University of Cincinnati '92, had been roaming the earth bridging water-gaps. He was a slide-rule and logarithm man. Privately, he was something more. There is a kinship between the rhythms and symmetries of math and the rhythms and contours of words. Skillful use of either calls for a leaping imagination. So, in secrecy, the engineer played at verse, though he knew it for a more exacting art than math or engineering because its practitioner never quite arrives at what he ultimately and absolutely wants to say, and is therefore never satisfied. But Joe's feet were on the ground even when his head was in the clouds like the bridge towers he was to build. Inventor, designer and patent owner of the concrete, counterweighted bascule lift bridges that have driven "turnstile" drawbridges out of business, he had pitched four hundred of his utilitarian devices over America's rivers. His ambitions transcended that. In college, he had designed a bridge for Bering Strait that, he dreamed, would connect America with Asia. In his heart he had probably spanned the Bosporus, Asia to Europe. In solid fact he had been consulting engineer to the mighty George Washington Bridge that overleaps the Hudson, and the Arlington Bridge over the Potomac. He had co-designed Montreal Bridge across the St. Lawrence, Longview Bridge over the Columbia, the Quincy, Illinois, bridge over the Mississippi, the Independence Bridge over the Missouri. He was not inexperienced.

So it was Joe Strauss, a tiny 120-pounder in his college days in Ohio, a portly but no taller figure forty years later, who decided to bridge the Golden Gate.

The financing: it would take tens of millions. The state wasn't ready for it. The state always follows behind traffic, seldom leads it. The economic necessity: undemonstrated. There were three-quarters of a million urban people on the south shore; but only a small suburban area and an endless but sparsely populated agricultural, dairy and timber region on the north—and the next large city Portland, but it was 700 miles away. The outcries of the beauty lovers were forceful. Who would not protest any desecration of that classic view where the mountains gather the setting sun into their arms and lower it into the sea—supreme symbol of day-is-done, of land's-end reached? But if they would listen to him, Joe Strauss, there would be no harshness done to Beauty. . . .

And then, the construction problems. But here Joe Strauss promptly grew ten, twenty, a hundred, eight hundred feet tall. People sensed it. While he struggled with the statistics— channel depths of more than 300 feet, currents of 6½ to 7 knots, winds up to 80 miles, mists up to a quarter of the time; the distance to be spanned, the tall masts to be cleared, the footings for towers, and the towers themselves, and the cables and the cable anchorages: while he wrestled with these details, well-wishers formed a highway district and voted the money, $35 million. (It would have to be $110 million today.)

At first the geologists battled. The Gate at its narrowest, 5,357 feet, was only six miles from San Andreas Fault, which had been rocking San Francisco for decades and splitting mountains for millions of years. Geology professors Bailey Willis of Stanford and Andy Lawson of the University of California locked over this one and smote each other hip and thigh, but majority opinion sided with Lawson and decided to take a chance. Nothing in the quarter-century since has refuted that decision.

Then, to get footings down into bedrock for the cable towers. The north pier was easy. Though the water was deep and the bedrock well below that, steel sheet piling was run down on three sides and buttressed with rock-filled cribbing. The pumps started, a wharf was run out from shore and it was just another construction job. The great red steel tower followed quickly, to a height of 746 feet. It could be seen from afar almost as clearly as Mount Tamalpais behind it, and it kept the taxpayers interested.

But that south tower-footing!

Here, 1,125 feet offshore, was practically open sea, exposed to all its storms, and subject to violent cross-currents. Four times the plan of attack was drawn up; four times changed. But the pier went down. Bombs excavated the bedrock for a concrete "fender" that would girdle the pier itself, and that fender, there in open-sea conditions, was poured. It was as big as a football stadium and twice as high. Like an island in the center of it, the pier then rose as swiftly as if it were a dry-land operation, for the fender had been de-watered and all was as handy within as in a drydock.

The south tower went up and up and up.

Between it and the shore a basketwork was erected to preserve the red-brick fort of Fort Point, that beloved landmark. The cables were hung, the roadway was suspended, and on May 27, 1937, the whole 123-million-pound, 8,981-foot structure was flung open to pedestrians. They swarmed across by thousands. They thrilled to its leap of 4,200 feet between towers, more daring than any span had attempted before. They observed that it was provided with two 10-foot sidewalks for those who would stroll and enjoy the sunlight on the hills, the ships on the water. They noticed that the fence or bulwark on each side was slit vertically to let riders in motorcars see the ships too, as well as let the wind through and keep the roadway from becoming a tossing hammock. And they rejoiced that Joe Strauss had done as he'd promised: he'd not despoiled the Gate.

By day the Bridge is a magnificently satisfying thing of strength and airiness. By night its amber lights gleam in two long arcs like a double necklace. Regrettably, thirteen men died in its building, twelve in one swoop when a workers' suspended conveyance under the roadway left its rails and a huge life net failed to hold the plunging weight. More than two hundred persons have leaped on purpose from its walkways 220 feet above the water. The bridge stands serene. It transports up to 75,000 cars a day, and more. It has brought the vineyards and orchards and America's illimitable forests to the doorstep of a city.

Seismographs at strategic points give daily record of any tremors underneath, and they have never been alarming; the bridge itself is built to sway 30 inches at its tower tops, its roadway to rise and fall 16 feet as temperature changes, and to crawl longitudinally over expansion joints for as far as the length of a man.

One wild night, in 1951, I chanced to be one of many who tried for the bridge at a late hour and was turned back by the police; the great span had been closed for public safety. Winds of unprecedented velocity were making war on its suspender wires and threatening to blow cars out of their lanes. When that gale was over, a substantial sum was spent in further stiffening the structure. Nothing else has ever threatened it, and its closing that night was only precautionary.

Once I was on the bridge of a ship passing below, an oil tanker, and its skipper gaily invited me to take over his own boyish pleasure of pulling the whistle cord as we passed under the Bridge. "It's the echo," he said. "I love the echo." And truly, from that spot on the sea below, the 90-foot width of the roadway high above our masts sent back a blast that was most satisfying, if one collects whistle blasts.

Besides attending to its own road lights and ship and air-craft light signals, the bridge operates a foghorn service that meshes with the Coast Guard's. When Morty Siem, chief electrician, or his deputy can't see a certain north shore rock-face from the southside toll plaza, a stubby lever is flicked within the bridge maintenance shops and all kinds of noise-makers begin to speak. There is a pair of tyfons at midspan 225 feet above water and two diaphones 12 feet above the water at the south tower's base.

Joe Strauss died just a year after completing his record-breaking structure. He'd kept faith with the beauty of the Gate. His artist's heart had controlled his engineer's head.

His poetic soul? One of its effusions hangs on a tree in the redwood forest far north of the Gate, and is appended here. But Joseph Strauss built the Bridge, and that's his Iliad.

There must have been a musician in him too. The vertical cables that hold the suspended roadway have turned out, some musicians declare, to be the strings to a pair of mile-long wind-harps.

Strauss didn't promise that. But he left the two wide walkways for those who would saunter and listen, as well as regard the view.

THE REDWOODS

Here, sown by the Creator's hand,
In serried ranks, the Redwoods stand;
No other clime is honored so,
No other lands their glory know.

The greatest of Earth's living forms,
Tall conquerors that laugh at storms;
Their challenge still unanswered rings,
Through fifty centuries of kings.

The nations that with them were young,
Rich empires, with their forts far-flung,
Lie buried now—their splendor gone;
But these proud monarchs still live on . . .

To be like these, straight, true and fine,
To make our world, like theirs, a shrine:
Sink down, Oh traveler, on your knees.
God stands before you in these trees.

—JOSEPH B. STRAUSS,
Builder of the Golden Gate Bridge

30 : THE MOUNTAIN ABOVE

MARINERS are told by that bible of Pacific shipmasters, the United States Coast Pilot 7 of the Coast and Geodetic Survey, "Mount Tamalpais, about 7 miles northward of Point Bonita, is a prominent mountain 2,604 feet high. . . . From southwestward and westward it shows three summits of which the westernmost is the highest and the easternmost is the sharpest. It is covered with brush and scrub trees, giving it a dark appearance which contrasts strongly with the surrounding hills, especially in summer when the hills assume a light reddish color."

In a state that has thirteen peaks of over 14,000 feet, Tamalpais is definitely a mere footstool. Snow only rarely powders it. No glaciers spangle it. No rivers spring from its flanks.

No matter. Hoary Tamalpais, product of twenty or forty million years of volcanic seethings and sedimentary settlings and liftings, is many things: a landfall for ships, a bender of winds, a cleaver of clouds, nourisher and protector of trees that were stalwarts a thousand years ago; it is a garden of ferns in its shadowy recesses and flowers on its meadows, and a robust workout for the walker. From the Bay towns below, it has been likened to Naples' Vesuvius without the smoke.

The mountain's triple summit is only thirteen miles from the heart of San Francisco. Seen across the Gate from the city, it is burly. It is, in fact, a whole range, rolling and tumbling about over forty square miles of landscape and ending on two sides in precipices that take the crash of the sea and the Gate. The gales on top of it sometimes reach hurricane grandeur, the rains give it a noble beating, and the sun paints it with green grass seven months of the year, then fries it for five, with great wet clouds of sea mist a cooling touch.

In some of the hollows about its base are forests of breathless beauty. Here the fog-loving coastal redwoods grow—primeval groves, less than an hour's drive from the hustle of a city. Crowns of some of these trees are 240 feet aloft and some trunks are 10 to 15 feet in diameter. Sunlight filters through, taking on a green-gold tint. In times of heavy ocean fog I have seen rivulets of condensation as thick as a man's finger running down the shaggy bark flutings, for the arms of redwoods reach for and gather the moisture and transmute it as if it were rain. Brooks trickle down through the brown leaf-mold; huckleberry fountains up out of old stumps; azaleas stand ready to explode into creamy bloom. The best of the redwoods have been perpetuated in Muir Woods, a 425-acre national monument. The brook which scampers through Muir Woods tumbles into the cove just north of the Gate where the *Tennessee* met doom in early times. That such an unspoiled and unique forest should stand within four or five beeline miles of a major town is just one of the unusual caprices of the Tamalpais area.

The upper half of the moated mountain usually stands above all fog. The sunny, golden topside of those billowy mists lies well below the old warrior's middle.

For decades the young in legs or heart used to make pilgrimages to this mountain by the hundreds. They came over on the 7:30 A.M. Sunday ferry, rolled their shirts and pants into bikinis, shouldered knapsacks and hit for the trails up

Blithedale Canyon, Old Pipe Line and Cascade Canyon, or
past the mill that Juan Reed built in 1834 for making lumber
for the Presidio of San Francisco; they thrashed through the
manzanita and mountain lilac, skimmed over the ridges and
debouched for Muir Woods, Steep Ravine and Stinson
Beach, or struck for the summit and finally stood there with
half of northern California and the Bay, the Gate, and 5,000
square miles of Pacific Ocean at their feet.

There was even a jolly little railroad. Called the Mill Valley & Mt. Tamalpais, proudly subtitled "The Crookedest
Railroad in the World," it wound by 281 curves and loops
from the verdant village of Mill Valley at its base to a tavern
near the top. The cars were of outdoor type, unwalled, with
transverse seats, and the powerfully low-geared Shay locomotive hauled the riders up with steam-whistle blasts that
made the redwoods rustle their cones in Blithedale Canyon
and left the bluejays speechless. The descent could be made
by gravity car, if desired, and a hairy trip that was. The railroad started business in 1896 and lasted until 1929, when veteran holiday engineer Harry Westcott put his locomotive in
the barn down in Mill Valley and retired with his memories.
These included his years as regular engineer on the suburban
line between Sausalito and Mill Valley, and passengers used
to ask him to halt the train in a marsh at the halfway point
while they shot a few brace of ducks from the car platforms.

It was an automobile road up the mountain that doomed
the railroad. Then the summit tavern burned up. And the
defeat of the old ferries by the Golden Gate Bridge completed the switch-over. Today there are fewer Sunday hikers
on the mountain, except on special occasions.

One of these is the annual Mountain Play. It is a pretty
thing. The idea of it was hit upon by three dedicated hikers,
one of them an actor and dramatic coach, as they chanced
to round a bend in the trail and came upon a natural amphitheater. Its backdrop was stunning—the Golden Gate and

its surf-fringed headlands, and the blue Pacific. The wings were ready-made: echeloned clumps of pine, redwood, oak, manzanita and madrone. "What a setting for a play!"

Amateur actors, talented and not so talented, sprang to the challenge. On a bright May morning of 1913, hundreds of spectators, many in town shoes and high-heeled pumps, labored over the rough trail. They blistered their feet and tempers, lugged picnic hampers, and arrived at that perch 2,000 feet above the sea to witness a thirteenth century miracle play and some scenes from *Twelfth Night*. A drama critic from the *Morning Call* sat with stones in his shoes and scowled at the whole thing, returned to the city badly sunburned, and wrote in his paper next day that such folly would never be repeated.

But the trail and the ground for sitting on have been raked and gentled, a better understanding of required footgear has been reached by the audiences, and the plays have gone on with scarcely a skip for fifty years.

Viewed from certain points south or southeast, the mountain has the outline of a sleeping maiden. This has given rise to legend. She was an Indian princess; a sun god wanted her; she preferred a brave of her own people; the god and the brave did battle over the lady and threw islands at each other; death or business elsewhere delayed the lover's return; and so she waits. The theme has been utilized with joy by the Mountain Players and their dramatists.

A literary researcher of the 1950's decided to dig into this bit of romantic folklore. How far back in time—to the wickiups of what tribe of Digger Indians, Pomo, Miwok or Nicasio —did the sad myth run? He delved into catalogues in the libraries. He came up with three published poems, two plays, eight newspaper articles and three unpublished manuscripts. The earliest of these was a Yale prize poem titled "The Legend of Tamalpais," published by that university in 1911.

In full cry now, the research scholar ran down the one-time sophomore who had put that tale to paper. Where had he got it? From an earlier published piece, or from Indians still extant? From none of those, said the astonished pen-pusher; from the sleeping maiden herself. As a member of a Sunday School mob of little boys he once had climbed her mountain, watching her silhouette as they ascended, and they all had slept out upon her elevated brow, bust and feet the whole starry night. There had been no previous rendering of the legend? None that he knew of. He made it all up? As far as he was concerned, yes. But why? Because there was a $50 prize involved for a poem about absolutely anything, and his landlady was becoming urgent about her board money.

The delving into aboriginal folklore, as far that disgusted researcher was concerned, died right there.

The best vantage points from which to see the Sleeping Maiden went out of business with the bay ferries. So now she rests less disturbed by word-weavers with vine leaves—or angry landladies—in their hair.

The spiritual and aesthetic influence of the mountain upon the dwellers below was summed up by R. L. Stevenson when he wrote, just before sailing out the Golden Gate on the *Casco,* "Though the other states were to put all their dollars together, they could not manufacture a Tamalpais."

31 : BEYOND THE HEADS

THE area beyond the Heads—the great vestibule to the Gate —is the Gulf of the Farallones, an almost rectangular seascape about 35 miles long and 23 wide stretching from Point San Pedro on the south to the Farallon Islands on the west and Point Reyes on the northeast, and south along the mainland shore for some 40 miles to Pedro again.

This gulf of some 700 square miles is comparatively shallow, from 4 to 48 fathoms. The deeps lie just beyond the outpost Farallones, plunging rapidly to 300 fathoms. The bar lies about three to six miles due west of the Gate. Its northern part, the shoalest, is known as the Potato Patch because schooners from Bodega Bay used to lose their deckloads of potatoes with regularity when crossing it.

From Point Lobos to Point San Pedro (not to be confused with San Pedro harbor 400 miles south), the coast extends 11 miles straight south. A dark, rocky promontory 640 feet high, Pedro was a conspicuous landmark for early navigators and is considered the southeast corner of the Gulf of the Farallones; but a point of equal prominence three miles farther south, Point Montara, was chosen to hold the lighthouse and fog signal.

Starting with a steam fog whistle in 1875 and an oil lens lantern on a post in 1900, Point Montara became a full-
214

fledged light in 1912 and the present tower went up in 1928. For a long while its keepers were a couple of hardy, dependable, God-fearing and gale-unfearing women. Right staunchly they lived up to the Instructions, which stated: "Light keepers must be of good character, of sober and industrious habits, and they are required to comport themselves in an orderly manner in their families and at the light stations to which they are attached." During thick or stormy weather keepers were required "To give their whole time and constant attention to the lights in their charge . . . the lights must never be left unattended by a keeper." And they never were, though while one lady did her stint beside the light, and presumably did her knitting, the other was at full liberty to be busy down in the lightkeepers' dwelling, making apple pies.

The Farallon Islands, twenty-one miles west, are a string of submerged reefs and outcrops. Early mariners gave them wide berth. In fact, the isles did quite as much as the fogs to keep the sixteenth- and seventeenth-century mariners from discovering the Gate. The Southeast Farallon, actually two islets separated by a watery chasm that is not for boats of any size, rises like a pyramid for 350 feet. It holds Farallon Light. Radio beacon and fog signal also are on this islet, and a small community of attendants and their families. The great circle route to and from Honolulu lies a mile and a half south of the light. Maintop, Sugarloaf, Hurst Shoal, Middle Farallon, North Farallon and Noonday Rock continue the stepping-stone chain for 9½ miles, Noonday being where a clipper ship of that name struck in 1862 and sank in sixty minutes.

Farallon Light has guided and warned ships since 1855. Solid rock 350 feet high was flattened on top to make a base for this historic lamp, and a suitable pedestal erected. But the lantern, when it arrived, wouldn't fit. The tower had to be rebuilt, and great was the swearing. The first-order Fresnel lens which finally went into service is now in the

Maritime Museum beside the waters of the Gate. In its day it sat 358 feet aloft, its beam visible for 26 miles. A successor lens still uses the 8-foot tower. The Southeast Farallon has a couple of more relics of past enterprise: ruins of the stone hovels that the Russian sea-lion hunters built, and a couple of stunted cypress trees that some lightkeeper's wife once planted and lovingly tended through drouth and storm.

At the building of Farallon Light, the U.S. Army engineers decided to harness and put to work a mighty blowhole that was a feature of the spot. Sea waves rushed into a cavern and a shaft in its ceiling sent them high, at times making the island spout like a whale. General Hartman Bache of the Engineers fell in love with the possibilities of this natural tuba or sousaphone. He walled the wind and water outlet with brick and capped it with a locomotive whistle and stood back to enjoy the effect. When a big wave rushed in and air shot up and found its voice constricted, it blew the general's brickwork about like bullets. Undaunted, the general tried again. There was some suggestion that a substitute be found in the mule which had been imported to carry building materials up to the tower, and which had a notable bray. But a mule needs feed and a budget and General Bache's natural tootle worked for nothing. He rebuilt that chimney and bolstered it with iron and cement. And that was fine if the waves were high; the whistle yelled like old No. 999 going around a curve. But on still days and nights the waves fell off to a lullaby, and the sentinel whistle slept. Still and all, it remained at its post for fifteen years, when a wild sea surged up thataway and carried the contraption overboard. It was succeeded by a steam siren.

The Southeast Farallon holds about twenty structures. The ten or a dozen denizens, all Coast Guard personnel, long were the most westerly group of citizens dwelling in the United States. When Alaska and Hawaii became states, the sequestered group on the Farallones lost that subtle distinction, if they'd ever known they had it. Much more important was whether the weekly boat would arrive as usual with the mail and groceries, and whether it would find good mooring and derricking weather or wouldn't. (Often it doesn't.)

Nearest neighbors are the men aboard the red-hulled San Francisco Lightship, 12 miles shoreward and west-southwestward of the main ship channel to the Golden Gate. As the lightship's gleam sweeps 14 miles, it paints the Farallon every fifteen seconds if the night is clear.

Often it isn't. The fog out here averages 950 hours a year and has been known to reach 2,018. Back in 1579, Francis Drake, who nosed up to Southwest Farallon for seal meat and sea-bird eggs, called it a spot "for heroicall spirits," and in the eleven decades since American occupancy, eleven ships have died on those rocks in spite of ever-growing "aids to navigation." Among these was the *Henry Bergh*, a Liberty ship homing from the wars with 1,300 navy people aboard in 1944. The morning of May 31 found the rocky chain in fog, and the groping *Bergh* unluckily blundered into a cone of silence west-northwest of the main islet and its south-ward-blaring signal. There the *Bergh* hit with a shrill crunching. The water happened to be quiet that morning, the discipline was admirable, and all hands swam, boated, rafted and daisy-chained ashore. For once the Southwest Farallon was really populous. Shards of the *Henry Bergh* still remain among the crannies.

The radio beacon and warning buoys of Noonday Rock stand eight miles due northwest in ten fathoms, with the Aleutians and Dutch Harbor, 3,000 miles away, the next break in the sea in that direction. Inboard, the Gulf of the Farallones here swings for Point Reyes Head directly north-east at about 13 miles. Here the Pacific Coast reaches its foggiest. Over a thirty-year period it recorded an average of 1,350 hours of the chilly damp stuff per year. In 1887, Point Reyes checked in 2,070 hours of the grey energizer and cosmetic and pointed to it as a record for any one year, but 1915 threw 2,145 hours at the San Francisco Lightship, and Reyes had to admit defeat.

However, it's a wild headland in its moments. Its light stands 612 feet above the water, visible 24 miles. The radio beacon is at the light, and the fog signal about 30 feet below. These give guidance for all vessels coasting north or south, and in further support they have a Coast Guard lifeboat station below and behind a sandspit on Drakes Bay. The boat station is frequently needed.

Storms around that head can be of size. Spray has been known to lash at the lighthouse windows. Following a tumultuous January 27, 1916, when a nor'-wester reached 104 miles an hour and stayed there all afternoon and night, the keeper reported the loss of a chimney, 140 feet of fence and a telephone post, all of which took wings. On one occasion a keeper heard human cries from below and, in an 80-mile wind, pulled three shipwrecked fishermen up 200 feet on a rope.

The light was installed in 1870. It is of the "first order," and the day it started flashing, a steam fog whistle also started. The same lens after more than ninety years is still doing business. In that period, more than thirty good-sized ships have died on the rocks and shoals of the vicinity. This has been partly due to some odd acoustics of the cliffs. They create dead spots whence the fog signal cannot be heard. To this day, after hard efforts by the government to engineer the muffling spots out of existence with concrete and steel, the United States Coast Pilot cautions, "From northward, vessels endeavor to make Point Reyes fog signal. This signal may not be heard in the bight north of the point, but soundings will indicate the ship's position. If inside the 30-fathom curve and the signal is not heard, the vessel should be put broad offshore. Under certain conditions, it has sometimes been found difficult to locate the fog signal owing to deflection in the direction of the sound, but by following the 30-fathom curve closely a vessel can round the point safely." This keeps a ship about two miles offshore during that 15 per cent of the hours when fog is in control—provided the skipper doesn't think he hears things that ain't, or vice versa.

All in all, the Gulf of the Farallones is a busy anteroom. If parts of it are rude to callers, the rest are full of friendliness, for it is buoyed and lighted and belled and whistled and radio-beaconed until about all a pilot in the sky has to know is his dits from his dats, and a skipper on the sea his reds from greens.

32 : THE ALWAYS READY
COAST GUARD

CERTAIN white-painted craft that dart in and out and about the Gate are conspicuous for their polite, businesslike friendliness. They range from motorized surfboats to swift 40- and 95-foot cutters; they also include buoy tenders, sea-going tugs and ocean-ranging steamships. Over them beat vigilantly co-operating planes and 'copters. They are the United States Coast Guard.

In 1790, eight years before the regular Navy was organized, the nation had a Revenue Marine of tiny wooden sailing ships. Their purpose was to stamp out smuggling. Later came a Lighthouse and a Life Saving pair of services. All are now unified as the Coast Guard. It has innumerable duties: to protect life and property at sea, to enforce federal laws at sea and on U.S. navigable waters, to serve in wartime as an integral part of the Navy and in peace as an arm of the Treasury; to maintain ice patrols, loran stations, aids to navigation; to search for and rescue the shipwrecked.

A vessel from overseas approaching the Golden Gate radios the Captain of the Port, twenty-four hours or more before arrival, for permission to enter. If it's deemed advisable to board him first, a swift cutter goes out. Permission granted, he moves in to quarantine, customs and immigra-

tion anchorage. "Captain of the Port" is the officer of the
Coast Guard charged with directing law-enforcement activities on all waters and waterfront facilities of an area reaching
from Point Reyes to Loma Prieta and inland to Stockton and
Sacramento. His office is a two-story structure at Pier 45½
perched directly upon a part of the planking of Fisherman's
Wharf. His officers and men survey and report upon the
condition of piers, maintain daily patrols, inspect manifests,
and screen waterfront personnel other than seamen. They are
on watch at the Captain's office and on bay patrol twenty-
four hours a day. They board ships for security purposes,
maintain waterside surveillance, watch for breaches of dangerous cargo regulations, and provide forces for disasters.

On the ninth floor of the Appraisers Building in downtown San Francisco is the office of the Commander, Twelfth
District, of the Coast Guard, and here is located the Rescue
Coördination Center, which not only directs search and
rescue throughout the district, but correlates the effective-
ness of adjoining districts centering at Long Beach, Seattle,
Alaska and Hawaii. It too is a throbbing, busy center on
watch twenty-four hours a day, seven days a week, and its
activities are always vital, often homeric. Minute by minute messages pour in and out at its Communications Room,
in crisp Coastguardese, and somewhere a cutter or a plane is
sent speeding on an errand that may mean life or death.

What's a typical day like at Rescue Coördination Center?
Translating the Coastguardese:

10:55 A.M.: 43-foot fishing vessel *Elena* advises he is sinking
½ miles from rocks, 10 miles from Point San Pedro. Number
of persons on board very hard for radio station to understand.
Coast Guard Air Station at San Francisco International Airport directed to assist. Air Station already has picked up
message and its helicopter is preparing to depart with towing
gear. Cutter 95311 also reports that it is en route after hearing
distress signal.

11:12: 'Copter there. Sights vessel.

11:22: 'Copter is attempting to place tow line aboard *Elena*, is having language difficulties.

11:25: Has line aboard. Is towing.

11:45: 'Copter has pulled *Elena* to safe distance from rocks. Cutter relieves it of tow and is en route with the damaged boat to Half Moon Bay.

12:25 P.M.: 'Copter returns to International Airport.

02:29: Cutter reports *Elena* anchored safely in Half Moon Bay. Three adults aboard. Case closed.

Often the Coast Guard receives valuable civilian help:

10:06 A.M.: Navy helicopter 302, four persons aboard, crashed on Mile Rock Light. Coast Guard Air Station, International Airport, directed to dispatch suitable aircraft; Fort Point Life Boat Station dispatches unit to assist.

10:15: Coast Guard 125-foot cutter *Ewing* en route.

10:21: Mobile radio unit advises four survivors have been picked up by commercial tug *Elizabeth Olson*.

10:35: rescued personnel transferred to cutter *Ewing*.

10:50: rescued personnel arrive at Fort Point; transferred to Presidio dispensary for check-up. Commander, Twelfth Coast Guard District, to *Elizabeth Olson*: "Your timely and seamanlike actions in helicopter crash appreciated and in best tradition of American merchant marine. No other assistance required."

01:31 P.M.: damaged Navy 'copter delivered to Oakland Naval Air Station.

Sometimes it's a big ship trapped and overwhelmed in a gale in breaking seas, calling for a classic old-time rescue complete with Lyle gun and breeches buoy. And sometimes a plane homing over the Pacific needs standby companionship:

07:57 A.M.: Word is flashed by Air Route Traffic Control of Federal Communications Commission that Air Force plane *Ethan 21*, Long. 127°55′ West, Lat. 32°32′ N., altitude 9000, destination McClellan AFB, Sacramento, has feathered her No. 1 and No. 2 engines; interception requested. Coast Guard cutter ordered to the Farallones; Coast Guard workhorse *Albatross* plane airborne; broadcast released to all ships.

02:23 P.M.: *Albatross* makes visual intercept of limping plane approximately 175 miles at sea; accompanies *Ethan 21* to destination.

04:02 P.M.: *Ethan 21* lands safely at McClellan Air Force Base.

Sometimes there is heartbreak ashore, as when three men of mature age set off from Seattle for Australia in a houseboat on pontoons, named *Leaky Tiki,* with a deck, a mast, a sail and food for two to three months. They made it to Eureka, sailed on, and were unreported at their next port, Santa Cruz:

07:36 A.M.: Coast Guard Radio Station, San Francisco, relays report from fishing vessel *Ruth Marie* of sighting mast with crowsnest, position 124°00′ West, 36°40′ North—well south of the Farallones.

01:45 P.M.: 54-foot Coast Guard cutter locates possible cabin top.

01:50: Fishing vessel *Defoe* reports itself alongside what appears to be *Leaky Tiki,* overturned. Position 92 miles south of Farallones.

11:22 P.M.: 95-foot cutter advises it has picked up various pieces of debris including a life ring with inscription *Leaky Tiki.*

Next day, 04:10 A.M.: Cutter advises no life aboard. Pontoons appear to have been flooded for several days. Weather still unsuitable for air search.

In spite of dense overcast, sea and air search continues throughout 2,400 square miles by cutters *Gresham* and *Active* and Coast Guard amphibian plane for three more days. Negative results. On ensuing days, search by air is continued from Cape Mendocino to the Channel Islands off

Santa Barbara. Regretfully, Mr. and Mrs. Jim Ball of Seattle are notified that their son Jerry, together with Charles Aylen and Don Trawitskie, must be considered lost.

Sometimes it is a stricken sailor or traveler at a point remote from medical aid. The United States Public Health Service in its great hospital at 15th Avenue and Lake Street, overlooking the Golden Gate, immediately transmits advice and directions upon receipt of calls for help through the Coast Guard Communications Room. A ship that has no doctor, but only a willing skipper and a patient in great distress, may be in the Persian Gulf, off Madagascar, or in the Banda Sea. Instructions crackle forth for removing that appendix, setting that broken jaw or delivering that baby half a world away.

And sometimes the sea provides merely another mystery.

On September 28, 1960, a radiotelephone message crackled through the fishing fleet a hundred miles southwest of the Gate, "I've been shot, boys, by the *Coho II*. This has been a good life. Good-bye, fellows."

The message was from the *Steelhead*, a one-man tuna boat operated by a popular fisherman known as "Dave" Davisson of Oakland. Of the more than two dozen fishermen who heard the message was the owner of the fishboat *Rogue*, who was near enough to investigate. Somewhere within the four hundred square miles of mistbound water that held the scattered fleet he came upon an overturned skiff and a hatch cover with a .22-caliber bullet hole through the center. The drain plug was pulled from the bottom of the skiff; its oars were lashed inside and evidently unused. But no *Steelhead*. And no *Coho II*.

"Strange," considered the skipper of the *Rogue*, "very strange." And he notified the Coast Guard. The Coast Guard air station at International Airport, the Fort Point Life Boat Station and the cutter *Ewing* were directed to make offshore search. Ceiling 400, results negative. Four hours after cutters and twin-engined Grumman amphibian search plane got off, the fishing vessels *Wendy* and *Christy* reported picking up more debris.

The whole fishing fraternity was alarmed. Coast ports and the F.B.I. were alerted for the missing *Coho II.* Meanwhile Helen Evans, who owned the dock at Oakland where Davisson usually unloaded his catch, said of that odd radio call that was Davisson's last message, " 'Shot' simply means 'fix.' Dave probably asked the *Coho* to locate him" —a navigational matter. Marvin Hoy, a fisherman who'd been working those same waters, disagreed with the dock keeper. "He would have called 'Mayday' and said he was sinking. He wouldn't say he was shot unless he was shot. I think there's something real wrong out there."

The *Coho* was located by Coast Guard search plane a few miles south of the Farallones. The cutter *Active* found one man aboard—a strongly built, middle-aged man named Ted Bean. He was known as a good fisherman. He had pulled three others out of the water in his time, saving their lives. "Direct, quiet-spoken and honest" was the verdict about him. The side of the *Coho* was heavily and freshly scratched, as if she had been raked or rammed by something. The guns aboard included a shotgun, a .22 rifle and much ammunition. But it is a commonplace for fishermen to carry weapons in order to kill sharks. Bean said that he had pulled alongside the *Steelhead* at 1 P.M. and given Davisson a letter to mail, as Davisson and *Steelhead* were at that time setting homeward for the Gate.

Lieutenant Jack Smith, skipper of the *Active*, was directed to bring Bean and his *Coho II* to San Francisco for questioning. "We couldn't arrest Bean or put a man on board," said a spokesman for the Coast Guard afterward, "because we have no conclusive evidence of a crime. Only reports of a frantic radio message." The two vessels, *Coho* leading and *Active* close behind, chugged northward through the fogbound night.

At 2:45 A.M. Bean radioed the cutter, "I'm so tired I can't think straight. I want to drift awhile and catch some sleep." So *Coho* and *Active* cut their engines and drifted until morning, when they got under way again.

This day, visibility was good in the Farallon Gulf. At 7:45, Bean was seen on the deck of his boat. At 10:30 the vessels neared the Gate. Lieutenant Smith, a salty and experienced officer of competence, didn't see Bean on the *Coho* so he tried to raise him by radio. No answer. That seemed odd. Smith used his lights, his whistle. Still no response. Instead, the *Coho* headed straight for Point Bonita.

Alarmed, Smith sped in pursuit. He caught up barely in time. Engineman Third Class George Mayfield, using one of the *Active's* boats, boarded the 50-foot *Coho* alone. Searching stem to stern, he found himself still alone. The wheel was lashed, the automatic pilot was set, the engines still throbbed. Down in the galley a cup of warm tea and a spoon rested on a table. On the foredeck was a single shoe.

Out at sea, the *Steelhead* and her owner lay in 2,000 fathoms. In the Gate, the *Coho* was saved from Bonita's rocks and brought through the Gate just as she ran out of fuel.

Had Ted Bean tied an anchor to his ankle and slipped over from the bow, concealed from the cutter's view by the cabin? Or had he tried a quiet getaway by means of a six-mile swim?

The *Steelhead* was said to have been heavy with tuna and low in the water when she turned homeward toward the Gate. Mused an F.B.I. man, "Fully loaded, the way the *Steelhead* was, it would take only a nudge in the right place to sink it. And the *Coho II* had a steel hull, and scratches on the sides."

Said one fisherman, shaking his head in disbelief, "I've

known both Davisson and Bean for years. They were both solid, calm, cool-headed. If you ask me, this whole thing didn't happen—they're still out there fishing."

Lieutenant Smith, a rugged type and an angry one, would have liked to think so too.

Only the sea knows what had really happened. "Closed," the Coast Guard reluctantly marked its fat file on the case.

The Commander of Twelfth Coast Guard District, Rear Admiral Allen Winbeck, who is also Commander, Western Area—from California, Oregon, Washington and Alaska to Hawaii and beyond—was born at Point Arena Life Boat Station. His cradle was virtually a surfboat. His blood pressure practically rises and falls with the tide.

The spray of the sea doesn't dash quite as high as the ninth floor, 630 Sansome Street, which is Twelfth District and Western Area Headquarters; but there is plenty of salt up there.

33 : HOME FROM THE SEA

THE splendid wooden clippers that once raced from Sandy Hook to Golden Gate died on far reefs, or rotted, or vanished in the mists. *Glory of the Seas*, a McKay masterpiece, was one of the very last. She was burned for her metal on a beach near Seattle in the 1920's. Nobody thought to save her. Nobody wanted her. She'd become a poor hulk, anyway.

A young man living a few miles north of the Golden Gate thought deeply about this vanishing heritage of America, this pageantry of windships. After pondering awhile, he acted. Without means, without friends in strategic places, armed with nothing but a burning idea, he came down to Gateside from a chicken ranch in Petaluma and set about salvaging suitable relics of past sea days, sail or steam. The thing was in his blood. He'd made a couple of voyages under sail himself, one of them around the Horn, and had come back as the mate of a steamship. Fired now with high purpose, he drove himself precisely as Lauchlan McKay once drove the *Sovereign of the Seas*, as Joe Creesy drove the *Flying Cloud*. Karl Kortum sought out and interested the publishers of four newspapers and some leading shipping people. He wangled from the city a first-rate building fronting Aquatic Park down near Fisherman's Wharf. He stocked the structure with an exciting collection of figureheads, log-books, anchors, windlasses, sextants, photographs and ship models. Then he went after bigger game. He foresaw a living museum of whole ships, one of each type and era, float-ing on blue water under blue sky outside his Golden Gate-facing doors. The Spanish caravels and galleons were gone but perhaps could some day be recreated. The clippers were gone and would have to wait for a large endowment to reconstitute a few. But there was one actual, tangible square-rigger remaining and she was almost in sight of his windows. She lay on the mudflats off Sausalito, be-hind the Gate's inside north corner. She was the last full-rigged Cape Horner. She was the last square-rigged ship to carry the American flag. And she hadn't rotted. She was built of steel. Her career had been varied and now nobody wanted her—except Karl Kortum.

This full-rigged ship, the last one available on the Coast, had been Clyde-built in the '80's for the Europe-Cape Horn-Golden Gate grain trade. Her original name was *Balclutha*. When the wheat trade waned, she'd become successively a world tramp, a lumber carrier to Australia, and a member of the great fleet which tied the Coast to the Alaska fish can-neries. Ousted from the sea lanes by steam after 43 years in and out of the Gate, she missed being sold to Japan for scrap by becoming a bedizened showboat with waxwork mutineers hanging at her yardarms. When that proved unproductive, she'd been tossed aside.

As a farer upon the seas, *Balclutha* had taken her lumps. Back in 1904, nineteen days out from the Gate, she felt her way along the midnight-misted coast of Alaska near Kodiak. With 20,000 square feet of canvas drawing, she struck. She had a thousand tons of supplies for the salmon canneries, and 100 people aboard including some Chinese close-packed be-tween decks. Somebody shot the bolt on the Chinese to keep them from creating panic on the deck. Four boats cleared the

white men off. With belaying pins at the ready, a rear guard
of officers and crewmen released the terrorized Chinese. Everybody reached shore, but *Balclutha* was left as a total loss.
She lay at a 45° angle on a reef of the Geese Islands, fifty
miles off her course.

The superintendent of a cannery paid $500 for her as she
lay, and salvage men dragged her off. They sent her homeward for the Gate on a towline. She didn't make it. Storms,
leaks and a mutiny interfered. She was left on a convenient
shore. In the following year, new salvage crews dug under
her, patched her plates, pumped the sand and water out of
her, and set her free. To show her pleasure in riding the
waves again, she reached the Gate in twenty days. Thoroughly rebuilt and refitted, and renamed *Star of Alaska*, she
then became the fastest full-rigger of the large Alaska Packers fleet. She put in more than two decades on that run,
retiring from commerce in 1930 and entering her mounte-
bank profession, which lasted another twenty years. When
Kortum eyed her, she had been about four years on the
Sausalito mud.

But Kortum saw beauty in the lines of that discarded ship
and could still hear the song of the trade winds in her tattered
rigging. Rust had eaten into the hull, the spars were forlorn-
looking, but there was a powerful sweep to her from the
figurehead of a noble Scotswoman and the yachtlike prow
clear to the fine sweet stern. She was 256 feet long and
measured 1689 tons. Above all, she was an honest-to-God
full-rigged ship.

So Kortum, a square-built able seaman himself, acquired
her from the showman's heirs as the nucleus for the outdoor
museum that would be the property of the San Francisco
Maritime Museum Association and of the people of California. The required $25,000 swept his treasury as clean as
a chewed bone. Restoring the ship would take $250,000 more.
That should have deterred him. But so should the gales of

Cape Horn have deterred the old-time mariners. Kortum went to work on this new problem. What he brought to it was vision, zeal and leadership.

The result was one of the most astonishing outpourings of community effort imaginable. Towboatmen, shipyard men, lumbermen donated material and services to get *Balclutha-Star of Alaska-Pacific Queen* (she'd borne all those names) off the tide flats and over the bay to drydock. Then behold what happened: in one of the most belligerent ports on earth, given to cat-and-dog labor-management rows, fourteen maritime unions buried the hatchet with each other and the shipping interests and volunteered the callused hands, technical skills, strong backs and free Saturdays of their members at no cost at all, but just for love of an almost dying ship. Those husky citizens gave up weekly holidays and swarmed over the grand old vessel. They sandblasted, redleaded, painted, plumbed, wired, carpentered, renewed and re-rigged the last of the Cape Horners for the public to enjoy, admire and appreciate. They and others from all walks of life donated more than 13,000 man-hours of work, while others donated sandwiches and coffee, and still others about $100,000 worth of materials and services. And with skilled superintendents watching over and coördinating all, they healed and made whole the tired old ship. And one day in the mid-1950's, with everything shining and ship-shape and her original name restored, *Balclutha* stepped down out of drydock like a bride going to a wedding, and tripped over the bay waters on the arm of a Crowley tug and into her permanent home at a pierside on the Golden Gate.

There she was joined soon after by a "baldheaded" schooner, the *C. A. Thayer*, which represents all the staunch little lumber-carrying windjammers of the early-day chute, loading-wire and gale-whipped doghole days. The *Thayer* was a sturdy alumnus of that bygone but once immense fleet. Kortum and some friends, all former mates and masters or other specialists, went up to Puget Sound for the *Thayer* and rerigged her and sailed her down the coast. Now she rides in the growing flotilla of the outdoor division of the Maritime Museum. Other types, now under repair, will follow.

They will rise and fall on the tides within a mile or so of where the *San Carlos* dropped anchor, two centuries ago; where Frémont made his crossing in a rowboat and gave the Golden Gate its name; where the *Rio de Janeiro* went down; and where the swinging lantern of Alcatraz lights today's ships homeward.

Sir Francis Drake's Bay, or Jack's Harbor

34 : THE WINDS OF CHANGE

NORTH of the Golden Gate, the land is virginal. Long given over to hidden gun emplacements, it is exactly as Captain Don Fernando Rivera y Moncado and Lieutenant Don Juan Manuel Ayala first beheld it. This is a spacious region, three miles airline-long from west to east and much more by its winding coves. Its shore is sheer wall; its ravines mount up and up, and back and back, until the whole embraces many square miles. Except for little pockets where Nike missiles lurk in clusters, and for radar and other installations, it no longer has much fortification value and it may well be declared government surplus. What then will become of it? Will it be turned into a sahara of tract homes? The mind recoils. Fortunately the public mood is for turning it into a Golden Gate State Park. Few places in the world are more sublime.

Around the northwest corner of the Gate and at goodly distance another public preserve is shaping up. Dairy farmers have held it intact for a century, and before that for three centuries it was just as early mariners once found it: a land of crestline forests, rolling hills, dunes, beaches and ocean-torn rocks and bluffs. At Drakes Bay in the hug of Point Reyes Head, little communities of week-end cottages have crept and the race is on between suburban development and

233

preservation of the natural scene, with the preservationists pulling ahead. It has been officially approved for inclusion in the national park system.

Elsewhere around the bay, population increases with ever-growing velocity. So the Gate, which successfully carried off the great experiment of being bridged for the first time, may have to be bridged again. Of late there has been a movement developing to bring back the ferries in some measure. That friendly, leisurely, economical mode of mass transportation would relieve at least a part of the growing burden on the Bridge.

Urban growth, or sprawl, seldom deals gently with any natural beauty that stands in its way. But some civic genius for the appropriate, or a lot of luck, has done well by the Gate's south rim. The chain of parks, strands, golf courses and embellishments begins with faded Cliff House and Sutro Heights on the west and is almost continuous to Telegraph Hill, the town's rocky green acropolis and the Gate's southeast hinge. The chain of pendants includes Fort Miley and the U.S. Veterans' Hospital, Lincoln Park and the Palace of the Legion of Honor, and the shining diamonds of James D. Phelan Beach, China Beach and Bakers Beach; the square ruby of Fort Scott almost hidden under the Bridge; the emerald Presidio; the Palace of Fine Arts parklet; the merry-masted Yacht Harbor and its tiny municipal lighthouse; the cool greensward of the Marina; the Victorian tranquility of Fort Mason; and Aquatic Park and Fisherman's Wharf. These are jewels of price, and they all adorn the Gate, each in its own way. But change is in the air.

First and foremost, it involves the Presidio. That broad sweep, once bristling with fortifications and strident with bugle calls, long has been a mere administration center for the western military frontier. Pressure is unceasing to have its woodlands, golflands and cemeteries declared surplus government property and sold off to the real-estate developers. But of gathering momentum is the civic determination to see that it is kept at least a park—just as, a few miles southward down the ocean front, Fort Funston has been adopted by the city.

A spot that is now in the bulldozer pathway of perhaps overimprovement is Fisherman's Wharf. The San Francisco Port Authority contemplates wholesale revision of the unkempt happy-go-lucky area from Grant Avenue to Van Ness. It proposes neat, shining malls, promenades, terraces, pedestrian overpasses, new quays, a "Palazzo del Pesce," a fishermen's chapel, all flanked by tree-lined office buildings, stores, hotels and apartment structures "gay and richly plastic"; with broad parking stretches—God be thanked—along with small parks, a plaza, and street kiosks for the crab cauldrons; the whole "woven as one cloth to reach a level of high civic purpose and human enjoyment." This is noble brochure-talk, though with a note running through it that the architects and civic planners, being of Olympian stock, know best. The Port Authority has already proved itself a success at passing bond issues. The principal trouble with the proposed new Grand Design for Fisherman's Wharf and its collateral activities is that—aside from the question as to whether cooked fish will taste better in a building resembling a Roman bath or a movie palace than it does in a shack on trembling piles—will the fishermen, when all is built, stay around? Fishermen, like fish, are independent fellows. They just possibly like certain sights and smells that the architects would lovingly get rid of. Perhaps, after giving the multimillion development a try, they will slip their painters and chug away for a less institutional, more congenial informality alongside some rotting pier that nobody thought was worth four dollars. And there, in a shack about the size of Andy's Lookout, somebody will start making *cioppino;* alongside it, A. Paladini will open a receiving shed; Boicelli & Boss will open a marine-engine shop and the Genoa Boat Building Company a boatway, and the proposed grandiose Il Palazzo del Pesce, "a fusion of carrousel and palace," will become as vacant and useless as the late Fox Theatre.

One doesn't know. The only thing that is certain is that the architects don't know. But the dream is exhilarating.

Meanwhile two things are slipping away from the southern side of the Gate that are more important than overpasses to reach the fish fries.

One is the steamship piers. They are tumbling into the water. One good yank of a Crowley tug would finish them. Though the public has voted $50 million for new facilities, time wastes, wharves decay, and steamship skippers wonder what they dare toss a hawser to.

The other is the intercoastal steamship lines. One by one they fold, or transfer away their ships. But the Gate has been the pathway of change for a century and it knows the changing winds. While rails and highways are beating the Panama Canal route at intercoastal freighting, American and foreign vessels of ever-new grace, size and beauty make the Gate majestic.

Its enigma abides. It still is hiding something from mankind.

It is one of the enthralling spots of this earth.

INDEX

Acapulco, 9
Accessory Transit Co., 68, 71
Alameda, 148, 164, 187; Fortman Basin, 150
Alcatraz Island (The Rock), 41, 75, 110, 164, 173, 177, 189-94; "Battle of Alcatraz," 193; citadel, 189; escape efforts, 192-93; Federal Bureau of Prisons, 191; fog signals, 81, 196-97; guns, 189-90; lighthouse, 195-97; Modoc Indians imprisoned, 190-91; "Spanish dungeons," 190; U.S. Army disciplinary barracks, 190
Aleut hunters, 36
American President Lines, 140
Andy's Lookout, 160, 235
Angel Island, 118; fog signal, 81, 196, 197
Anian, Strait of, 19, 25, 87
Año Nuevo Point, 27
Anza, Juan Bautista de, 24, 28, 32; Golden Gate reached by, 24
Aquatic Park, 228, 234
Arctic Oil Works, 148
Arellano, 9
Argüello, Concepción (Concha), 34, 38
Argüello, José Darío, 33
Argüello, Luís, 33
Aspinwall, W., 67
Ayala, Juan Manuel de, 27, 141, 233; given command of San Carlos, 26

Bache, General Hartman, 216
Bahia de San Francisco, 12, 20
Bakers Beach, 234
Baldwin, E. J. (Lucky), 116
Ball, Jerry, 224
Baránof, Alexander, 33
Barbary Coast, 126, 173, 188

Battery Davis, 119
Bay Bridge, 82, 197
Bean, Ted, 225-27
Bear Flag Republic, 39
Beetle, J. C., 148
Benges, Heinie, 183-84
Benny the Chinese, 170-71
Bering, Vitus, 32
Berkeley, 22
Bernston, Albert, 99-100
"Big Four," railroad builders, 78
Black Point, 110, 118, 173, 197. See also Fort Mason
Blossom Rock, 173, 177
Bodega Bay, 6, 15, 36, 214; Russian port, 35-36
Bodega y Quadra, Juan Francisco de, 26
Boicelli-Boss, 160, 235
Bolinas Bay, 6, 15
Bolton, Herbert E., 16
Brannan, Sam, 44
Bridges, Harry, 175
Bucareli, Antonio Maria, 21, 24, 29
Bucket of Blood, 186

Cable cars, 5, 154, 158
Cabrillo, John Rodríguez, 7, 130; Alta California discovered by, 8
Caldeira, William, 17
Canizares, Jose de, Bay explored by, 28-29; Golden Gate entered by, 27
Cape Mendocino, 9, 12, 223
Capone, Al, 191-92, 194
Captain of Port, 220-21
Carey, Capt. J. J., 100
Carmelo River, 27, 141
Carmeño, Sebastian Rodríguez, 11-12, 20, 24
Carquinez Strait, 200, 201
Carson, Kit, 40, 41, 162

237

Carson, Mrs. Mary, 130
Castagnola, Tom, 160
Castillo de San Joaquin, 41
Cavallo Point, 81
Central Pacific, 78, 151-52
China Basin, 65
China Beach, 234
Chinatown, 194
Chirikof, Alexei, 32
Chrysopylae, 42
Clark, Capt. Charles Edgar, 108-09
Clark, John, 101
Cliff House, 5, 83, 85, 86, 87, 144, 234
Clipper ships, 152
Coast Artillery, 120
Coast Range, 200, 201
Coast Seamen's Journal, 126, 127
Coast Seamen's Union, 126
Cobb, George D., 98-99
Coblentz, E. D. (Cobbie), 101-02
Cochituate Company for California, 45
Colorado Desert, 24
Colorado River, 5, 25
Columbia River salmon boat, 156
Comstock Lode, 123, 124
Conquistadores, 7, 21, 25
Corte Madera Cove, 8
Corte Madera Creek, 16
Cortez, Hernán, 6
Coyote Creek, 22
Crab Boat Owners Association, 154
Creesy, Capt. Josiah, 60, 62, 228
Crescent City, 141
Crespi, Father Juan, 21; Gate seen by, with Fages, 22; interior explored by, 23
"Crookedest Railroad in the World," 211
Crowley, David (Hook-On), 172-74
Crowley Launch & Tugboat Co., 174
Crowley, Thomas, 97, 173-75, 179, 185

Daily Alta, The, 49, 52, 53, 55, 90, 91
Daly, John, 92
Dana, Richard Henry, 45, 126
Davidson, George C., 11, 15

Davisson, "Dave," 222-27
Dewey, Commodore George, 107-08
Diamond Head, 140
Dickie, James, 136-37
Dickie, John, 136-37
Dolla, Capt. Robert, 139-40, 175
Donahue, Peter, 163
Doolittle, James, 112
Drake, Francis, 10, 13-18, 22, 32, 37; "Plate of Brasse," 11
Drakes Bay, 6, 11, 15, 218, 233
Dumaresq, Capt. Philip, 59
Duxbury Point, 100
Duxbury Reef, 91, 176

El Camino Real, 21
Embarcadero, 186
Englehardt, C. F., 95-96
Eureka, 11

Fages, Lieutenant Pedro, 21, 23, 24
"Falange Americana," 70
Farallon Gulf. See Gulf of Farallones
Farallon Islands, 4, 12, 22, 37, 60, 87, 155, 214-19; passed by Ferello, 8; Russian base on, 36; sighted by Ayala, 27; visited by Drake, 11
Farnham, Eliza Woodson, 48
Farquhar, Francis P., 17
Feluccas, 155
Ferrelo, Bartolomé, 7, 8, 14, 202
Ferries, restoration of, 234
Ferry tower, 165
Filibustering, 66-73
Fire of 1906, 159
Fisher, Al, 84
Fisherman's Cove, 159, 160, 161
Fisherman's Wharf, 5, 75, 76, 77, 106, 155, 156, 161, 228, 234; reconstruction plans, 235-36
Fitzgerald, J. P., 64
Fletcher (Drake's chaplain), 15
Fort Baker, 120
Fort Cronkhite, 80
Fort Mason, 118, 234. See also Black Point
Fort Miley, 119, 120

Fort Point, 84, 92, 118, 206; anchoring of *San Carlos* on, 28; Castillo de San Joaquin, 41
Fort Ross (El Fuerto de los Rusos), 36, 37, 171
Fort Winfield Scott, 117-18, 234
Francis, Phil, 111
Frémont, Jessie, 41
Frémont, John Charles, 13, 39, 40, 43, 45; Alcatraz Island bought for public by, 189; Gate crossed by, 41; Gate named by, 42; "Geographical Memoir" by, 42
Fulton Iron Works, 137
Furuseth, Andrew, 125-28

Garrison, Cornelius Kingsland, 68, 69
Garrison & Morgan, 71
General Steamship Corp., 106
Genoa Boat Building Co., 235
"Geographical Memoir," Frémont's, 42
Gielow (Fireman of ferry *Sausalito*), 167
Gila Valley, 24, 25
Goat Island, 22, 82, 197; Civil War fortifications on, 118
Gold Street, 159
Golden Gate Bridge, 5, 80, 117, 120, 167; fog signals, 81; opening of, 145-46
Golden Gate Ferry Co., 165
Golden Gate Life Saving Station, 99
Golden Gate Park, 87
Golden Gate State Park, 233
Gomez, Izzy, 185-88
Gordon, Capt. George, 57
Gormand (Engineer of ferry *San Rafael*), 167
Grain trade, 151-53; first California wheat ship, 151; 1868 wheat-shipping port, 151
Grand Opera House, 154
Greytown, 68, 71
Grizzly Peak, 22
Gulf of Farallones, 214-19, 226
Guns, 116-21; barbette, 119; disappearing, 119
"Gurdy" reel, engine-powered, 159

Hall, Samuel, 59
Hall-Scott marine engine, 160
Hamilton, Edward H., 110
Hawaiian Islands, 9; annexation, 137; whaling haven, 147
Hawkins, John, 10
Heads of the Gate, 6, 55, 66, 79, 89, 109, 129, 156, 214; fogs, 199-200
Hecate, Bruno de, 26
Hicks, Frank, 159
Hicks marine gas engine, 154, 159
Hogan, Capt. W. J., 93
Hole in the Rock, 92
Howes, Commander, 91, 92
Hudson, Capt. William H., 56
Humboldt Bay, 12
Hyde Street, 160, 165

International Seamen's Union, 126
Irons & Grinnell, 60
Isham, Capt. J. B. G., 53, 55
Islais Creek, 29

Johnston, James A., 193
Jordan, Fred, 94

King Kalakaua, 139
Klondike rush, 174
Knowles, Capt. Josiah, 132-34
Kortum, Karl, 229-31

Lands End, 86, 119, 197
Law, George, 67
Lawson, Andy, 205
Life Saving Service, 220
Lighthouse Service, 220
Lime Point, 28, 81, 197
Lincoln Park, 234
Linderman, Gus, 176
Lobos. *See* Point Lobos
London, Jack, 167
Long Wharf, 52
Lopez, Joe, 187
"Lumber Street," 75

McAdie, Alexander, 200, 201, 202
McCarthy, Edward F., 184
McKay, Donald, 60, 61, 134, 288
McKay, Lauchlan, 61, 62, 228
MacKenzie, Capt. Jack, 166

Mahoney, Andrew F., 178-79
Maloney, Sergeant, 82
"Manifest Destiny," 39
Manila galleon, 9
Mare Island, 177
Marin County, 79, 164
Marina, 234
Marine Exchange, 76, 183, 184
Maritime Museum, 133
Mark Twain, 136
Marshall, James, 44
Martin, Alex, 84
Matson, Capt. William, 138-39, 175
Matson Navigation Company, 153
Maxwell, Mike, 102
Meiggs, Henry, 74-78
Meiggs, John C., 75, 76
Meiggs Wharf, 65, 75-77, 129, 156, 163, 173, 174, 179, 183, 184; *Hanalei* survivors' arrival, 102; "Meiggs' Folly," 78
Melville, Herman, 128-29, 131
Mendocino Cape. *See* Cape Mendocino
Mendocino County, 146
Mile Rock, 81, 89, 91, 197
Mile Rock Light, 197-98
Mill Valley & Mt. Tamalpais Railroad, 211
Mission Bay, 29
Mitscher, Capt. Marc, 112-13
Montara Point, 214-15
Monterey, 24, 25, 27, 29, 34, 45; Alta California's first presidio, 22; Alta California's second mission, 22
Monterey Bay, 6, 8, 20, 21, 141
"Monterey hull," 156
Morgan, Charles, 69
Morton Alley, 126
Mother O'Brien's, 186
Mountain Play, 212-13
Mrs. Hare's Firemen's Boarding House, 186
Muir Woods, 210-11

Napoli, John, 104-06
Nelson, Capt. Norman, 181-83; *Hanalei* wreck, 101-02
New Albion, 11

Nicaraguan (Vanderbilt) Line, 91
Niemeier, Dad, 187
Nike-Ajax, 121
Nike-Hercules, 121
Nootka Sound, 34
North Beach, 75, 155, 160
Northern Mystery, 25. *See also* Anian, Strait of; Northwest Passage
North Pacific Coast Railroad, 163
Northwest Passage, 19, 87
Nutter, Joe, 100, 102

Oakland, 22, 128, 285
Oakland Creek, 148, 150
Oceanic Commercial Society of Hamburg, 138
Oceanic Steamship Co., 138
O'Connell, Dan, 172
Old Ben, 87
Olson & Mahoney, 178
Olson, Oliver J., 178
Ortega, Sergeant, 20, 22
Osborne, Fanny, 128-29
Osborne, Sam, 129
Oxenham, John, 10

Pace, Charles P., 179
Pacific Coast Artillery District, 119
Pacific Mail Steamship Co., 51, 53, 56, 58, 68, 89, 91, 126, 127, 137; *Rio de Janeiro* wreck, 94; Vanderbilt acquisition, 72
Pacific Steam Whaling Co., 134, 148
Pacific Street, 173, 186
Palace of Fine Arts, 234
Palace Hotel, 123-25, 157
Palace of the Legion of Honor, 234
Paladini, Achille, 157-59
"Palazzo del Pesce," 235-36
Pálou, Father, 140
Panama Railroad, 62, 72
Parrott, Jack, 164-65
Parsons, Capt. William S., 114
Patten, Capt. Joshua, 62
Patten, Capt. Mary, 62
Pearl Harbor, 111
Pearson, Capt. R. H., 56
Pérez, Juan, 26
Peterson, Henry Clarence, 184-85

Phelan Beach, James D., 234
Phelps, Capt. William D., 40
Pier 45, 77, 160, 197
Piers, condition of, 236
"Plate of Brasse," 14-16
Point Arena, 8, 143, 169, 226
Point Bolinas, 20
Point Bonita, 4-5, 49, 79-85, 125,
    183, 197, 226; fog records, 202;
    fog signals, 82; lifeboat station
    83-84; lighthouse, 79, 83
Point Diablo, 81
Point Lobos, 4-5, 28, 49, 55, 59, 85-
    87, 99, 104, 125; semaphore to
    Telegraph Hill, 52
Point Lobos Road, 86
Point of Pines, 27
Point Reyes, 11, 12, 20, 27, 100,
    144, 214, 234
Point San Carlos (Lime Point), 28
Point San Pedro, 214
Portolá, Gaspar de, 19, 21, 22
Portsmouth Square, 128
Potato Patch, 176, 214
Potrero district, 148
Presidio of San Francisco, 39, 116,
    234-35; founding by Juan Bau-
    tista de Anza, 25

Ralston, William C., 122-25
"Red Record," 126-27
Red Stack Tug Co., 174
Redwoods, 210; "dogholes," 145;
    falling and logging, 145; Meiggs'
    sawmills, 142; "redwood fleet,"
    142. See also Muir Woods; Steam
    schooners
Revenue Marine, 220
Rezánof, Nikolai Petrovitch, 33, 34,
    35, 38
Rincon Hill, 64
Rivera y Moncada, Fernando, 20, 21,
    22, 86; Gate reached by, via land
    route, 23
Rolph, James Jr., 65
Ross, Harold, 181
Roumainzoff, 36
Russia, 25
Russian American Fur Co., 33, 34
Russian hunters, 216

Russian River, 163

San Andreas Fault, 205
San Antonio, 22
San Blas, 25, 27
San Diego, 21, 25; Alta California's
    first mission, 20
San Diego Bay, 19
San Francisco, 5, 20, 24, 37, 44, 63;
    chief whaling port, 148; down-
    town climate, 202; presidio site,
    25
San Francisco Bar pilots, 170-71
San Francisco Bay, 5, 7; Ayala's re-
    port on, 29; discovery of, 20; pos-
    sibility of visit by Drake, 10
San Francisco Herald, 52, 55, 69
San Francisco Lightship, 217-29
San Francisco Maritime Museum As-
    sociation, 230
San Francisco Port Authority, 235-
    36
San Gabriel Valley, 25
San Gregorio Pass, 25
San Jacinto Mountains, 24
San Jose, 45
San Juan del Sur, 28, 71
San Miguel Island, 8
San Pedro Cove, 20
San Rafael, 16, 164
Sandwich Islands, 62
Sanguinetti, Joe, 160
Santa Barbara, 8
Santa Fe railroad, 164
Santa Lucia Mountains, 8
Sargent, Capt. Henry, 64
Sausalito, 40, 80, 90, 91, 162-63,
    229; Sausalito Land & Ferry Co.,
    163; whaling haven, 147
Schmidt, Alexis von, 177
Schmidt, Edward A. von, 177-78
Schultz, Dutch Louie, 191
Seal Rocks, 5, 81, 84; Seal Rocks
    House, 86
Sea otters, 36, 37
Serra, Father Junípero, 20, 21, 24,
    29
Sharpe's rifle, 70, 73
Shinn, Beryle, 16

Sitka, 33, 34; mission bells cast in, 38
Slater, John, 99
Slavyanka, 36
Sleeping maiden, 212-13
Sloat, Commodore, 39
Smith, Capt. Dick, 171
Smith, Lt. Jack, 225-27
Smith & Dimon, 57
Sonoma, 39
Southeast Farallon, 215-16
Southern Pacific, 164, 165
Southern Pacific Golden Gate Ferries, Ltd., 165
Spanish Armada, 17, 18
Spreckels, Claus, 138
Spreckels, John D., 138
Starr, Walter, 17
Steam schooner, 142-46
Stevenson, Robert Louis, 128-30, 213
Stoddard, Charles Warren, 128-29, 134
Stoll (surfman), 101
Strauss, Joseph B., 203-08
Sutra, Adolf, 86-87
Sutro Heights, 87, 234
Sutter's Fort, 37
Sweeny & Baugh, 55, 59

Tamalpais, Mt., 4, 11, 205, 209-13; Legend of Tamalpais, 212-13
Tehuantepec, Gulf of, 53
Telegraph Hill, 75, 78, 128, 140, 156, 165, 173, 186, 194, 234; semaphore, 52, 59
Temperature, vicinity of Gate, 201
Tennessee Cove, 90
Tennessee Point, 90
"The Countess," 187
Tiburon, 163-64
Tiburon ferry, 162-63
Tivoli Opera House, 154
Tomales Bay, 6, 15
Tonquin Shoal, 75
Tortorici murder, 179
Trawilskie, Don, 224
Treasure Island, 81, 197
Treaty of Guadalupe Hidalgo, 41
Tribble, Capt. Bill, 167

Union Iron Works, 108, 137
United States Coast Guard, 108, 137, 218, 220-27; Air Station, San Francisco International Airport, 221-22, 224; Alameda base, 83; Captain of Port, 221; Commander, Twelfth District, 221; Commander, Western Area, 221; Communications Room, 224; Fort Point Station, 81; Rescue Co-ordination Center, 104
United States Mail Steamship Co., 67
United States Veterans Hospital, 234

Vanderbilt, Commodore Cornelius, 67, 68. See also Pacific Mail Steamship Co.
Vigilante activities, 93
Vizcaino, Sebastian, 19, 20; Monterey Bay discovered by, 12

Waddell, Capt. James, 118
Wagner, Henry Raup, 15
Wakeman, Capt. Ned, 48
Waldo tunnel, 4
Walker, John, 126
Walker, William, 66-73
Waller, Cyrus, 167
Ward, Capt. William, 94-96
Washington Street Market, 157
Waterman, Capt. R. H., 61
Wells Fargo Express, 137
Weule, Louis, 179-81; Louis Weule Co., 180
Whalebone, 148-49
Whale Whisker Kelly's, 186
Whaling, peak year for Gate, 148
White, Charles G., 142
Whitehall boats, 171-74; whitehaller, 133
Willis, Bailey, 205
Winbeck, Rear Admiral Allen, 227
Winship, Capt. Jonathan, 35
Women light keepers, 215

Yacht Harbor, 234
Yellow Bluffs, 81
Yerba Buena Cove, 29, 39
Yerba Buena (Goat) Island, 22
Yermak, 32
Yuba Manufacturing Co., 159

SALTY COMPANY

Active, revenue cutter, 118
Active, Coast Guard cutter, 225-26
Ada Iredale (Annie Johnson), 134
Alabama, CSS, 118
America, pilot boat, 170
American, 76
Andrew Jackson, swift clipper, 60
Angelique, bride-ship, 49
Angelo Petri, wine ship, 85
Annie Johnson (Ada Iredale), 135
Antelope, ferry, 163

Balclutha (Star of Alaska, Pacific Queen), 229-32
Barracouta, 118
Bear (Bear of Oakland), 76
Benevolence, military hospital ship, 103-06
Boston, USS, 108
Bounty, 132
Bridgemaster, 138
Brooklyn, first passenger ship through Gate, 44
Brooklyn, USS, 109
Brother Jonathan, steamer, 69
Buffalo, USS, 109

C. A. Thayer, 231-32
Caleb Curtis, lightship, 172
California, first steamer through Gate under own power, 49, 50
Casco, 129, 213
Celestial, clipper, 58
Challenge, clipper, 51, 61, 64
Charmer, clipper, 151
China, steamer, 138
Civilian, 45
Claremont, 178
Clark, 93
Coho II, 224-27
Comet, 51, 64

Constitution, 52
Crusader, clipper, 63

Dashing Wave, 64
Democrata, 136
Diana, ferry, 163
Dirigo, 144
Dresden, German cruiser, 110-11

Eclipse, clipper, 59
El Principe (Santiago), 26
Elizabeth Olson, tug, 222
Escambia, 152
Esther Johnson, last wooden steam schooner, 144
Eureka, 84
Euterpe, 92
Ewing, cutter, 224
Excelsior, 143

Fanny, pilot boat, 170
Farragut, USS, 165
Felicidad, 26
Flying Cloud, immortal clipper, 60, 61, 64, 228
Flying Fish, clipper, 64
Flyaway, clipper, 64
Francis, 93

Gaelic, 107, 108
Galatea, clipper, 172
Gay Head, 148
Gjöa, 87
Glory of the Seas, last clipper, 63, 134, 228
Gneisenau, German cruiser, 110, 111
Golden Age, ferry, 165
Golden Age, mail steamer, 53
Golden Bear, ferry, 165
Golden City, ferry, 165
Golden Coast, ferry, 165

Golden Era, ferry, 165
Golden Fleece (San Carlos), 43
Golden Gate (Golden City), ferry, 165
Golden Gate, pilot motorship, 171
Golden Gate, steamship, 52-53
Golden Hinde (Pelican), Drake's flagship, 10, 13, 16, 43
Golden Poppy, ferry, 166
Golden Shore, ferry, 165, 166
Golden State, ferry, 166
Golden West, ferry, 165
Goliath, tug, 54, 55, 169
Governor, 93
Gracie S., pilot boat, 170
Granada, 91
Greenfield, first California wheat ship, 151

Hanalei, 100-02
Helen W. Almy, 93-94
Henry Bergh, 217
Herald of the Morning, clipper, 64
Hesper, 136
Hood, HMS, 174-75
Hornet, USS, 112-13
Houqua, clipper, 64

Indianapolis, USS, 113-14
Isabella, 36
Isthmus, 52

Jenny Lind, 93
John Gilpin, clipper, 64
John L. Stevens, 53
Juno, 33, 34

La Victoria, Ferrelo's ship, 8
Lady Mine, pilot boat, 170
Leaky Tiki, 223-24
Leipsig, German cruiser, 110, 111
Little Sitka, 48
Llewellyn J. Morse, 150
Los Tres Reyes, 12
Louis Weule, steamer, 181
Louise Morgan, 93

McCulloch, USS, revenue cutter, 100, 102, 169

McPherson, quartermaster steamer, 191
Mandarin, clipper, 64
Manga Reva (Pyranees), 136
Marietta, USS, 109
Mariposa, 138
Mary Luckenbach, 103-06
Memnon, clipper, 57, 58
Merrimac, USS, 118
Milo, whaler, 118
Monacacy, USS, 108
Monitor, USS, 118
Moscow, 40
Moses Taylor (Rolling Moses), 137

N. B. Palmer, clipper, 59
Neptune's Car, clipper, 62
New World, river steamer, 48
New York, 125
Newsboy, 139
Nightingale, clipper, 64

O'Cain, 35
Olympia, USS, 107
Ontario, 151
Oregon, USS, 108-10, 164
Oxford, 93

Parallel, 87
Peacock, 35
Pelican (Golden Hinde), 10, 13
Petaluma, ferry, 163, 164
Petrel, USS, 108
Phantom, clipper, 64
Pomona, 144
Prince Alfred, 93
Princess, ferry, 162-63
Pyranees (Manga Reva), 135, 136

Quang Se, first Gate wheat ship to Europe, 152

Race Horse, 64
Raiatea, 138
Rainbow, famed clipper, 63, 64
Raven, clipper, 60, 61
Reindeer, clipper, 179
Rio de Janeiro, steamer, 94-97, 198, 232; legends, 96-97
Romance of the Seas, clipper, 65